Playing with Religion
in Digital Games

DIGITAL GAME STUDIES

Robert Alan Brookey and David J. Gunkel, editors

PLAYING with RELIGION in DIGITAL GAMES

Edited by

HEIDI A. CAMPBELL

and

GREGORY PRICE GRIEVE

INDIANA UNIVERSITY PRESS   *Bloomington & Indianapolis*

This book is a publication of

INDIANA UNIVERSITY PRESS
Office of Scholarly Publishing
Herman B Wells Library 350
1320 East 10th Street
Bloomington, Indiana 47405 USA

iupress.indiana.edu

Telephone orders 800-842-6796
Fax orders 812-855-7931

∞ The paper used in this publication
meets the minimum requirements of
the American National Standard for
Information Sciences–Permanence of
Paper for Printed Library Materials,
ANSI Z39.48–1992.

Manufactured in the
United States of America

Cataloging information is available from
the Library of Congress

ISBN 978-0-253-01244-9 (cloth)
ISBN 978-0-253-01253-1 (paperback)
ISBN 978-0-253-01263-0 (ebook)

1 2 3 4 5   19 18 17 16 15 14

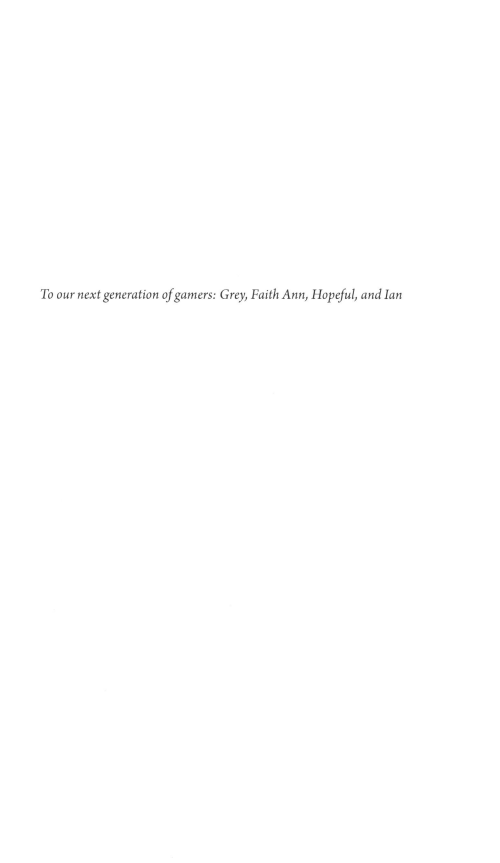

To our next generation of gamers: Grey, Faith Ann, Hopeful, and Ian

Contents

Acknowledgments · ix

Introduction: What Playing with Religion Offers Digital Game
Studies · *Heidi A. Campbell and Gregory Price Grieve* · 1

PART 1. EXPLORATIONS IN RELIGIOUSLY THEMED GAMES

1. Dreidels to *Dante's Inferno:* Toward a Typology of
Religious Games · *Jason Anthony* · 25

2. Locating the Pixelated Jew: A Multimodal Method for Exploring
Judaism in *The Shivah* · *Isamar Carrillo Masso and Nathan Abrams* · 47

3. The Global Mediatization of Hinduism through Digital Games:
Representation versus Simulation in *Hanuman: Boy Warrior*
Xenia Zeiler · 66

4. *Silent Hill* and *Fatal Frame:* Finding Transcendent Horror in and
beyond the Haunted Magic Circle · *Brenda S. Gardenour Walter* · 88

PART 2. RELIGION IN MAINSTREAM GAMES

5. From *Kuma\War* to *Quraish:* Representation of Islam in Arab and
American Video Games · *Vít Šisler* · 109

6. Citing the Medieval: Using Religion as World-Building
Infrastructure in Fantasy MMORPGS · *Rabia Gregory* · 134

7. Hardcore Christian Gamers: How Religion Shapes
Evangelical Play · *Shanny Luft* · 154

8. Filtering Cultural Feedback: Religion, Censorship, and Localization
in *Actraiser* and Other Mainstream Video Games · *Peter Likarish* · 170

PART 3. GAMING AS IMPLICIT RELIGION

9. The Importance of Playing in Earnest · *Rachel Wagner* · 192

10. "God Modes" and "God Moods": What Does a Digital Game
Need to Be Spiritually Effective? · *Oliver Steffen* · 214

11. Bridging Multiple Realities: Religion, Play, and Alfred Schutz's
Theory of the Life-World · *Michael Waltemathe* · 238

12. They Kill Mystery: The Mechanistic Bias of Video Game
Representations of Religion and Spirituality · *Kevin Schut* · 255

Gameography · 277

Contributors · 281

Index · 285

Acknowledgments

WE WISH TO THANK THE DIGITAL GAME STUDIES SERIES editors, Robert Alan Brookey and David J. Gunkel, for their support of this project, and we are grateful for the wonderful editorial support and oversight offered by Raina Polivka at Indiana University Press. Heidi A. Campbell wishes to thank the fellow scholars working in the overlapping areas of media, religion, and game studies, especially Mia Lövheim, Patrick Burkhart, and Srividya Ramasubramanian for their support and encouragement related to this project. Gregory Price Grieve would like to thank Anne Blankenship, Vincent Gonzalez, Rabia Gregory, Shanny Luft, Brian Moynihan, and Pamlea Mullins Reaves. It was their innovative panel, which Grieve presided over at the American Academy of Religion Conference in 2007, that opened up the field. He would also like to thank Christopher Helland – because what happens in the magic circle stays in the magic circle.

Playing with Religion
in Digital Games

What Playing with Religion Offers Digital Game Studies

Heidi A. Campbell and Gregory Price Grieve

THE PERPENDICULAR GOTHIC SPIRES OF A THIRTEENTH-CENTURY medieval cathedral tower over the strangely empty English countryside. Inside, the richly decorated choir stalls are empty; the sun filters through the stained-glass windows, streaking the dust-filled air and illuminating the gilded nave and the hallowed halls, which are covered with a veneer of centuries of prayer. Suddenly, there is a blood-curdling screech, and the cathedral is filled with the scurry of hundreds of spider-like creatures that fill the shadows. A blast shatters the silence, and multiple flashes of gunfire light the darkness. An archway begins to crumble; tracer bullets fill the air, leaving behind red puffs of blood. For a moment there is near-silence, with only strange growling whispers to be heard. Then, the click of reloading, and the shooting begins again.

Of course, this is not happening in the actual world, but in a digital game. The violent shootout is under way between the alien race called the Chimaera and the last vestiges of humankind in Sony's first-person shooter game *Resistance: Fall of Man* (Insomniac Games, 2006). Set in an alternative history where Europe has been invaded by aliens, a virtual copy of Manchester Cathedral in England is utterly destroyed at the hands of warring soldiers and, of course, the gamer.[1]

Soon after the release of the game in the United Kingdom, the Church of England claimed that the digital depiction desecrated the actual physical cathedral and violated copyright.[2] As the digital recreation of Manchester Cathedral and the controversy its virtual destruction caused illustrate, religion has a significant presence in the digital context. Indeed, since the 1990s everyday religious practices have become increasingly intertwined with new forms of media. In the twenty-first century, scholars have noted how people use digital media to recreate religious practices: they visit online shrines, take virtual pilgrimages, and incorporate social media and the internet into their spiritual routines. Despite this, the study of religion and gaming has not received much attention in the study of religion and the internet and remains one of the most understudied elements of such digital environments.

In this book, digital gaming is explored as a field filled with potential for new insights into the place, presentation, and impact of religion within popular culture. As the contributors elucidate, digital games are not a superficial phenomenon peculiar to an uncharacteristic cultural activity. Rather, digital games are an important site of exploration into the intersection of religion and contemporary culture that helps us understand what religion is, does, and means in a changing contemporary society. In fact, *Playing with Religion* contends that just like films helped to illuminate and expose the religiosity of the twentieth century, digital games now depict the religious within the twenty-first century.[3] This volume also offers a space for discussion of the nature of "play" within our notions of religious participation and spiritual searching.

Careful study of the symbolism found in popular games such as *Resistance: Fall of Man* reveals that digital games often rely on important cultural and religious content to drive both the narrative and gameplay, utilizing these modes as unique forms of cultural communication and valence. Further, and as the chapters in this volume demonstrate, references to religious and cultural practices in digital games inform the role religion plays in the organization of contemporary society. As Walter Ong argues in *The Presence of the Word: Some Prolegomena for Cultural and Religious History,* different media may make different religiosities possible.[4] Ong suggests that religion began in an era of orality, was transmitted into visual form through manuscript writing as well as print, and has now entered the world in a new way via electronic media. This volume contends that digital games both reflect and shape contemporary religiosity, creating a fertile ground for research into what it means to be human in the fullest sense.

We suggest that studying the intersections between digital games and religion has often been neglected for four reasons: games are widely considered simply a form of young people's entertainment; video games are often seen as artificial or unvalued forms of expression; technology is thought to be secular; and virtual gaming worlds are seen as unreal. Because games are assumed to be merely frivolous childish fun, mixing religion and gaming is problematic for many people. Nonetheless, as Jason Anthony indicates in this volume, religion and games have a long intertwined history. Echoing the work of the Dutch historian and one of the founders of game studies Johan Huizinga, Rachel Wagner shows that games and religion share many of the same structural elements.

While some still perceive the average digital game player as a young male playing alone, just wasting time, a large gap exists between the public perception of who plays video games and what the research demonstrates.[5] Statistics show that video games are not a ghetto of adolescent boys: the average gamer is thirty-five years old and has been playing for thirteen years.[6] Forty percent of all game players are women; boys age seventeen or younger account for only 18 percent of players.[7] Moreover, gamers do not play alone, but typically play with others – either face-to-face or online.[8] The perceived connections between the availability of video games and an epidemic of youth violence do not have a solid foundation, and research has not conclusively proved that video games desensitize players.[9]

A second reason that religion is frequently overlooked within digital games is that some assume games to be shallow, unable to carry or communicate important ideas. This means that they are seen as an inferior medium of expression, whose messages are playful and not to be taken seriously. Such assumptions have been expressed by religious groups as well as by some technologists and game designers. For example, in 2012, Apple stated in its "App Store Guidelines," "We view Apps different than books or songs, which we do not curate. If you want to criticize a religion, write a book."[10] The guidelines explain that applications containing critiques, controversial framings of religious groups, and offensive references to or misquotations of religious texts will be rejected. Religious content "should be educational or informative rather than inflammatory." While Apple's stance appears to be an attempt to limit what could be perceived as offensive content to dissimilar groups, it also innately communicates that games are not able to provide critical reflection or arguments about topics such as religion, which the company feels should be covered in text-based or electronic books. Furthermore, even though the designer sought to provide a space where play could reveal wider implications of multiple outcomes, in 2012 Apple rejected the game *Endgame: Syria* (which is based on the real civil war in the Middle Eastern nation) because of its perceived targeting of "a specific race, culture, a real government or corporation, or any other real entity."[11] While this can be seen as simply an attempt at ethical policing of app content, it also points to assumptions about the controversial nature of religion in popular media content, and that certain media platforms, such as games, should be neutral spaces avoiding not only stereotyping, but also complex narratives related to religious history and tradition. This limiting of how religion is dealt with in app and digital culture is something not seen in game development in general, since many popular games draw on religious narratives, characters, and symbols as central themes directing gameplay. The move toward serious gaming has meant that games often deal with very complex historical and cultural framings as religious and political narratives often underlie gameplay.

Reflecting an implied secularization theory, a third reason religion tends to be ignored in relation to gaming is that digital media are seen as the epitome of modernity and therefore imagined as anathema to religious practice. Such secularist assumptions draw from the work of early sociologists such as Karl Marx and Max Weber, who have been repopularized by authors such as Dawkins and Hitchens, who claim that society is becoming increasingly secularized; this work also contends that scientific progress, especially technological progress, will bring about religion's eventual decline.[12] Some have argued that because digital media and networks bring different traditions in close contact with one another, allowing alternative voices to have a global platform, this will ultimately dissolve traditional faith structures. Indeed, some frame the internet in particular as a catalyst for the potential secularization of society. Nonetheless, as the scholar of religion and digital media Christopher Helland claims, "Religion on the internet is a unique phenomenon. Due to its massive online presence, it challenges traditional academic theories that link the secularization process with developments in modernity and technology."[13] In fact, there is no one evolution of technology. Since the mid-1990s, many religions and religious actors have used digital information technology in radically different ways to spread and practice their faith.[14] Consequently, as the chapters in this volume demonstrate, claims that the growth of technology and of secularization go hand in hand are unfounded.

Finally, the claim is often made that because digital games are a "virtual" medium, that means they are unreal or do not reflect reality. Indeed, the question of whether digital games can be viewed as an authentic form of expression has been raised in the courts. In April 2002, the U.S. district judge Stephen N. Limbaugh Sr. ruled that digital games are incapable of conveying ideas based on reality, and that digital images are not "real" and therefore enjoy no constitutional protection. As evidence, St. Louis County presented the judge with videotaped excerpts from four games, all in the first-person shooter genre. In June 2011, the U.S. Supreme Court overturned the ruling, and declared that digital games are covered under the First Amendment: "Like the protected books, plays and movies that preceded them, video games communicate ideas – and even social messages – through many familiar literary devices (such as characters, dialogue, plot, and music) and through features distinctive to the medium (such as the player's interaction with the virtual world)."[15]

Soon after *Resistance: Fall of Man*'s release, the Church of England claimed that the digital depiction desecrated the actual physical cathedral and violated copyright.[16] To prevent further virtual desecrations, the cathedral announced its "Sacred Digital Guidelines," which included provisions that game designers "respect our sacred spaces as places of prayer, worship, peace learning and heritage," and "do not assume that sacred space interiors are copyright free."[17] While publicly apologizing, Sony responded to the controversy by arguing that "throughout the whole process we have sought permission where necessary" and, furthermore, that the game "is entertainment, like Doctor Who or any other science fiction. It is not based on reality at all."[18] It is clear that a number of issues and assumptions have framed religion and gaming as a contentious meeting, at odds with one another. But the study of this intersection is not only fruitful and worthwhile, but in our minds, it also contributes new depth to current explorations in game studies.

THEMES IN THE STUDY OF RELIGION AND GAMING

Because of the relatively brief history of digital gaming and its neglect by scholars of religion and media, the academic study of religion in gaming has a correspondingly short genealogy. Scholarly work began to surface in the middle of the first decade of the twenty-first century and gained momentum through discussions hosted at the American Academy of Religion's annual meeting later in the decade. In 2007, in a panel called "Born Digital and Born Again Digital: Religion in Virtual Gaming Worlds," scholars presented work on religiously themed games, the problematic of violent narratives in religious gaming, and the rise of the Christian gaming industry. In 2008, the panel "Just Gaming?: Virtual Worlds and Religious Studies" considered the use and presence of religious rituals and narratives in mainstream video gaming. These presentations drew attention to the need for more focused and systematic study of religion in gaming and virtual worlds. To date, only two full-length books have been dedicated solely to the critical study of religion and gaming. The edited volume *Halos and Avatars: Playing Video Games with God* offers a variety of religious critiques and responses regarding the nature and content of video games from scholars, religious practitioners, and game producers. William Sims Bainbridge in *eGods: Faith versus Fantasy in Computer Gaming* (2013) looks at conceptualizations of the sacred in massively multiplayer online role-playing games.

In considering the current state of scholarship on religion and gaming, it is important to note that research has often focused on a few specialized topics. One of the first areas of scholarly inquiry focused on religious education research as it related to video games, including pedagogical reflections on using gaming within religious education,[19] and how video games may be used to contribute to religious identity formation and the development of critical reflection.[20] Such work has frequently focused on the symbolism and narratives of explicitly religious-themed games. Related to this work, some scholars have considered how specific religious groups, especially within the Christian tradition, have approached or responded to games and gaming culture. Here we see studies unpacking the cultural and theological stories underlying popular games such as *Left Behind: Eternal Forces* and those seeking to provide frameworks for a critical evaluation of games based on the boundaries of specific faith communities.[21] Clifford Scholtz emphasizes that the study of games by religious groups and for religious education highlights a number of themes that are shared with the broader field of game studies; these include the exploring of identity negotiation, ritual, and flow theory in media environments.[22]

Researchers have also examined specifically how popular mainstream video games, such as *Halo* or *Assassin's Creed,* use religion as a narrative tool or plot device.[23] In this case, the focus has been on the role played by religion and on religious intertextuality in reading video games. The incorporation of religious symbols and characters may have unintended consequences for gameplay. For instance, Mark Hayse has argued that "religion within video games tends to suffer from a narrative and procedural incongruity," since mixing religion and gaming can be inherently problematic.[24] He notes, as similarly observed by Bogost, that the adoption of the procedural rhetoric, especially as it relates to violent narratives in mainstream games, informs religious narratives in ways that challenge the traditional framing of morals and codes of behavior.[25] Issues such as these have been studied in detail in the rising scholarship around Islamogaming, which has questioned how gaming narratives and environments may enforce religious and ethnic stereotypes or be used to present alternative identity representations.[26] Vít Šisler, a pioneer in this area, has demonstrated the intentionality of Arab game designers to subvert and refashion traditional Western framings of Arab characters as villains. This demonstrates how religious representation can be used to create "serious games," thereby turning gameplay into an important arena for religious and political discourse.[27] Such inquiries into the consequences of certain game narratives and structures on player beliefs and behaviors are of interest not only to this subfield, but also to game studies in general.

More recently, scholars have taken an interest in the relationship between virtual play, the sacred, and the performance of religion in gaming.[28] Considering, for instance, how games present and offer rituals that mimic attributes of religiosity, which add purpose and meaning to gameplay in this context, emphasis is frequently placed on the gaming environment and the experiential nature of gaming.[29] Drawing on Huizinga's concept of the magic circle as the way to explore the relationship between play and symbolic and religious ritual and magic, some work in this category has additionally considered the nature of the sacred and magic in gaming. Notable here is the work of Rachel Wagner, who has explored in detail the ways video games evoke the "otherworldly" and encourage an escape from the daily or mundane in the same way that religious ritual invites practitioners into a space of play and re-imagination.[30] Wagner has also produced a monograph giving significant attention to the relationship between religion and gaming, dealing with gaming in a broad context of religious imagination and virtuality.[31] Her work explores what she calls "first-person shooter religion" as a theoretical frame to discuss how the boundaries of computer and gaming culture configure the gaming experience in a manner similar to the ways religious culture and tradition frame behavior in a religious space.[32] As Wagner illustrates in "God in the Game," such implicit religion is even more apparent in the proliferation of handheld digital devices, which offer an almost religious vision by imposing order on a chaotic environment driven by information overload.[33] Implicit religion recognizes that seemingly secular practices may serve a religious role in people's everyday lives,[34] which means that traditional religious language and notions can be transposed onto actions and artifacts previously seen as nonreligious.[35] Therefore, this area of research adds to innovative theoretical thinking on issues arising from gaming studies, and considers how the nature of serious games and the gamification of culture may impact and have application to wider social relationships and contexts.

OVERVIEW OF THE BOOK

This book brings together a range of compelling and important contributors on religion and gaming to offer an overview and synthesis of key questions and approaches being taken in this growing area of research: the study of religiously themed games; considering the role religion plays in mainstream games; and finally – though at first glance it may seem a completely secular enterprise – reflection on how gaming can be seen as a form of implicit religion in terms of experience and expression. Although scholars have paid attention to the dominant narratives in religiously themed games, further work is needed on the implications of such constructs for gamers and each community's presentation of religious identity. Mainstream games such as *Halo* and *The Legend of Zelda* frequently evoke or rely on religious narratives, symbols, and rituals to frame and facilitate gameplay. The ways in which video games and virtual world environments, such as *Second Life* and *World of Warcraft*, might offer players religious experiences has received some attention. However, this raises additional issues about the extent to which religious themes underlie digital storytelling, and the implications this has for the gaming experience. Religious-like experiences or gaming encounters can indeed be described in religious terms. Furthermore, the question of how gaming practice and culture might be discerned and understood as a form of implicit religion emerges especially when secular activities take on a sacred role or meaning for individuals. *Playing with Religion* draws together a range of studies from innovative scholars, which coincide with these three common areas of inquiry, in order to map and evaluate how studying religion in digital gaming contributes to a fuller understanding of gaming culture.

The chapters in part I, "Explorations in Religiously Themed Games," discuss the implications of deliberately using various religious narratives and themes as the basis for designing gameplay. The production of religiously themed games raises many interesting and important questions regarding how digital gaming may influence the presentation and perception of different religious identities in contemporary culture. It also raises issues about how religious groups may react to the integration of such themes at the core of gameplay.

Jason Anthony in "Dreidels to *Dante's Inferno:* Toward a Typology of Religious Games" maintains that digital games entangle the mind with many of the same mysteries as religious practice. He argues, however, that game studies do not yet possess the critical apparatus to interpret religiously themed digital media productively. Using Greece as a backdrop, Anthony's chapter offers a seven-dimension typology, which achieves two goals. On the one hand, it creates for game studies a unified language that bridges religious games, past and future. On the other hand, it will assist game designers in creating more sophisticated religious characters, themes, and moods.

Isamar Carrillo Masso and Nathan Abrams in "Locating the Pix-elated Jew: A Multimodal Method for Exploring Judaism in *The Shivah*" ask the question, "Where has the pixelated Jew gone?" They maintain that while images of Jews have been examined in almost all other popu-lar media, they have not yet been fully explored in the realm of digital gaming. Using the point-and-click, single-player, hard-boiled Jewish de-tective video game *The Shivah* as a case study, they uncover and discuss representations of Judaism by taking a semiotic approach derived from film studies and combining it with a new corpus-based critical discourse analysis: the multimodal approach. Their emergent method explores the representation of Judaism and questions of religious-based beliefs, behaviors, values, ethics, and faith in the religious adventure game. This study is significant because it reforms the understanding of the role that Judaism in particular, and religion in general, plays in video game ecologies.

Xenia Zeiler in "The Global Mediatization of Hinduism through Digital Games: Representation versus Simulation in *Hanuman: Boy War-rior*" discloses the negotiation of Hindu authority and identity in digital gaming contexts. *Hanuman: Boy Warrior* (Sony Computer Entertain-ment Europe, 2009) is the first entirely India-developed digital game based on Hindu mythology. However, instead of being applauded, the game has caused heated debates on the appropriateness of incorporating Hindu deities into gaming environments. The chapter discusses both the game's narrative and its representations of Hanuman, in relation to rec-ognized Hindu texts and narratives and the intense international debate the game instigated. Zeiler argues that in order to position and sustain themselves in diaspora environments, diaspora-based religious organi-zations and communities require and often utilize out-of-the-ordinary means for self-representation and authority negotiation. *Hanuman: Boy Warrior*, in particular, allows an American audience an easily decipher-able way to understand the broader religious issues and values of Hindu identity.

Finally, Brenda Gardenour Walter in "*Silent Hill* and *Fatal Frame*: Finding Transcendent Horror in and beyond the Haunted Magic Circle" discusses the formalized religions and rituals constructed within two Japanese survival horror game worlds. In *Silent Hill*, the rules and rituals of the Order, the game's primary cult, are vital for the deciphering of the plot and the survival of the main character and therefore the player. In *Fatal Frame*, the player journeys to sacred sites such as Shinto shrines and Buddhist temples and uses ritual objects such as sacred mirrors, masks, and plaited ropes in the performance of conflated and scrambled Shinto and Buddhist rituals. While the religious structures within these different game worlds are dissimilar, both use transcendent horror and go beyond what Walter calls the "haunted magic circle." Through trans-media storytelling, the magic circle is unbound, thereby allowing the player-pilgrim to find individual and communal alternative religious experiences, identities, and narratives beyond traditional formal religion.

The chapters in part II, "Religion in Mainstream Games," focus on the ways mainstream games rely on or utilize religious strategies or characters to frame gameplay, and the implications this has for the gaming experience. Attention is given to how religiously infused digital storytelling may shape player perceptions and experiences of the game world and the unintentional consequences of such integration.

Vít Šisler in "From *Kuma\War* to *Quraish*: Representation of Islam in Arab and American Video Games" maintains that game studies needs to understand the symbolic and ideological dimensions of how Islam is represented. Šisler discusses American and Arab video games, analyzing the ways in which they (a) construct virtual representations of Islam and Muslims; and (b) communicate these representations to their audiences. The chapter compares and contrasts the audiovisual, narrative, and procedural elements of two different games of a similar genre (one American and one Arab).

To offer a model for conceptualizing the virtual realities and complex identities of contemporary gaming, Rabia Gregory in "Citing the Medieval: Using Religion as World-Building Infrastructure in Fantasy MMORPGs" analyzes the role of "neomedievalism" in *Shadowbane* (Wolfpack 2003). The chapter proposes that "game designers . . . incorporate elements of medieval religion into their products because neomedieval religious elements can narrate a game world's story without direct involvement from game masters or lengthy scripted dialogues from non-player characters." Gregory indicates that neomedieval religious systems and cosmologies invented for video games are not just replicas of historical religions. Instead, they reflect contemporary values, resonate with modern audiences, and guide players into and through gaming worlds.

In "Hardcore Christian Gamers: How Religion Shapes Evangelical Play," Shanny Luft explores how evangelicals share their faith in different online chat rooms related to gaming. He shows that their religiosity is overt, as members engage in online Bible study, post prayer requests, and share spiritual testimonies with one another. Luft finds it interesting that most of the games discussed on these forums have a common characteristic of overt depictions of violence. Elucidating some of the ways in which religion impacts evangelical engagement with video games, Luft considers how these Christians intertwine religion and gaming.

Peter Likarish in "Filtering Cultural Feedback: Religion, Censorship, and Localization in *Actraiser* and Other Mainstream Video Games" explores how the content and language of a game are adjusted before it is released in a country in which it was not produced. The chapter examines why religious content, and even symbolism that is only tangentially religious, is susceptible to alteration. Likarish argues that "cultural feedback" is what makes religious terminology and iconography so very sensitive.

The final part, "Gaming as Implicit Religion," looks at the ways digital games and gaming environments facilitate or encourage forms of religion-like practice, in which secular activities may take on sacred roles or meanings for individuals. These chapters consider how the act of gaming itself, and the meaning-making processes brought by gamers to such digital experiences, evokes emotions and processes that emulate implicitly religious behavior, which in turn have interesting implications for our understanding of gameplay. This understudied area may be the most productive for future research.

Rachel Wagner in "The Importance of Playing in Earnest" argues that the error usually made when thinking about games and religion is to assume that religion is "serious" whereas games are "fun." Wagner maintains that games and religion share a fundamental similarity: both are order-making activities that offer a mode of escape from contemporary life, and both demand, at least temporarily, that practitioners give themselves over to a predetermined set of rules that offer a system of order that is comforting for its very predictability. Furthermore, the greatest offense to both religion and play is to break the rules, that is, to become an apostate or a cheater. Wagner suggests that, whether we are religious or not, thinking critically about play affords us the freedom to take responsibility for the games we choose to play.

To illustrate the religious effectiveness of digital games, Oliver Steffen in "'God Modes' and 'God Moods': What Does a Digital Game Need to Be Spiritually Effective?" explores the short horror game *The Path*. Steffen wonders if certain categories of games satisfy the same psychological needs as religion satisfies and suggests that the feelings associated with flow and disempowerment in *The Path* might be religiously relevant to some users. Steffen's chapter is significant because it suggests that digital games tend to offer the "god mood" that characterizes the popular notion of spirituality, which is focused on "mystical experiences," among other variables.

Michael Waltemathe in "Bridging Multiple Realities: Religion, Play, and Alfred Schutz's Theory of the Life-World" uses the first-person shooter game *Resistance: Fall of Man* to ask, "What is the relationship between play, religion, and virtual worlds?" Often, religious spaces in video games are dismissed as inconsequential, but Waltemathe argues that because both the religious experience and play relieve us of the tense and fundamental anxiety of what Schutz calls "paramount reality," play bridges the worlds of video games and the actual world. The chapter demonstrates that a sociophenomenological approach is crucial for understanding religion and games because it takes the individual player's perspective into account and describes the structure of human-machine interaction from this perspective. For Waltemathe, what makes a video game religious is the relationship between playfully experiencing symbolic universes and transposing those experiences to other parts of the life-world.

Finally, Kevin Schut in "They Kill Mystery: The Mechanistic Bias of Video Game Representations of Religion and Spirituality" maintains that the construction of the digital medium itself has an impact on the manner in which games handle religion. On one hand, because digital games can give players supernatural powers, they can easily offer the experience of being a god. But the systematic nature of game rules and computer programming produces a bias in the video game medium toward a mechanical, demystified representation of religion. The chapter's argument is not that the designers and players of video games are locked in an iron cage of rationalized religion. Instead, it is worth being aware that, uncorrected by any contrary force, video games have a tendency to mechanize faith, presenting an impoverished vision of what religions mean to their adherents.

EMERGING THEMES IN RELIGION AND DIGITAL GAMES

As illustrated in this collection, scholars in religious studies have begun to explore how video games can be seen as religious texts, can be framed in relation to religious experiences, or can serve as an extension of religious practice itself. Media scholars have noted that many games employ religious characters, narratives, and symbols, which shape gameplay in distinctive ways and create representations of various religious and cultural groups that are worthy of in-depth study. Therefore, this volume carefully considers a range of different religious narratives and symbols employed in religiously themed video games, as well as the impact and implications of video games created for religious markets.

Playing with Religion fills an important gap in the field of game studies by demonstrating that careful attention to the study of religious narratives, rituals, and behaviors within gaming can offer a fuller understanding of the social and cultural impact of the gaming experience on contemporary society. It also offers focused reflection on how video games might potentially inform or reform different individuals' and groups' understandings of the practice of religion.

This collection offers an overview of the variety of ways religion plays a role and is present in digital games through various methods, including case studies, ethnographic research, content analysis, and interviews with game designers and gaming communities. These explorations provide a broad and rich foundation for theoretical reflection on key themes, including how religious gaming is constructed ideologically, and how different expressions of religion and religiosity are manifested in different gaming genres and narratives. *Playing with Religion* also demonstrates a range of ways in which gaming can be analyzed as a religious-like act.

The contributors argue that the study of religious symbols, representations, and narratives reveals how gaming may have larger cultural and religious implications, which are frequently unforeseen by both game designers and players. This is seen in Walter's findings that presenting a "haunted magic circle" in gameplay, which associates religious narratives with the horror genre, can frame religion in ways that are both innovative and problematic. This is further seen in Šisler's study of Arab stereotyping in digital games and Zeiler's demonstration that employing sacred narratives can be highly problematic for different religious and cultural groups, since nontraditional religious interpretations may unintentionally make gameplay a source of cultural "othering," or Orientalization.

Another question raised in this collection is why religion is present at all within gaming, and why we may need to examine the implications this integration has for our understanding of play and playfulness in game theory more carefully. The work of Anthony specifically emphasizes that across history, religion and play have gone hand in hand as a way to instruct, inform, affirm, and inculcate players into specific narrative and world views. Consequently, the gaming enterprise can be seen as simultaneously playful and providing the inculcation of certain beliefs and behaviors; gaming must therefore be studied as a culture-building sphere. Steffen further argues that gameplay evokes unique patterns of flow, empowerment, and disempowerment that are associated with religious feelings. Because gaming may lead players to draw on broad religious narratives to explain their emotions and experiences, understanding religious language and tradition becomes essential in interpreting the process of gaming. This innate link between religion and play also raises interesting questions about how religion is framed or possibly extricated from a particular gaming context in order to avoid controversy, as emphasized in Likarish's work on gaming companies attempting to erase religion from contexts in which they perceive potential cultural conflict.

This volume also provides reflections on why gamers and game designers often read religion into the gaming context. Wagner suggests that it may be because religion and play exhibit shared qualities and encourage similar conditions, such as a need to define the cultural boundaries of a given space in order to break the perceived rules. Luft suggests that religious gamers often draw similar connections between games and religion in order to justify their participation and engagement in such a space and culture.

Finally, *Playing with Religion* offers a range of theoretical and methodological approaches for studying games. From Steffen's approach to studying ludological structures in light of spiritual efficacy as a way to explore gaming as a form of implicit religion, to Isamar Carrillo Masso and Nathan Abrams's development of a multimodal approach to game analysis to investigate meaning-making pathways in gameplay, we suggest that the study of religion and gaming can offer new tools and methods that can be applied to other areas of game studies. Overall, by highlighting what the integration of religion into digital games and gaming environments may mean and the larger cultural, social, and religious impact of such actions, this volume seeks to enliven discussion of the relationship between video games and religion.

CONCLUDING THOUGHTS

Playing with Religion draws much-needed attention to an emerging field of scholarship that combines the best elements of game studies and religious studies. We suggest that studying digital gaming is not merely an end in itself, but a means of displaying and unlocking the meaning of religion in contemporary society as a whole. Digital games are not simply mirrors that reflect culture. Rather, they frequently eschew or alter, like a funhouse mirror, assumptions about religion. This means they have the potential to inform or interpret religious practice as it is reflected back at us, with a selectivity determined by the source. Digital games do not simply mediate religion, but they also "mediatize" it. Stig Hjarvard in "The Mediatization of Religion: A Theory of the Media as Agents of Religious Change" describes the concept of mediatization: "the media have developed into an independent institution in society and as a consequence, other institutions become increasingly dependent on the media and have to accommodate the logic of the media in order to be able to communicate with other institutions and society as a whole."[36]

We suggest that game studies should not ignore how religions can and do shape gameplay. Together, these chapters share an understanding that gaming is a serious pursuit and that religion should also be taken seriously in public discussions related to digital games. Although in writing about the Manchester Cathedral, Ian Bogost in "Persuasive Games: The Reverence of *Resistance*" defends Sony's use of the cathedral, he criticizes the corporation's response as a self-defeating statement, which while addressing gun violence, does not speak to how the cathedral plays into the game itself. Bogost maintains that the need "to defend the artistic merits" of the game "is now left to the critic. For my part, I think the cathedral creates one of the only significant experiences in the whole game, one steeped in reverence for the cathedral and the church, rather than desecration."[37] To make sense of this terrain, game critics and scholars need to consider the different layers of how religion shapes not just the gaming experience but also the institutional and public response to it. This nuanced and multifaceted investigation of religion in gaming offers game studies, as Anthony's work argues, a unified language to understand how religion informs gaming. It also offers tools for deciphering the framing and impact of religious characters, themes, and moods.

Conversely, religious studies cannot ignore how games can and do shape faith practices. Despite the popular conception that religion and games do not mix, or at least do not mix well, this book shows how digital games have both intentionally and unintentionally become spaces to grapple with complex cultural histories, existential meanings, and religious narratives. Often, such interaction is intensified through what Likarish calls "cultural feedback," which refers to how content from one culture is appropriated and reinterpreted by game developers in a second culture, only to be reintroduced into the original culture in a recognizable, but discordant form. On the other hand, it could be, as Schut argues, that digital games have a bias toward what he calls "mechanized religion," a kind of mechanical theology that sees gods as technologies to be manipulated for power. In either case, as the controversy surrounding *Resistance: Fall of Man* shows, gaming has become an important sphere for cultural discourse that cannot be ignored. As Manchester resident Patsy McKie from Mothers Against Violence maintained, the game is "something that needs to be taken seriously first by the Church but also by parents."[38]

For the Church of England this was a matter, to borrow a phrase from Wagner's chapter, of utmost earnestness and thus of ultimate concern. For Sony, the cathedral was just part of a game. The church wanted to ignore the game. Sony wanted to ignore religion. As Schut suggests, this lack of nuance may be indicative of the relative adolescence of the medium; indeed, film took quite a few decades to mature as a tool for art and expression. Nonetheless, *Playing with Religion* adds to the public conversation something that is missing from much of the discussion concerning digital religious games: analysis of the games themselves, especially how religion plays out in them. We see the importance of exploring why video games use religious structures such as churches and cathedrals as central narratives and the implication of reading religion through the processes of play. By emphasizing the diverse ways in which religion potentially shapes the gaming experience, we hope to make space for a broader conversation between the scholars of media and of religion and to encourage a rich interdisciplinary exchange.

Demonstrating how religion offers important cultural meaning-making resources and symbolic scripts that still play an important role in contemporary popular culture, *Playing with Religion* provides an apologetic for religion in digital games. As Wagner illustrates, what makes the connection between religion and games defendable is that both provide order-making activities and escapes from the everyday; religion and gaming provide similar tools and map out overlapping world views. This book also defends the study of digital religious games because they provide important insights regarding contemporary culture and religion beyond the narrow confines of current debates. Zeiler demonstrates that religious organizations and communities often utilize tools offered by popular media culture to enact and affirm their distinctive religious identities for global audiences. In a similar fashion, Masso and Abrams stress that religious groups may seek to present themselves in video game ecologies in order to establish or negotiate their role in the wider culture.

Digital religious games have strong popular appeal and economic relevance, even if they have been a neglected area of study. We argue that because religion in gaming can have an impact on the collective imagination, studying such forms of popular culture is crucial.

NOTES

1. BBC News, "Cathedral Row over Video War Game," http://news.bbc.co .uk/2/hi/uk_news/england/manchester /6736809.stm.

2. BBC News, "Fantasy Meets Reality in Church Row," http://news.bbc .co.uk/2/hi/uk_news/england/man chester/6736809.stm.

3. We would like to thank Paul Emerson Teusner for his important input regarding the introduction as a whole and particularly the framing of the first paragraph.

4. Walter Ong, *The Presence of the Word: Some Prolegomena for Cultural and Religious History* (Minnesota: University of Minnesota Press, 1967).

5. Karen Sternheimer, *It's Not the Media: The Truth about Popular Culture's Influence on Children* (New York: Westview, 2003).

6. Entertainment Software Association, http://www.theesa.com.

7. Ibid.

8. James Gee, *What Video Games Have to Tell Us about Learning and Literacy* (New York: Palgrave, 2001).

9. David Grossman, "Teaching Kids to Kill," *Phi Kappa Phi National Forum 2000*, http://www.killology.org/article _teachkid.htm; Marjorie Heins, Brief Amica Curiae of Thirty Media Scholars, submitted to the U.S. Court of Appeals, Eighth Circuit, *Interactive Digital Software Association et al. v. St. Louis County et al.* (2002), http://www.fepproject.org /courtbriefs/stlouissummary.html; Henry Jenkins, "Lessons from Littleton: What Congress Doesn't Want to Hear about Youth and Media," *Independent Schools* (2002), http://www.nais.org/pubs/ismag .cfm?file_id=537&ismag_id=14.

10. "App Store Guidelines," reposted at http://www.cultofmac.com/58590 /heres-the-full-text-of-apples-new-app -store-guidelines/#p6smqGUzOLVFkS gv.99.

11. Jeffrey Grubb, "Apple: 'Want to Criticize Religion? Write a Book' – Don't Make a Game," *Venture Beat* (January 15, 2013), http://venturebeat.com/2013 /01/15/apple-want-to-criticize-religion -write-a-book-dont-make-a-game /#YrZCyRBPJbrTCQ1m.99h.

12. Richard Dawkins, *The God Delusion* (Boston: Houghton Mifflin, 2006); Christopher Hitchens, *God Is Not Great: How Religion Poisons Everything* (New York: Twelve/Hachette, 2007); Graeme Smith, *A Short History of Secularism* (London: Tauris, 2007).

13. Christopher Helland, "Online Religion as Lived Religion: Methodological Issues in the Study of Religious Participation on the Internet," *Heidelberg Journal of Religions on the Internet* 1, no. 1 (2005).

14. Heidi Campbell, "Spiritualising the Internet: Uncovering Discourses and Narratives of Religious Internet Usage," *Heidelberg Journal of Religions on the Internet* 1, no. 1 (2005).

15. *Brown, Governor of California v. Entertainment Merchants Association et al.*, http://www.supremecourt.gov /opinions/10pdf/08-1448.pdf.

16. BBC News, "Fantasy Meets Reality in Church Row."

17. Ruth Gledhill, "Manchester Cathedral Says Sony Apology Not Enough and Issues New Digital Rules," *Times Online*, July 6, 2007 (accessed March 3, 2009).

18. "Sony Apologises over Violent Game," *BBC Online*, June 15, 2007 (accessed October 17, 2008).

19. Scholtz, "Religious Education and the Challenge of Computer Games."

20. Hayse, "Religious Architecture in Videogames."

21. Schut, *Of Games and God.*

22. Scholtz, "Fascinating Technology."

23. Corliss, "Gaming with God"; Love, "Not-So-Sacred Quests."

24. Hayse, "Education (Religious)," 182.

25. Bogost, *Persuasive Games.*

26. Šisler, "Representation and Self-Representation"; Campbell, "Islamogaming."

27. Šisler, "Video Games, Video Clips, and Islam"; Šisler, "Palestine in Pixels"; Šisler, "Digital Arabs."

28. Plate, "Religion Is Playing Games."

29. Pargman and Jakobsson, "Do You Believe in Magic?"

30. Wagner, "Our Lady of Persistent Liminality"; Wagner, "Religion and Video Games."

31. Wagner, *Godwired.*

32. Wagner, "First-Person Shooter Religion."

33. Wagner, "God in the Game: Cosmopolitanism and Religious Conflict in Videogames," *Journal of the American Academy of Religion* 81, no. 1 (March 2013):249–261.

34. Bailey, "Implicit Religion of Contemporary Society."

35. Heidi A. Campbell, "Understanding the Relationship between Religion Online and Offline in a Networked Society," *Journal of the American Academy of Religion* 80, no. 1 (2011):64–93.

36. S. Hjarvard, "The Mediatization of Religion: A Theory of the Media as Agents of Religious Change," in *Northern Lights 2008: Yearbook of Film & Media Studies* (Bristol, England: Intellect Press, 2008), 11.

37. http://www.gamasutra.com/view/feature/1689/persuasive_games_the_reverence_of_.php.

38. Quoted in BBC News, "Cathedral Row over Video War Game."

REFERENCES

Bailey, E. "The Implicit Religion of Contemporary Society: Some Studies and Reflections." *Social Compass* 37, no. 4 (1990):483–497.

Bainbridge, William Sims. *eGods: Faith versus Fantasy in Computer Gaming.* New York: Oxford University Press, 2013.

Bogost, Ian. *Persuasive Games: The Expressive Power of Videogames.* Cambridge, Mass.: MIT Press, 2007.

Campbell, Heidi. "Islamogaming: Digital Dignity via Alternative Storytellers." In *Halos and Avatars: Playing Video Games with God.* Edited by C. Detweiler, 63–74. Louisville, Ky.: Westminster John Knox, 2010.

Corliss, Vander. "Gaming with God: A Case for the Study of Religion in Video Games." 2011. http://digitalrepository.trincoll.edu/theses/5.

Detweiler, Craig, ed. *Halos and Avatars: Playing Video Games with God.* Louisville, Ky.: Westminster John Knox, 2010.

Hayse, Mark. "Education (Religious)." In *Encyclopedia of Video Games: The Culture, Technology, and Art of Gaming.* Edited by Mark J. P. Wolf, 181–183.

Santa Barbara, Calif.: ABC-CLIO, 2012.

———. "Religious Architecture in Videogames: Perspectives from Curriculum Theory and Religious Education." Ph.D. diss., Trinity Evangelical Divinity School, 2009.

Love, Mark Cameron. "Not-So-Sacred Quests: Religion, Intertextuality, and Ethics in Video Games." *Religious Studies and Theology* 29, no. 2 (2010):191–213.

Pargman, Daniel, and Peter Jakobsson. "Do You Believe in Magic?: Computer Games in Everyday Life." *European Journal of Cultural Studies* 11, no. 2 (2008):225–243.

Plate, Brent. "Religion Is Playing Games: Playing Video Gods, Playing to Play." *Religious Studies and Theology* 29, no. 2 (2010):215–230.

Scholtz, Christopher. "Fascinating Technology: Computer Games as an Issue for Religious Education." *British Journal of Religious Education* 27, no. 2 (2005):173–184.

———. "Religious Education and the Challenge of Computer Games: Research Perspectives on a New Issue." In *Towards a European Perspective on Religious Education.* Edited by Erin Steuter and Deborah Willis, 256–267. Sweden: University of Lund Press, 2004.

Schut, Kevin. *Of Games and God: A Christian Exploration of Video Games.* Grand Rapids, Mich.: Brazos, 2012.

Šisler, Vít. "Digital Arabs: Representation in Video Games." *European Journal of Cultural Studies* 11, no. 2 (2008):203–220.

———. "Palestine in Pixels: The Holy Land, Arab-Israeli Conflict, and Reality Construction in Video Games." *Middle East Journal of Culture and Communication* 2, no. 2 (2009):275–292.

———. "Representation and Self-Representation: Arabs and Muslims in Digital Games." In *Gaming Realities: A Challenge for Digital Culture.* Edited by M. Santorineos and N. Dimitriadi, 85–92. Athens: Fourmos Center for Digital Culture, 2006.

———. "Video Games, Video Clips, and Islam: New Media and the Communication of Values." In *Muslim Societies in the Age of Mass Consumption.* Edited by Johanna Pink, 231–258. Newcastle: Cambridge Scholars, 2009.

Steuter, Erin, and Deborah Wills. "Gaming at the End of the World: Coercion, Conversion and the Apocalyptic Self in *Left Behind: Eternal Forces* Digital Play." *Reconstruction: Studies in Contemporary Culture* 10, no. 1 (2010). http://reconstruction.eserver.org/101/recon_101_steuter_wills.shtml.

Wagner, Rachel. "First-Person Shooter Religion: Algorithmic Culture and Inter-Religious Encounter." *Cross Currents* 62, no. 2 (2012):181–203.

———. *Godwired: Religion, Ritual and Virtual Reality.* London: Routledge, 2012.

———. "Our Lady of Persistent Liminality: Virtual Church, Cyberspace, and Second Life." In *God in the Details,* 2nd ed. Edited by Michael Mazur and Kate McCarthy. London: Routledge, 2010.

———. "Religion and Video Games." In *Understanding Religion and Popular Culture.* Edited by Terry Ray Clark and Dan W. Clanton Jr., 118–140. New York: Routledge, 2012.

PART ONE

Explorations in Religiously Themed Games

Dreidels to *Dante's Inferno*

TOWARD A TYPOLOGY OF RELIGIOUS GAMES

Jason Anthony

IT'S HARD TO IMAGINE TWO MORE DIFFERENT ARENAS THAN games and religion. Games strike us as a pleasant distraction, a space where amiable conflicts play out to a conclusion which, tomorrow, won't matter much. Religious activity is clearly quite different. It calls for utmost seriousness and a minimum of conflict, and our commitment will yield consequences that can last a lifetime – or longer, depending on the views we hold on eternity.

So goes the conventional wisdom. Yet games and religion share a long, rich, and intertwined history, even in the digital age. Consider a brief snapshot of the events at the 2011 Game Developers Conference. The world's top designers, developers, and game studios have gathered to discuss the state of their art. Design guru and director of the NYU Game Center Frank Lantz steps up to the podium. In a highly anticipated talk, he advocates at length for the "sublime" in games. He explains that the venerable game of Go held a place in Confucian practice, and asks why poker and other complex games could not attain a similar stature: "Why can't a video game be a spiritual discipline?" And he continues: "I want more video games that give me a space in which to entangle my mind with the mysterious infinite secrets of the universe. And this doesn't have to be precious. Poker proves that it can have something vulgar and violent and dirty and shameful and dangerous and addictive. And if it's deep enough, it can slingshot you all the way around to new orbits of insight and higher levels of consciousness."[1]

In the days that follow, the conference takes up this gauntlet. Eric Zimmerman – who had been working with Deepak Chopra on the con-

sole meditation game *Leela* (discussed below) – coordinates the annual
game design challenge. He gives three prominent designers the task of
coming up with a new game that addresses the theme "Bigger than Jesus:
Games as Religion." The previous year's winner, on a totally unrelated
challenge, had been *Heavenville*, "a sort of stock market that measures
the social currency of dead people."[2]

The result of Zimmerman's challenge made headlines. Jason Rohrer
came up with *Chain World* – a whole universe on a flash drive. The game
could only be possessed and played by a single person at a time. Each
player would live a life, be born and die, then pass the game on, leaving
traces of their short virtual life to be discovered by the next possessor
of the artifact. Because Rohrer's game evoked a meditative practice, em-
braced a closed and fervent community, and presented a position on the
ephemerality of life, *Wired* magazine devoted a feature to the question
of whether Rohrer had designed a new religion.[3]

This kind of work would seem to be the purview of priests and shamans. And the attitudes of game designers on this frontier of religious
thinking remain complex; Rohrer is a professed atheist, and Lantz has
been vocal in his criticism of organized religion.[4] Yet their fascination
with religion is extensive and takes many forms. Games are exploring
ways to tap the mind's capacity for transcendent experience. Major studio titles regularly use religious characters and themes from existing
traditions. Players are invited to immerse themselves in worlds where
new religions can be explored.

The critical work to be done here is daunting. This chapter offers one
strategy for parsing that wide field: a backward look. Can we understand
more about the religious dimensions of digital games by looking broadly
at the history of pre-digital games in religion? I make the following case:
games have intersected deeply with religious practice across centuries.
These intersections may be broadly placed into four types, each a different strategy for engaging with the "divine" or with the central object
of a religious tradition. The four categories will then be held up to the
current digital gaming landscape. Some of the four historic types will
have direct corollaries; others will not. Those digital games that don't
follow a historical precedent may prove to be of special interest, pointing
the way toward the unique aspects of the digital medium and the digital

moment. In short, how do we understand something like Rohrer's *Chain World* – bold, inventive, and puzzlingly unique? A historical typology of sacred games might allow scholars to place such a development within a larger historical and critical story.

Such an undertaking comes with obvious reservations. An exhaustive survey of religious games is difficult if not impossible. The ludic arts present challenges, both historiographical and contextual, since they are often popular, plastic, and ephemeral performances. Most gravely, placing religious games correctly – and without offense – within a nexus of religious practice, meaning, and relative cultural importance is prone to missteps, especially for traditions that are foreign to the researcher or are no longer extant.

That said, such a typology's value might outweigh its limitations. I argue that religious games in history have functioned in one (or more) of four ways: as educational mechanisms; as festal elements in public or private rituals; as divinatory methods; and occasionally, as orthodox forms of worship in and of themselves. Digital games have begun to expand these functions in many ways, and three new directions are mapped here. The first opens new virtual spaces in which traditional religious activities can unfold. The second creates alternative realities in which players engage with new metaphors of the religious. The third offers players the chance to try on the perspective of the divine itself. Before getting into the specifics of these categories, I briefly contextualize the reach, history, and definition of games in religion.

GAMED RELIGION: THE GREEK CASE STUDY

The London Summer Olympics have captured the world's attention at the time of this writing (2012). Though they are no longer religious events, today's Olympics still carry an echo of public ritual, as historian John MacAloon has carefully explored. The modern Olympics come cloaked with a quasi-religious gravitas, from the torch run that "[initiates] the period of public liminality" to the "rites of closure and reaggregation with the normative order."[5]

For the ancient Greeks, the holiness of the games was gloriously explicit. Athletes swore oaths to fast and to observe chastity as they trained, offered sacrifices upon their success, and atoned when they cheated. During the games, debts among spectators were paid and crimes forgiven. Gods were invoked in poetry composed and read for the victors.[6] In Philostratus's description, the players themselves were woven into the rites. To open the games, runners were placed one *stadion* away from the altar, the priest waved a torch, the race began, and the winner "put fire to the sacred portions,"[7] creating an inseparable fusion of game and ritual.

Olympic races represented an engagement with the sacred for player, priest, and spectator. Yet these were far from the only games that Greeks wove into their religious lives. Events at Delphi, Nemea, and Corinth helped make up a vast athletic liturgical calendar, which also included funeral games, like those staged for Patroclus in *The Iliad*.[8] Among non-athletes, devotees might compete at carding wool (an early step in the weaving process), playing the flute, or singing at sacred festivals in Delphi and Athens.[9] Western drama itself comes from a contest central to the springtime festivals for Dionysus. (Some scholars, ancient and modern, argue that the word "tragedy" derives from the root word for he-goat, perhaps the prize given to early winners.)[10] The word used for dramatic scenes between characters – *agones* – is the same word used for Olympic events. It's not far wrong to see the whole sober canon of Athenian tragedy as a series of contests within a contest, games within a holy game.

Narratives of Greek divinity also reflect this theme. Atalanta made a footrace the basis of her courtship, and Orion met his death in a contest played between Apollo and Artemis. Arachne met her doom in a contest against the goddess Athena. The Trojan War itself began with an *agon;* three goddesses made Paris the judge of a beauty contest between them, similar to the beauty contests held on the island of Lesbos in the sanctuary of Zeus, Hera, and Dionysus.[11]

The West at one time had a thriving tradition of sacred games. That tradition waned considerably with the rise of Christianity, for reasons we can only conjecture.[12] Yet puzzles, games, and competitions have surfaced even in Christian traditions; and when we look more broadly across other traditions, regions, and epochs, examples of gamed engagements with the divine are never hard to find.

Before delving into examples, the term "religious game" needs some defining. For the purpose of the first typology, this chapter will consider a game *religious* if it is practiced in conjunction with a religious body, holiday, or ritual. This casts a wide net, and captures games with vastly diverging levels of ritual importance. A game with real political and symbolic consequences, such as the egg races of Rapa Nui, seems an altogether different encounter than, say, unsupervised children spinning a dreidel in a Reform Jewish congregation.

So much for *religious* – what do we mean by *game*? Definitions of what constitutes a game are slippery, and many of them might encompass a good many religious rituals. Consider dharma combat in the Zen traditions, or structured debates in Tibetan Buddhism. These are ritual discussions about sober metaphysics, yet their rules and enactment can be surprisingly lively. In the Tibetan tradition, two contestants face each other: a sitting defender and a standing challenger. The showdown can attract spectators who cheer and jeer. There is a strict rule set and a declared victor.[13] Voices are raised and animated, hands clap in a raucous and ritual rhythm. Smiles are common, as is playful mockery. This sounds game-like. And this ritual model of two opposing forces is hardly an uncommon one. But to avoid chaos in defining what is a game and what isn't, this chapter will use a more utilitarian approach. Games here all replicate or exhibit a marked similarity to games played outside of religious contexts. For instance, dreidel spinning, footraces, and the Mayan public ball game of *ulama* are (or were) played as games both inside and outside of religious contexts. In contrast, Tibetan debates are not "played" anywhere outside of the monastery, and so are not considered religious games here.

Finally, the category names below are new and mostly neologisms from Greek roots. This is both to avoid confusion with English terms, and to playfully offer a nod to the Greeks' contribution to this history.

Didactic Games

The first category may be the most familiar to modern readers. Didactic games – from the Greek διδάσκειν, "to teach" – are games that instruct players about a religious doctrine or history. Games are powerful teaching tools, both because they are an easy avenue for communicating with children and, as Stephen Sniderman points out in "Unwritten Rules," because they inherently teach about larger societal rules and norms.

Didactic religious games are also often distinguished by their limited ritual role. They generally focus on passing along rules and concepts, rather than offering a sacred experience. Such games may take place in sacred space, such as a worship center, but are rarely seen as sacred events. In a phrase, didactic games embrace the "divine as lesson," mostly pointing to the sacred without participating in it. A familiar archetype might be Bible camp in the Christian tradition: scripture charades, crossword puzzles, chapter-and-verse freeze tag, and the like. Super Bowl Sunday School, credited to Leah O'Connell, has students answer Bible trivia to march down the length of a classroom to reach the "eternal endzone."[14] Such games are often adapted from secular play for religious purposes, layering doctrinal teachings onto a more profane structure.

A more ancient example might be the game of dreidel, a welcome institution of the Chanukah holidays. According to the story, devout Jews would use dreidel to disguise their Torah studies from the approaching forces of the Seleucid monarchy by hiding their scrolls and pretending to play. The gambling game is still played by the original rules, yet children are taught that the letters on the sides of the dreidel also stand for the phrase *Nes Gadol Hayah Sham,* which means "a great miracle happened there." (Or, for dreidels manufactured in Israel, *Nes Gadol Haya Po,* "a great miracle happened *here.*") Some scholars teach that the four letters point to the four Jewish exiles, under Babylonian, Persian, Greek, and Roman rule. Layers of teaching elements on a secular game make this a good example of didactic play.

Hestiasic Games

This term comes from the Greek word ἐστιάω, "to offer a feast or festival." It connotes sacred events celebrated at home, rather than at the temple. This category broadly embraces games that occur as a lighthearted part of a sacred celebration, the sort of games that might be played at some distance from a formal site of prayer or contemplation. Such religious games might be those that most closely and exclusively aim for "fun," the ineffable quality that, according to Johan Huizinga in *Homo Ludens*, "characterizes the essence of play." Hestiasic games, then, might be thought of as lively games that take place with the divine as context or occasion.

Consider Ramadan games. In parts of Iraq, the nightly game of mhaibis is considered a welcome part of the season. After the nightly feasting, teams square off, and one player hides a ring in his fist (*mhaibis* means "little ring"). It is up to the other team to guess who is holding it. They discern this through a close scrutiny of facial gestures and body postures, and star players gain great acclaim. Veteran mhaibis champion Lateef Moussa claims to have correctly guessed the holder of the mhaibis from among four hundred players.[15]

Such seasonal games are common. During Russian Christmastide (Svyatki), divination games about the coming year are a familiar rite. Hindu wedding games, where the romantic future of the couple is playfully divined, might function similarly. Clifford Geertz, in his classic study of Balinese cockfights, explains how these popular and rowdy contests sometimes occur as an integral counterpart to Njepi (Day of Silence) celebrations.[16] Like didactic games, hestiasic games are rarely proffered as ritual means to access the sacred in a sober, orthodox way. Rather, they are lighthearted elements of religious seasons or festivals.

Poimenic Games

Poimenic games represent a sharp departure from this casual approach. They propose instead that the divine is an active, interested player. The term comes from the Greek ποιμὴν, which means "shepherd" in the sense that this word is used in Matthew 25:32 of the Christian scriptures. There, the Son of Man is described as separating the nations in the way that a shepherd separates sheep from goats. In a poimenic game, the divine makes an active selection between two or more contestants, or between two or more courses of action. This is the "divine as player."

The annual *Tangata Manu* competition on Easter Island was a well-documented example. The bird-man for the coming year was selected by means of an elaborate obstacle course. Each contestant would appoint a representative to try to collect the season's first sooty tern egg, laid on outlying Motu Nui island. The path was treacherous; contestants would wait for the birds in a cave, scale the cliffs to reach the nests, then descend and swim back through shark-infested waters. Many were killed. The first to return with an intact egg won the right for his sponsor to be the bird-man for the coming year. The position carried a number of honors and responsibilities: the *Tangata Manu* lived in a ceremonial house for a year, he received tribute, and his clan had the sole right to collect the eggs from that outlying island. As the winner, he was regarded as having earned a special favor from the god Make-Make.[17]

Here, the very structure of a game – an uncertain situation that is resolved in favor of a single winner – makes it a formal fit for divine intervention. Another example was the embrace of trial by combat in Northern Europe. Litigants in a range of legal matters squared off. The ritual was overseen by priests, and might include other elements, such as touching blades to a patch of contested soil. The winner earned his vindication from God (the official term for such an outcome was *judicium dei*, "God decides").[18]

Poimenic games also include more lighthearted contests, such as the annual diving competition during Eastern Orthodox Epiphany celebrations. However, they are often gravely serious, as in the *Ullamaliztli* games of the Aztec Empire where, by some accounts, one team lost their heads after the game. In short, poimenic games are staged in the hope that the divine will become involved directly in the play, and show favor or reveal its favor for the winning side.

Praxic Games

The fourth type of game represents yet another departure. If didactic and hestiasic games have an informal air in a divine context, and a poimenic game is one in which the divine intercedes to show favor to only the winner, then the praxic game is an outright engagement with the sacred, win or lose. Praxic games are stand-alone practices of devotion. The term is taken from the Greek πρᾶξις, which means "action," and carries the Eastern Orthodox Christian connotation of praxis, a term for a material practice of the faith, rather than an explanation of belief or theology. Such a game might be described as the "divine as experience."

The game of *WeiQi,* or Go, has already been mentioned. As early as the first century, historian Pan Ku argued in *The Book of Han* that becoming bound to the rigors of the game of Go would provide insight into the Tao. Play involves strategically placing black and white (or yellow) stones on a marked grid, which is filled with symbolism:

> There are on the Go board 360 intersections plus one. The number one is supreme and gives rise to the other numbers because it occupies the ultimate position and governs the four quarters. 360 represents the number of days in the [lunar] year. The division of the Go board into four quarters symbolizes the four seasons. The 72 points on the circumference represent the [five-day] weeks of the [Chinese lunar] calendar. The balance of Yin and Yang is the model for the equal division of the 360 stones into black and white.[19]

The Zen koan might also fit this definition of praxic game. Chinese court riddles of the fourteenth century were elaborate and poetic forms of wordplay; riddles might be posed and pondered for weeks. Some historians argue that these are the forerunners of koans, the poignant and enigmatic stories and riddles posed to initiates in Zen monasteries. By playing a variant of a classic riddle game, monks engaged in a pursuit at the heart of Zen Buddhism – chasing truth and the sudden, dramatic liberation of consciousness.[20]

Sumo provides a more muscular example. The game dates back at least fifteen hundred years, and maintains strong ties to Shinto worship. When the athletes enter the arena, the space is consecrated through a purification that involves a ritual pouring of sand. Both wrestlers theatrically raise and lower their feet, and the stomping is thought to drive away malignant spirits. One myth says that the sport was not intended to test the mettle of individual athletes, but instead to provide entertainment for the *kami,* or spirit gods. In this way, each contestant is fulfilling a divine purpose, and spectators are steeped in the rituals of preparation, such as the tossing of salt into the ring before a match, which take far longer than the sometimes brief fights in the ring. The arena itself is covered with a canopy that intentionally echoes the roof of a Shinto shrine.

In all of these examples, the praxic games are canonical engagements with the sacred. They are distinguished from poimenic games largely because they omit the element of divine favor. Simply playing such a game is an act of devotion.

THE DIGITAL COROLLARIES

What happens when we apply this thinking to the world of digital games? Some categories hold up neatly; others don't. Didactic games are widespread, as many traditions now playfully teach and evangelize through online games. On the other hand, poimenic games – those mostly pretechnological games where the divine chooses a winner – offer few digital counterparts.

Digital media also seem to chart new territory, offering new ways to explore and engage with sacredness. A parallel reality game, like an MMORPG, lets a Christian group go to an online fantasy world and fellowship in alternative identities. Deep RPGs let players play at worshiping new gods. How do these fit in with the outline above? The following sections explore the four categories just discussed, and three new ones are added to the mix: the allomythic, the allopolitical, and the theoptic, each defined below. While these new categories may not inhabit the same devotional space, each shows a new way of treading religious territory, made possible or popular by digital media. Other avenues may exist or may be invented, but these three have been most broadly adopted at the time of this writing.

Digital Didactic Games

The "divine as lesson" games – which educate about religious ideas or themes, but don't usually purport to offer a sacred experience – include hundreds if not thousands of digital examples. Religious gaming sites for children are common across the major traditions. The Christian market dates back to the dawn of the home computer in the early 1980s. The popular *Computer Bible Games* by John Conrod hit the shelves in 1984. Simple educational games in the book included offerings like *Daniel and the Lion's Den*, which lets players use prayers to shut the mouths of hungry lions. The most famous Christian game might be *Left Behind: Eternal Forces* (Inspired Media Entertainment, 2006). This relatively large-budget game offers an RTS experience of the book of Revelation, as interpreted through the popular rapture fiction series created by Tim LaHaye and Jerry B. Jenkins.

Jewish educational games have also shown an enterprising reach, and they exist all along the ideological spectrum. They follow narratives derived directly from the Tanach, such as the popular *Ehud's Courage and the Cunning Blade,* to more pensive explorations of Jewish traditions. *The Shivah* (Wadjet Eye Games, 2006), an award-winning game created by Dave Gilbert, follows Rabbi Russell Stone as he wrestles with faith, community, and an unsolved murder. His weapons include a highly nuanced dialogue system, which tries to capture the cadences of rabbinic disquisition, and he faces unique obstacles that subtly teach players about the tradition. Should the protagonist violate *shabbos* laws to pursue an assassin on a subway platform?

To stretch the definition, could we also apply the term "didactic" to games that evangelize – that directly or indirectly educate players about a specific tradition that is not their own? Many major releases have done this in recent years. *Dante's Inferno* (Electronic Arts, 2010) is loosely based on the fourteenth-century Italian poem about a journey to the Christian heaven, and *Enslaved* (Namco Bandai Games, 2010) is a retelling of a sixteenth-century Chinese story of a similar trip in a Taoist and Buddhist context. The Wii release *Cursed Mountain* (Deep Silver Vienna, 2009) is billed as a "survival horror" game, but relies entirely on the Tibetan Book of the Dead for its setting and plot. Players are educated about Buddhist traditions, and in-game prayer, meditation, and lighting incense are necessary to progress. *Asura's Wrath* (Capcom, 2012) offers another major studio's immersion in Buddhist ideas, taking up a traditional wrathful spirit, the Asura, as its protagonist. Visual designer Richmond Lee Chaisiri drew heavily on devotional Buddhist sculpture for his character design and blogged: "So what's Buddhist about *Asura's Wrath*? Everything. The characters, the environments, the ultra-violence, the cosmic scope."[21] If that is true, *Asura's Wrath* may be the most critically and commercially successful example of a didactic video game to date.

Whether these games succeed in the way that, say, a Sunday school game succeeds in enriching one's relationship to faith is open to question. The case of *Hanuman: Boy Warrior* (Sony Computer Entertainment Europe, 2009) is telling. Touted as the first major console game developed entirely in India, it took as its protagonist Hanuman, a Hindu deity and a central figure in the *Ramayana*. The gameplay itself received tepid reviews, but that was overshadowed by greater formal concerns of impiety. Should a deity be a playable video game character? The Universal Society of Hinduism objected vehemently to the game, and asked that Sony withdraw it. Despite this, didactic games have largely thrived, with the "divine as lesson" games largely conducive to the structure and aims of the digital age.

Digital Hestiasic Games

Hestiasic games engage the "divine as context." They are often a traditional part of sacred holidays or festivals. Since the digital traditions are so young, no examples could be found of digital games finding a niche in established holidays. However, there are precedents for new forms of media entering that space. Films like *It's a Wonderful Life* or *The Sound of Music* and other programming have become quasi-rites of the Christmas season. Churches often gather to watch the Super Bowl. In an age when digital gaming is becoming more social – the Entertainment Software Association claims that "sixty-two percent of gamers play games with others"[22] – digital games might at some point enter the realm of public ritual.

Digital Poimenic Games

Poimenic games are those in which the divine intercedes to show favor to one player or to a course of action. These are also difficult to locate in digital space. One set of examples might be teased out by looking at the evolution of divination rituals into a gamed space. Smartphone apps have sprung up around dozens of traditional divination methods. Users can download Yoruba *Ifa* divination with virtual palm nuts, *I Ching* readings, Nordic rune tosses, Buddhist Guanyin sticks, tarot card readings, Celtic ogham letter divination, Russian fortune-telling cards, and many others along those lines. Some of these apps caution users that the medium may cause some interference. The famous Wong Tai Sin Taoist temple in Hong Kong has issued an app that offers the traditional Kau

Cim fortune sticks, but asks users to choose the sticks physically at the temple itself to ensure their efficacy.[23]

Rituals of divination do not fit the definition of religious games stated above, namely that a religious game is a game that is recreationally played elsewhere. However, by translating rituals into the heavily gamed space of a smartphone, in a lighthearted context, it might be argued that the new medium causes these divinations to exist in a grey area, game-like. If so, the shape of such games is strongly poimenic. Other than these, digital poimenic games – in which the "divine as player" chooses a winner or a winning course of action – seem to still be in the wings.

Digital Praxic Games

The praxic games – which are in themselves a devotional practice – show the most compelling promise of what is possible, and follow most directly on the sort of "deep" games that Frank Lantz discussed at the Game Developers Conference. Take the popular *Dance Praise* (Digital Praise, 2005), a variation by a Christian publishing house on the synchronized movement game *Dance Dance Revolution*. Players must execute deft moves set to Christian music. While the tone is lighthearted, the title strongly suggests that players are invited to use the game devotionally. Records of sacralized dance in the Christian church date back at least to the ninth century,[24] and while this practice has waxed and waned in popularity and canonical acceptance, *Dance Praise* seems to offer an interesting gamed twist on this tradition.

Other faiths are certainly represented. Deepak Chopra, a New Age author who writes widely about the intersections of Western medicine and the ayurvedic treatments of his Hindu tradition, developed *Leela* (THQ, 2011), a game based on chakra philosophies. Players may choose from several games, each of which allows them to focus on and "balance" a chakra. Tasks vary from moving the chest in order to collect "energy" for the heart chakra, to moving the eye chakra in the head, allowing the player to navigate through a twisting tunnel, which is supposed to assist in developing intuition. According to the website of lead designer

Eric Zimmerman, "The game . . . explores the idea of play as meditation. The Kinect version includes seven unique games, each based on one of the chakras from yoga. It also includes a meditation mode where the Kinect tracks your breathing in the lower, middle, and upper torso in real time."[25] This is a clear, innovative attempt to offer gaming as a form of ritual practice.

Okami (Capcom, 2006), a widely acclaimed game from Clover Studio in Japan, may at first blush seem to belong to the didactic category. In the setting of ancient Japan, players take the role of Ameratsu, the sun deity of the Shinto tradition. Incarnated as a white wolf in a world ravaged by pollution, Ameratsu must purify each region of the planet, then confront Orochi, the eight-headed dragon of Shinto myth. Players solve puzzles and attack demons, but the mechanism for leveling up – unlocking new abilities for Ameratsu – is inventive and thematically apt. Ameratsu must gather "praise" by healing trees and nature and by feeding woodland animals. When she does so, players are transported to a tranquil environment and contemplate a scene of natural harmony. This kind of meditation on balance and nature plays into traditional Shinto worship, and it is a jarring departure from the button mashing typical of the genre. Music plays in these scenes, and Clover Studio based its award-winning soundtrack on traditional works. The defining mechanism of *Okami* is mastering "divine brushstrokes," a repetitive motion that has a parallel in Japanese contemplative calligraphy. All of these are ingeniously designed to harmonize play with traditional meditative praxis.

One final type of game might fit this category. Jason Rohrer's *Chain World*, mentioned in the opening of the chapter, is a stand-alone meditation on mortality, responsibility, immediacy, and congregation. It exists on a single flash drive and calls on players to pass it among themselves, self-consciously creating both a ritual and a community of play. A similar approach is taken by the immensely popular *Journey* (Thatgamecompany, 2012), a beautiful online pilgrimage that deliberately evokes a language of shared ritual from start-up to power down. Though neither game hews to a religious tradition, they both consciously strive for a gamed experience of an engagement with the sacred. Since the praxic digital game is one where playing counts as an act of worship – engaging with the "divine as experience" – they might be considered praxic games within a stand-alone tradition.

DIGITAL RELIGIOUS GAMES: NEW PARADIGMS

What about a game that lets you play *as* a god? Or a game that lets a player practice her tradition in another body or identity? The digital age has proven to be a fertile ground for revolutions in our ideas around identity, authority, authorship, and authenticity. It's no wonder that gaming – a chief space of engagement in the digital age – has extended these to religion. The three categories outlined below explore only the more robust branches. They differ from the categories already discussed by seldom being recognized by mainstream traditions. However, their preoccupation with religious themes and practices merit their inclusion in a discussion about the medium's future.

Allomythic Games

Games that explore nonexistent traditions make up one aspect of this evolution. We might call them allomythic, from ἄλλος ("other") and μῦθος ("story"). Like science fiction before them, allomythic games postulate new religious landscapes, and go a step further by providing a first-person way to step into these traditions and practice them. Virtual worship can be shallow – healing at an in-game "shrine" is commonplace – but in some titles, players may be forced to go on pilgrimages, engage in religious dialogue, or offer critique or support for the game's invented faiths. The deepest examples of these belong to longer fantasy and sci-fi RPG environments, where deep narrative is key to gameplay.

The *Mass Effect* series (BioWare, 2007–) may be one of the best examples of this type. Some have noted that the overarching game riffs on the Christ narrative; the protagonist, a space warrior named Shepherd, dies and is reborn to save humanity. But the game's engagement becomes deliciously complex as it fleshes out the belief systems of its many sentient species. The lizard-like Krogans embrace a nihilistic stoicism, but retain shamans, burials, and rites of passage from their tribal past. The courtly Hanar, a race that looks like outsized jellyfish, practice a cargo-cult faith based on the long-absent Protheans who once visited their world. The one-gendered Asari race is pantheistic; the name of their religion translates to "all is one." But their aesthetics of fleeting beauty are reminiscent of Japanese Buddhism, and remnants of an ancestral Asari religion called Athame hold a clear relationship to neo-paganism, both through their worship of a three-phased goddess and through the fact that their name is taken from a ritual dagger used in that tradition. The three-fingered Quarians, on the other hand, riff quite clearly on Jewish themes. An intellectual race that prizes the wisdom of their ancestors, they roam the universe in exile from their homeworld. They were driven out by the Geth, an intelligent race of machines that they created to help them wage war – a close parallel to the narrative of the Golem of Prague.

The *Elder Scrolls* series (Bethesda Softworks, 1994–), an RPG of the swords and sorcery type, fleshes out a divine cosmology to which Gnosticism may be the closest parallel. The world is overseen by nine Divines, gods and goddesses; they rarely engage directly in worldly affairs. Players are much more likely to run into Daedra, supernatural and largely malicious beings who, unlike the Divines, have their fingers in human plots. They reward players for acts of (largely depraved) service. Religious wars are frequently part of gameplay, and characters are healed of disease by prayer and ritual, which can become quite complex. This cosmology weaves through each *Elder Scrolls* installment, and the antagonism between Divine and Daedra creates a moral friction, which helps to propel the choose-your-own-path ethos of the RPG narrative.

Allomythic games might also include games that borrow a religious cosmology from history, but that cannot be said to portray it in any faithful or didactic way. *El Shaddai: Ascension of the Metatron* (Ignition Entertainment, 2011) features a cast of angels based loosely on the apocryphal book of Enoch, but the plot and character of the angels takes it far afield from any canonical understanding of scripture.

How do allomythic games fit into the outline I described in the first part of the chapter? Perhaps they can be said to explore the "divine as metaphor" – engaging religious ideas from entirely outside any existing tradition through new stories, characters, and symbols.

Allopolitical Games

A sixth category of digital religious games is the allopolitical, from the Greek ἄλλος ("other") and πόλις ("city" or "society"). These games hinge on digital social space – a community that exists only online, where identities are mediated by screen names or avatars. Here, reality is not necessarily metaphorical. People gather to interact, transact, and discuss news and ideas of the outside world in different skins.

A classic example might be *Second Life* (Linden Lab, 2003), and much has been written about the religious communities that form, meet, and worship there. However, these kinds of spaces are widespread and diverse. Gamed tasks can play a larger or smaller role. The PlayStation Home, a virtual meeting space accessible through all PS3 consoles, has a largely social aim. Players are encouraged to host hangout and discussion spaces in private clubhouses. The users of the clubhouse Home Tabernacle meet for Christian music, fellowship, and worship every Sunday.

Other sites mesh religion with gameplay more directly. The *Neopets* website is a successful meeting place for children, which its developers claimed logged its trillionth page view in June 2011. Players feed, house, and battle their virtual pets; fulfill quests; and play mini-games to earn neopoints, a site currency. A guild option was added to the site for players to share tips and interests in small groups. Although the terms of use prohibit "controversial" topics such as politics and religion, many faith-affiliated guilds thrive. The Road to Emmaus serves Christian players, the As-Salāmu 'Alaykum guild serves Muslims, and many Wiccan guilds are drawn to such virtual neighborhoods as the Witches Tower or the Haunted Forest. These guilds can go beyond simple intra-faith affiliation. The Coven of the Blood Rose, one of the Wiccan guilds active at the time of this writing, offers information about upcoming sabbats, how to perform spells, and Wiccan history lessons. Allopolitical games feature game space serving a role traditionally held by devotional space. Perhaps this is succinctly described as offering an experience of the "divine as wired" – that is, accessible through avatar communities online.

Theoptic Games

The last category is taken from the Greek words for "god" and "vision," and embraces the category of "god games." The classic god game has the player assume the role of an all-seeing power, who controls the environmental circumstances of the game world. That game world is populated by computer-generated inhabitants, whose destiny the player affects, but they ultimately retain free will over their actions. While this definition may be broad enough to encompass strategy/planning games such as *Sim City* (Maxis, 1989–), which allow player-mayors to inflict "acts of God" on their populations, this category in this chapter speaks more specifically to games that have players explicitly assume the role of a divine god.

That premise may seem deeply irreligious, and the games are hardly presented as devotional opportunities. Yet practices that encourage a close identification with divinity have a long ritual lineage. The practice of deity yoga in various branches of Vajrayana Buddhism teaches practitioners to imagine a close nonduality with the Istha-deva, or meditation deity. Shamanic trances may involve an invitation to become possessed by spirits. And even in the influential *Spiritual Exercises* (1548) of St. Ignatius of Loyola, initiates are encouraged to spend days closely putting themselves (quite literally) in the shoes of Jesus Christ: picturing the feel of the road from Bethany under his sandals, and the size and composition of the room where the Last Supper was held.

Torching virtual villages doesn't fall into the same devotional vein. Theoptic games, however, work best when they present a very practical exploration of divinity and the human relationship to it. In *Black & White* (Electronic Arts/Feral Interactive, 2001), one of the more critically noted examples, the god player must try to gain disciples through his actions. He can assist villagers by answering prayers or rain down destruction. Two distinct strategies evolve: one earns worship through terror, and the other through mercy. Neither is privileged in the game, and players may win objectives using either tactic, exploring the logic and advantages of both.

A well-received example, *From Dust* (Ubisoft Montpelier, 2011), uses the same dynamic of earning the praise of villagers. But the gameplay is almost entirely focused on managing the physical aspects of the world, in effect gamifying the first verses of Genesis in which the land and sea are made. On the other end of the spectrum, the quick and irreverent *Let There Be Smite* (Pippin Barr, 2011) humorously explores theodicy and why a god dispenses destruction on humankind.

More traditional real-time strategy games – those in which the player has control over a whole world, but does not play an explicitly god-like role – have also begun to explore their theology more explicitly. The *Civilization* franchise of games, started in 1991, invites players to create a civilization that is strong and widespread. *Civilization V* (Firaxis, 2010) offered a major expansion, which lets players customize the religion of their virtual peoples. There are eleven options of historical religions, and each can be customized with "beliefs" that give players various bonuses in play. (For example, opting for the "evangelism" bonus allows the player to send missionaries abroad.)

So theoptic games offer the player the experience of the "divine as avatar," though it must be noted that such games can rarely be understood as engaging the divine. As with allomythic games, these games are largely opportunities to engage with ideas about religion, rather than with religious experience itself. However, should the *Spiritual Exercises* ever be gamified in digital space, they might define the potential of this category.

CONCLUSION

At the Game Developers Conference in 2011, Eric Zimmerman offered a koan to the game design community: How is a game like a religion? That community continues to respond with broad experimentation and flashes of insight. They create narrative commentaries on religion, use backdrops inspired by religious texts, pursue deeper, "higher consciousness" gameplay, and create overtly devotional game experiences.

I hope that the typology I have offered does two things. On the one hand, it may be of use to scholars, by creating a unified language that bridges religious games, past and future. Such a historical view might open doors to applying critical tools and methodologies from anthropology, ritual studies, sociology, and other fields to digital gaming. If we can agree that didactic religious games share a certain functional DNA, what is to stop us from using Lea Shamgar-Handelman's work on games in Israeli kindergartens to study the games on TorahTots.com? For the richly interdisciplinary field of digital game studies, I hope that a typology that connects a very new medium with a very old past may spark new critical insights and connections.

There is a second hope for this critical tool: to help create a higher level of sophistication in games that engage religious characters, themes, or methods. A close study of gamed religious experience offline might offer fresh sources of inspiration on consoles, smartphones, and PCs. The study of religious games in particular is an invitation to remember that games have historically played meaty roles at the center of cultural explorations of meaning, and may indeed continue to do so for centuries to come.

NOTES

1. Lantz, "Life, Death and the Middle Pair."
2. Fagone, "*Chain World* Videogame Was Supposed to Be a Religion."
3. Ibid.
4. Lantz is quoted in the *Wired* article (ibid.) about the *Chain World* episode: "[It] reflects the deep sickness unto death that is religion, a lethal blend of megalomaniacal solipsism, paranoid-schizophrenia, platonic idealism, banal pyramid schemes, authentic grassroots collectivism, and good old-fashioned ressentiment [*sic*]."
5. MacAloon, "Olympic Games and the Theory of Spectacle."
6. Burkert, *Greek Religion*, 105–107.
7. Philostratus, *Gymnastikus,* ch. 5.
8. Homer, *The Iliad,* ch. 23.
9. Burkert, *Greek Religion,* 106.
10. The Marmor Parium inscription, dating to about 534 BCE, states: "From when Thespis the first poet acted, who

produced a play in the city and the prize was a goat."
11. Burkert, *Greek Religion,* 105.
12. Early Christians were sometimes targeted by the grand Roman spectacles, which shared a lineage with the Greek public games. Some Christians ended up *damnatio ad bestia* (thrown to wild animals). In the third century, Tertullian in *De Spectaculis* advised his fellow Christians for this and other reasons to avoid the public games altogether. In the Jewish world, a parallel backlash seemed to unfold. The Jerusalem Talmud in the fourth century introduced the idea that the inhabitants of Mount Simeon were punished by God for their ball playing.
13. Purdue, *Debate in Tibetan Buddhism.*
14. Sunday School Network, "Super Bowl Sunday School."
15. Mawtani, "Iraqi Mhaibis Champion Shares His Memories."

16. Geertz, "Deep Play."
17. Crikey, "El Ritual del Hombre-Pajaro."
18. Neilson, *Trial by Combat.*
19. Chang Nui, *The Classic of Go* (ca. 1049–1054 CE).
20. McRae, *Seeing through Zen.*
21. Kotaku, "Everything About This Game Is So Buddhist."
22. Entertainment Software Association, "Game Player Data 2012."
23. Asia One, "HK Temple Fortune Tellers Cynical."
24. Backman, *Religious Dances in the Christian Church.*
25. Zimmerman, "Leela."

REFERENCES

Asia One. "HK Temple Fortune Tellers Cynical of Fortune-Telling App." http://www.asiaone.com/News/Latest%2BNews/Science%2Band%2BTech/Story/A1Story20120122-323402.html (accessed January 24, 2012).

Backman, E. Louis. *Religious Dances in the Christian Church and in Popular Medicine.* Westport, Conn.: Greenwood, 1977.

Burkert, Walter. *Greek Religion.* Cambridge, Mass.: Harvard University Press, 1985.

Conrod, John. *Computer Bible Games.* Denver, Colo.: Accent, 1984.

Crikey. "El Ritual del Hombre-Pajaro – The Bird-Man Cult of Rapa Nui." http://blogs.crikey.com.au/northern/2009/05/19/el-ritual-del-hombre-pajaro-the-bird-man-cult-of-rapa-nui (accessed May 19, 2009).

Entertainment Software Association. "Game Player Data." http://www.theesa.com/facts/gameplayer.asp (2012).

Fagone, Jason. "*Chain World* Videogame Was Supposed to Be a Religion – Not a Holy War." http://www.wired.com/magazine/2011/07/mf_chainworld/3 (accessed May 19, 2012).

Geertz, Clifford. "Deep Play: Notes on the Balinese Cockfight." In his *The Interpretation of Cultures.* New York: Basic, 1973.

Huizinga, Johan. *Homo Ludens: A Study of the Play-Element in Culture.* Boston: Beacon, 1955.

Kotaku. "Everything About This Game Is So Buddhist." http://www.kotaku.com.au/2012/01/everything-about-this-game-is-so-buddhist (accessed January 30, 2012).

Lantz, Frank. "Life, Death and the Middle Pair: Go, Poker and the Sublime." Speech given at the Game Developers Conference, San Francisco, Calif., 2011.

MacAloon, J. J. "Olympic Games and the Theory of Spectacle in Modern Society." In *Rite, Drama, Festival, Spectacle: Rehearsals toward a Theory of Cultural Performance.* Edited by J. J. MacAloon, 241–280. Philadelphia, Pa.: Institute for the Study of Human Issues, 1984.

Mawtani. "Iraqi Mhaibis Champion Shares His Memories." http://mawtani.al-shorfa.com/en_GB/articles/iii/features/iraqtoday/2011/08/13/feature-05 (accessed August 13, 2011).

McRae, John. *Seeing through Zen.* Berkeley: University of California Press, 2003.

Neilson, George. *Trial by Combat.* 1890. Clark, N.J.: Lawbook Exchange, 2009.

Purdue, Daniel E. *Debate in Tibetan Buddhism.* Ithaca, N.Y.: Snow Lion, 1992.

Salen, K., and Zimmerman, E. *Rules of Play: Game Design Fundamentals.* Cambridge, Mass.: MIT Press, 2004.

Sniderman, Stephen. "Unwritten Rules." *The Life of Games* 1, no. 1 (1999):2–7.

Sunday School Network. "Super Bowl Sunday School." http://www.christian crafters.com/game_superbowl.html.

Zimmerman, Eric. "Leela." http://eric zimmerman.com/portfolio/leela.

TWO

Locating the Pixelated Jew

A MULTIMODAL METHOD FOR EXPLORING
JUDAISM IN *THE SHIVAH*

Isamar Carrillo Masso and Nathan Abrams

THE VIDEO GAME *THE SHIVAH* (WADJET EYE GAMES, 2006) opens with the epigraph: "A Goy [non-Jew] came up to Rabbi Moishe to ask, 'Why do rabbis always answer with a question?' to which Rabbi Moishe replied, 'Why not?'" In a similar Talmudic style, this chapter opens with a question: "Where has the pixelated Jew gone?" In popular culture, images of the Jew have been examined over many formats – art, film, television, cartoons, comics, graphic novels, online, and so on – but to date, despite their prevalence, images of Jews in video games have yet to be fully explored. This is partly because, in general, representations of race and ethnicity in video games are relatively unexplored and thus undertheorized.[1] Furthermore, given the volume of research dedicated to analyzing the Jewish contribution to American visual culture, such as film,[2] it is surprising to note that comparatively little work has been done on Judaism as a distinctive set of religious practices, behaviors, beliefs, and values. As a consequence, it is possible to read entire books on these subjects that have almost no references to Judaism qua Judaism.

Using the hard-boiled Jewish detective video game, *The Shivah,* as a case study, this chapter uncovers and discusses representations of Judaism by taking a semiotic approach derived from film studies combined with a new corpus-based critical discourse analysis: a multimodal approach.[3] This emergent method, specifically developed for the study of games, is used to explore the representation of Judaism and questions of religious-based beliefs, behaviors, values, ethics, and faith in the religious adventure game. Using a project-specific multimodal corpus,[4] we argue that *The Shivah* explores Jewish faith through gameplay, as well as a Jewish identity that is not based on Othering stereotypes.

The Shivah is a point-and-click, single-player game where the user plays a detective in the form of the character Rabbi Stone. David Gilbert, the game's creator, said in an interview that unlike other games, which rely on violence to solve problems, "questioning is the rabbi's power."[5] In a similar fashion, and because our method is still emergent, we also interrogate this game and video games more generally: Does the game format ("modality" and "mediality")[6] allow for an unlimited and unlimitable range of representations to be produced in contrast to other media, where notions of photorealism or greater censorship might apply? How can metaludic and metalinguistic practices in *The Shivah* inform our understanding of Judaism and Jewish identities, as portrayed in the game? What discourses on religion are present in the game, and how do players enact them? What is the relationship between these issues of identity and representation, and the epistemology of games? And how do video/digital games inform or reform our understanding of Judaism within digital and gaming culture?

Our exploratory study shows why an analysis of *The Shivah* can reform our understanding as ludologists, semioticians, theologians, and critical discourse analysts of the role that particularly Judaism, and religion in general, plays in video game ecologies.

CONTEXT: POST-DENOMINATIONAL
AND POST-ETHNIC JUDAISM

To locate the missing pixelated Jew, we explore the religious (Judaic)[7] factor in contemporary video games by unpacking specific religious aspects of Judaism. The chapter will show how *The Shivah* reflects the wider societal introduction of a normalizing spectrum into the representation of Judaism that moves beyond the Reform-*Haredi* dyad. We start from the premise that there is a clear distinction between Jewishness as a racial, ethnic, political, or cultural identity, and Judaism as a religion and set of beliefs, behaviors, and values.

Scholarship has largely tended to focus on ethnicity (Jewishness) as the analytic category for the study of Jewish representations and industry participation. Hitherto, where Judaism was represented in media, it tended to fall into one of the binary categories: Haredi[8] or Reform. Since Haredism is "the most obviously distinctive and colorful" branch of Judaism,[9] it works as shorthand for an instantly recognizable Jewish religious status. Indeed, Haredism tends to stand as a metonym for all of Orthodox Judaism. In contrast, since Reform Jews are represented as no different from the vast majority of Americans, they are rarely explicitly described or delineated as Reform.[10] Furthermore, such Jewish representations often display downright ignorance about the Judaism of Reform Jews. Rather, Reform Judaism is inferred by the lack of outward markers that identify a male Haredi Jew, such as a yarmulke, *tzitzit* (Heb. fringes), *peyot* (Heb. sidecurls), and distinctive black hat and clothing. Almost without fail, whether Reform or Haredi, Jews are represented as Ashkenazi (Eastern or Central European).[11]

However, as Nathan Abrams's study of Jewishness and Judaism in contemporary cinema argues, some media are now depicting Jewish identity both ethnically and religiously. Abrams shows how contemporary Jewish culture's comfort with an increasing range of religious identification beyond the Reform-Haredi binary was the product of the revitalization of Jewish religious beliefs, practices, and literature in the United States (and beyond) during the 1980s and 1990s. This change was a result of a number of factors, including greater enrollment in Jewish day schools, improvements in Jewish education at all levels, the expansion of Jewish studies at the university level, the publication of Jewish literature, an increase in the number of secular Jewish organizations observing Jewish holidays, and the Jewish programming offered in Jewish community centers.[12] It was also a reflection of a growing post-denominationalism in which committed, younger Jews increasingly refused to be labeled by existing religious institutions and rejected established branches of Judaism in order to create something more fluid and qualitatively "better."[13]

Rather than discard Judaism wholesale, or "engage in community structures they find alienating or bland," post-denominational Jews use their creativity and commitment to organize independently, to build Jewish experiences that are meaningful to them, and to create ritual on their own terms, outside community institutions but within their own

organic communities of friends and family.[14] Twenty- to forty-year-olds
in the United States (and Europe) are increasingly indicating a sense
of alienation from Jewish communal organizations and experiences,
which are perceived as boring and uninviting.[15] The result has been a
general decline in synagogue membership, financial contributions, and
denominational affiliation, as greater numbers of younger Jews have begun to identify as "just Jewish" rather than as Reform, Conservative, or
Reconstructionist like in the past. Rather than following their parents
into the halls of synagogues and Jewish federations, a significant segment of younger Jews has sought to create new avenues and opportunities for Jewish involvement that do not replicate older patterns of Jewish
communal participation. Instead, they have begun exploring their own
opportunities for Jewish experiences outside and independent of the
existing communal infrastructure.

It is possible now to lead a varied and spiritually fulfilling post-denominational Jewish existence outside of and unrelated to mainstream
organizations and institutions. One does not need to go to a synagogue
to be Jewish anymore. Known as "do-it-yourself Judaism" or what David
Graham calls "pick 'n' mix Judaism," this trend emerged from a post-
modern mix-and-match tendency in general. This reflects an environment that is, as Graham writes in "European Jewish Identity at the Dawn
of the 21st Century," "open and welcoming and encourages choice and
personal preference above rules and dictates."[16]

Contemporary culture has reversed the previous binary model of
Judaism to produce a multiplicity of religiously defined Jews onscreen.
Not only have these representations increased, but they have also taken
on different forms, marking a departure from the past toward more un-
selfconscious, self-critical, deeper, subtle, nuanced, playful, and even
outrageous representations of Judaism. There is even some attempt to
understand and explore religious beliefs and the ideas and philosophy
behind these rituals, as well as to mock, mimic, and reverse them. Film
now not only represents subjective Judaic experiences, but also serves an
overt educational purpose. Jews are increasingly being identified through
religious rather than simply ethnic (names, physical looks, professions,
locations) markers.[17] Key points in the Jewish religious calendar, other
than just Chanukah and Passover, are depicted.[18] In this way, contempo-

rary popular culture has been moving toward a more sophisticated understanding of Judaism and its beliefs, rituals, and practices, portraying a fuller range of Jewish denominational affiliations (rather than just secular, Reform, and Haredi) and intra-Jewish conflict such that contradictory and "multiple cultures are shown to thrive within Jewish life itself."[19]

METHODOLOGY: A MULTIMODAL
APPROACH TO GAME ANALYSIS

The multimodal approach is an emergent method that Isamar Carrillo Masso has been developing since 2006. In this chapter, we apply and refine it in relation to *The Shivah*. Because of their interactive nature, video games present a number of problems that make their study difficult. Until relatively recently scholars have been reluctant to allow video games to be studied as texts using tools that have been traditionally used to study other media.[20] The most problematic aspect of video games as texts is the feature of interactivity. This means that the text to be studied is the complex product of the game's rules, the experience of gameplay, and the content of the game, including its user interface. To further complicate matters, the content of the game itself and the deterministic choices already made for the players by the game designers are semiotically and semantically loaded.

For reasons of space, we will give here only a brief account of our methodology for studying *The Shivah*. The first step was playing the game itself; both researchers played the game, and our gameplay was recorded using screen-capture software called Camtasia Studio, version 7.0 (TechSmith, 2010). Camtasia allows for the capture of sound and video from a screen and can produce outputs in MP4 files. It also has the capacity for video editing and annotation, which makes it very useful for multimodal PC game corpus building. This allowed us to better understand the game's affordances and to make the game more malleable for analytical purposes. We arrived at four different endings, producing four separate gameplay videos. We then transcribed verbatim all the spoken text in the game. This transcript constituted the textual part of the corpus accompanying the video clips of our gameplay. We then examined the video clips and the text produced using Transana, which

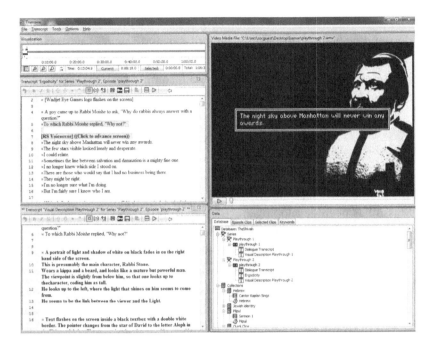

2.1. "The Night Sky above Manhattan." A screenshot of the multimodal corpus of *The Shivah* in Transana, showing both a verbatim transcript and a visual description.

allows the user to synchronize transcript(s) and video, making it easier to qualitatively examine large amounts of data in detail.

Once the data were processed into different transcripts, with annotations varying in granularity, the data were revisited from a critical discourse analytical perspective, a research approach in applied linguistics that uses an eclectic methodology to look at the way language and discourses work, especially in relation to operations of power. This was done to contextualize the game within the wider field of media studies, particularly focusing on the intertextuality of the elements deployed. In a different game context in which prayer was used, two more sets of transcriptions were added: one using a form of Labanotation for movement notation,[21] and one for sound, using the software tool *Tattoo* (Audio Damage, 2012) and making it compatible with Transana.

One intertextual element is the "trajectory," which is used in this chapter as a general term to describe the meaning-making pathways that

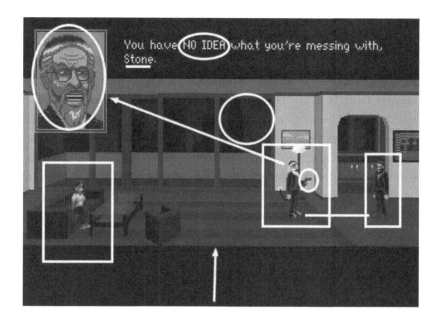

2.2. "You have NO IDEA." A sample annotated screenshot from a scene in *The Shivah*, recorded using Camtasia Studio and annotated with ScreenCAP to show visual clusters and to highlight points of interest for analysis.

are created when players move through a game, including the movement within one screen/level, and from one level to another. A meaning-making trajectory in this sense refers to the progressive integration over time of the semiotic resources that are encountered as the player progresses from one linked object, space, or level to another. A trajectory may last minutes or hours; it may occur over much longer periods of time; or it may be picked up and continued on separate occasions. Trajectories encompass both potential and actual playpaths. Transcriptions of trajectories included descriptions of local resource configurations, such as semantic clusters, as in figure 2.1.

By examining the platform's affordances and positioning the game in question within a wider context of PC games, the method of analysis takes into account the nature of the different semiotic resources that are used and the ways they are used to create a particular video game, both as individual text and as part of a genre. This includes the player's "reading" pathway, that is, the "potential playpath" that can be taken

through a particular game, as opposed to the "actual playpath" taken
by a particular player, in a particular instance, as a user creates and ne-
gotiates the meanings offered by that particular game along with other
particular meanings, making a fixed trajectory out of a more or less fluid
set of potentials. Both of these contrast with what Carrillo Masso terms
the "preferred playing" of a game (based on the idea of the "preferred
reading" of a text, extrapolated to games).[22] Thus a video game, in toto,
comprises a series of potential playpaths, all virtually possible but existing as unrealized potential until the game is actually played. Each
iteration of play produces an actual playpath, which is the chronological
series of the player's actions and choices during the game. This actual
playpath, recorded for analysis and studied as a sum total of meaning-
making activities, is called the player's "trajectory."

The multimodal transcription and analysis of such trajectories can
reveal the ways in which the trajectory integrates diverse semiotic resources into itself as it develops and unfolds. In time, possible trajectories are offered by the resources, both technological and semiotic,
of video games. By the same token, the recording and analysis of trajectories will provide insights into the ways in which players experience
games and their possible meanings through actual play pathways. It also
can show the extent to which trajectories have generic and individual
characteristics in their semiotic makeup, as the preferred playing that
the designers envisioned can be compared to both the potential pathway
and the actual one. It is important to note here that the acts of recording
and transcribing are in themselves analytical decisions, since the nature
of the transcript and the tags assigned to different elements of the analysis will influence the outcome (see figure 2.3).

The notion of the visual transitivity frame is logocentric, that is, it
is centered on words as labels.[23] Thus when we label or tag for analysis a
segment of a player's trajectory, or actual playpath, it becomes a visual
transitivity frame. Specifically, visual transitivity frames are based on the
experiential dimension of meanings and visual texts. Visual transitivity
frames are an important analytical tool: tagging visual meanings and
texts for the purpose of creating a multimodal corpus made up of various
kinds of units in a visual grammar, and for recording purposes. In the

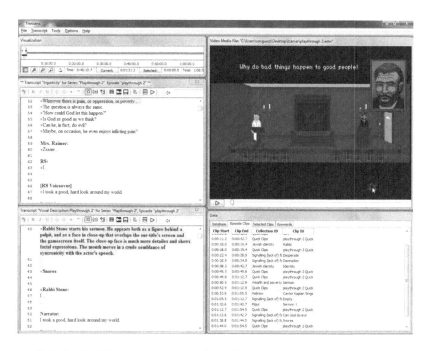

2.3. "Why Do Bad Things Happen to Good People?" A screenshot of the multimodal corpus of *The Shivah* in Transana, showing both a verbatim transcript and a visual description.

context of Transana, they can be seen as the transcription and analysis that centers around a single "collection" – the smallest unit of analysis, consisting of a small portion of video and its transcription with one or more labels attached to them. On occasion, visual transitivity frames coincide with a single shot; they can also be distributed across more than one shot. The former are intra-shot transitivity frames; the latter are inter-shot transitivity frames.[24]

Our previous experience and knowledge of these objects are, above all, intertextual, that is, these are all texts – auditory, verbal, visual, and so on – that we have all encountered in other contexts. In addition, there is a clear visual intertextual tie to many point-and-click adventure games of the 1980s (as suggested by Carrillo Masso in "Grips of Fantasy" in 2011), as well as to serious games as a pseudo genre, and to film noir in terms of aesthetics. As Dovey and Kennedy write in *Game Cultures:*

By and large, the game interface is still representational; for many games, perhaps most, representation has not disappeared and cannot easily be argued away. Even though the representation content may only be an interface to the simulation of the game engine, even though action might be more significant than connotation, even though the textual meaning of the representation is secondary to the compulsive engagement with improved game performance – despite acknowledging all this, researchers working within these frameworks insist that *most games still use representation*; despite "the Tetris Defence," it hasn't gone away. *Whilst games use representation, they remain contextually aligned with operations of power;* however, this alignment is certainly of a different order to the relations of meaning production encountered in novels, cinema or television.[25]

Undoubtedly, there is such a thing as representation within video games. Studying the representation of Jewish characters in video games using a hybrid theoretical framework to study video games as media texts is thus not only possible, but also a necessary feature of this type of study, at least for the present. Partial analyses of the content of games have studied the portrayal of violence; the representation of racial minorities and the Other; the representation of female characters; ideological assumptions; and fractal recursivity operationalized in game discourses. However, Jewish characters in games and the meaning of Judaism in this new medium have yet to be systematically analyzed.

In video games as a medium – because of their affordances – variability, fluidity, and context specificity are emphasized over global order and stability of meaning. In other game studies, scholars have drawn attention to these features. What is absent in most discussions, however, is any detailed account of the meaning-making process that accounts for the appointment of semiotic and material resources that takes place during this process. The process is simply taken for granted and celebrated as such. And yet the premises for a better understanding of video games are often ill defined, without any basis in the detailed analysis of their ludological aspects and their associated activities.

The following analysis is based on close playing and on following three separate playpaths. This is how the game trajectory – the sum total of meaning-making devices located in game choices and moves – was teased out of the potential playpaths, and a closer understanding of the text was produced.

THE SHIVAH

Judaism is both the theme and the setting for *The Shivah*, which promotes itself as "a rabbinical adventure of mourning and mystery." The game's protagonist is New York City rabbi Russell Stone (voiced by Abe Goldfarb), who ministers to a poor synagogue on the Lower East Side of New York City, congregation B'nai Ben-Zion (Heb. "the sons/children of Ben-Zion"). Membership is declining and the resulting lack of funds means that his temple is on the verge of closure. The opening scene, for example, depicts Stone delivering a sermon to a near-empty synagogue in which the sounds of a sleeping congregant can be heard. Although he is devout, the bleakness of his situation has embittered Stone, who has progressively become more cynical with time and is, as a consequence, struggling with his faith. Full of doubt and about to resign, Stone receives a visit from a policeman (strangely mimicking the hardboiled cop from 1940s film noir), who informs him that a large sum of money has been bequeathed to him from a former member of his congregation, Jack Lauder. Lauder was murdered three days earlier, but Stone has not seen him in eight years. Stone decides to investigate the circumstances relating to his congregant's death, turning into the noir-ish, albeit yarmulke-wearing, hardboiled antihero detective, complete with his own foulmouthed (e.g., "bull," "crap") voiceover narrative. The investigation takes him on a journey across Manhattan to uncover the truth of the murder, revealing a deep conspiracy between an opposing rabbi, Amos Zelig, and the Mafia. They are fleecing unwitting businesspeople through large and unrepayable loans.

As Stone digs into his and Lauder's shared past, the game depicts his actions as a stubborn, conservative rabbi, particularly when he interacts with a less hard-line rabbi at a much wealthier Reform synagogue. Stone's history with the murder victim is gradually uncovered as the story progresses, and draws the player into Stone's identity and the reasons for his bitterness. In this way, *The Shivah* ponders issues of how to portray faith through gameplay itself, as well as "the nature of ethics in the post-religious age."[26]

The Shivah is an unusual game in several respects. It uses an old-fashioned, 1980s-style, 2D format known as "point-and-click," lacking what some might perceive as the sophisticated graphics of contemporary games. Furthermore, while we as players may "drive" and "direct" Stone, we do not "occupy" him. It is not our hand-eye coordination that propels the character; it is our choices, based on knowledge and intelligence. Rabbi Stone is not an empty vessel; he has a past, he has made mistakes, and his choices are based on who he is. He also has religion-based prejudices, having refused to officiate at Jack Lauder's wedding because he was marrying a non-Jew.

The transcript is liberally peppered with Hebrew and Yiddish, pointing to a metalinguistic portrayal of both Judaism and Jewishness. It uses suggestive and untranslated phrases (although a dictionary is provided), as well as the rhythms and cadences of Hebrew and Yiddish, with seemingly little concern as to whether players understand the words or not (e.g., *bubkis, mensch, putz, kibitz, momzer, yenta, shikse, tuches*). Indeed, the very name of the game is the Hebrew term referring to the seven-day mourning period after someone dies. In this way, the game fits into a contemporary paradigm in which younger Jews are increasingly representing themselves without the mediation or biases that older, more assimilationist Jews may deploy. In today's multicultural, post-ethnic, pluralist, and post-pluralist world, such Jews are less focused on Jewishness as a marker of an oppressed, diaspora-conscience minority. Where Yiddish (and Hebrew) was once perceived by a generation of Jews as an obstacle to acculturation, the language of the game is more ethnically inflected, more "Jewish." Where once such utterances were confined to older characters or set in the past, today words in different languages and dialects are voiced by younger characters and often set in the present. And these characters sound normal; they speak like everyone else, not as if they just got off the boat from Eastern or Central Europe. These are not Jews for the gentile world, that is, stereotypically exaggerated versions of reality familiar to a non-Jewish society. All of this indexically marks Gilbert's own metaludic discursive position on Judaism: one that is not overly concerned to reach out in an interfaith fashion, or with what its co-religionists might think. One significant thing about *The Shivah* is its refusal to use the game to any edifying effect. Gilbert seems not to care whether the import of such references is readily decoded or if they

prove too subtle for players. If *The Shivah* is a cautionary tale, one has to
ask: to what effect?

The game's marketing promotes its original features: a Yiddish dictionary, "rabbinical conversation methods, a unique method of fighting, an original score, and three different endings!"[27] (This last feature
reminds us of the old quip about two Jews and three opinions.) Furthermore, unlike many other video games, "words replace weapons" in *The
Shivah*. A Talmudic line of questioning propels the narrative forward,
replacing violence. Talmudic tradition is often one of questioning and
analysis, and typically a rabbi answers questions with more questions.
Thus when Stone confronts and questions Rabbi Zelig, he is answered
with a question. Furthermore, typically the player is given three (or
more) options, and the wisest course to follow is often (although not
always) the one labeled "rabbinical"; indeed, the game can only be won,
in its later stages, by consistently choosing the option that answers a
question with a question. Subsequently, when confronted with an as-
sailant, the player can choose either to ask another question or to throw
a punch, thus enacting on a very basic level the traditional discourse on
questioning. If the rabbi gives a rabbinical response, answering a question with a question, then he is immune to any physical action. But if he is
a "poor" rabbi and does not respond with a question, the blow connects.
In another scene, a key character in the game attacks Stone with a knife;
violence does not protect the rabbi nor help him to solve the mystery.
Rather, the only way to ward off the mugger is by asking him questions.
"Questioning is the rabbi's power," said Gilbert.[28]

Perpetuating the stereotypical link between Jews and superior intelligence, Gilbert marketed *The Shivah* as more "cerebral" than the typical gaming fare. Indeed, the look of the game – *The Shivah* harks back
to old-school video games that were popular in the 1980s and 1990s in
which the graphics looked retro and the games emphasized character
and dialogue – emphasizes the flatness of this characterization. At the
same time, however, *The Shivah* goes against the grain. As argued by
Atkins, there exists "an unspoken tacit agreement between player and
text to make fewer demands of game fictions than films or novels – no
one expects great dialogue in a game fiction; no one looks for depth

of characterization; no one judges the success of a game fiction on the sophistication of its back story."[29] Transcripts of *The Shivah*'s dialogue clearly show signs of thought, and a deeper characterization and back-story compared to most games.

The type of religion invoked is the Ashkenazi variety of either modern Orthodox or Conservative Judaism, on the one hand, and Reform Judaism, on the other. Neither rabbi is shown in the dress typical of a Haredi Jew. In Stone's congregation, the evening service concludes with the hymn, in Hebrew, *Adon Olam* (Heb. "Eternal Lord" or "Infinite Lord"), a regular part of the daily and sabbath liturgy since the fifteenth century. His synagogue is dark and rundown, and there is even a distinct crack in one of the walls. In contrast, Rabbi Amos Zelig's synagogue (Temple Beth Tikvah; Heb. "House of Hope") is brightly lit, with large stained-glass windows, and clearly wealthy. While distinctive Eastern European klezmer music plays in the background of Stone's shul (synagogue), organ music is heard at Zelig's temple. Unfortunately, the designer unhelpfully chose to use the term "temple" as an all-encompassing designator, confusing and blurring the denominational boundaries.

CONCLUSION: LOCATING THE JEWISH
FAITH AND IDENTITY IN GAMEPLAY

The Shivah is not an educational or didactic game. It makes no attempt to instruct on Judaism. Rather, it presents a pluralistic discourse on Judaism, embodied in widely differing characters, all of them flawed in some way according to normative rabbinic standards. Judaism is both backdrop and setting, but also the reason for the game. Judaism is not simplified, diluted, or presented in a fashion that elides its more troubling or unpleasant facets, here its traditional antipathy toward exogamy or out-marriage, which Rabbi Stone opposes, hence his refusal to marry Jack and Mrs. Lauder (née Sharma), a non-Jewish woman, in his synagogue – the cause of the subsequent rift between Lauder and Stone. In the denouement, Stone elaborates on his reasons: "For thousands of years we've struggled to keep our place on this planet and you talk of concessions! As a rabbi, I do everything I can to help. And if that means refusing an interfaith marriage, then *so be it*. I can still look at myself in the mirror and call myself a rabbi." But Judaism is not represented as monolithic: while Stone opposes the Lauders' marriage, Zelig marries them, since Reform takes a less hard-line attitude toward intermarriage than do Orthodoxy and Haredism.

Furthermore, building upon Michael Chabon's *The Secret Yiddish Policemen's Union* (2007) and anticipating *A Serious Man* (directed by Joel and Ethan Coen, 2009), these Jews are not one-dimensional or even pretty. Stone is portrayed as tough: he spent four years on the B'nai Brith Yeshiva (Heb. "Sons of the Covenant" Religious Seminary) high school boxing team. He does not flinch at foul language and confronts his attackers, even though they are armed, head on. At the same time, he is described as a particularly dogmatic, "Zionist," "pig-headed," and "arrogant" rabbi, who "never learned to make concessions." In this way, the game is critical of normative rabbinic Judaism's stance on intermarriage. Yet the Reform rabbi comes off no better. Zelig may have married Jack and his wife, but he is a corrupt, greedy cleric in league with the Mafia, who thinks nothing of kidnapping, extortion, and even murder, including that of innocents. As Stone puts it, he is "a common criminal, who consorts with gangsters and assassins." In the final analysis, *The Shivah* leaves us with a form of Judaism that has been normalized rather than subjected to complete hagiography, on the one hand, or demonization, on the other.

The Shivah, although not monolithic, does not allow for an unlimited and unlimitable range of representations to be produced, although its affordances do make for some leeway in terms of how Rabbi Stone's particular brand of either modern Orthodox or Conservative, but certainly non-haredi and non-Reform, Judaism is enacted. Because of how it is played, *The Shivah* gives a nuanced depiction of contemporary American Jewish faith and identity. Play is an aspect of human life, as much as religion is. The reason that video games are now studied separately from other types of play is essentially that, with the aid of computers, the sets of rules that make up video games have grown a thousandfold, and it is impossible now to separate the aspect of play itself from the rest of the content of this medium.[30] Play does not make for an infinite array of experiences, however. The possible outcomes/endings in a video game are restricted to the number and types of outcomes that were included by the game's designers, as well as by the number of choices available to the player. In this view, the behavior of a player is "programmed" or "modeled" (in the semiotic sense) by a "series of limitations of choices of operations," which produce the "text" as gameplay. A number of games follow this simple narrative style, which can be linked to multiple-ending story books (for example, the *Choose Your Own Adventure* series, popular in the 1980s), and therefore many of the analytical tools that apply to narrative can be recycled and adapted to this genre.

As the multimodal method displays, there is often a high degree of self-consciousness in game design, meaning the focus is not just on the aesthetic appeal of the game but also on the semiotic principles of its design and functioning. There is a clear reason for this: video games appeal to and require players to understand their semiotic modus operandi as a normal routine whenever they interact with the game. Finding, selecting, purchasing/downloading, and subsequently installing a game are in themselves important game-related activities, as is access to specific sources of information, such as a walkthrough or the game's backstory. In this sense, understanding religion within a game can be very much like understanding religion within a painting: one can get a certain amount of enjoyment from interacting with the image itself, but to truly understand it, one needs to understand the semiotic resources used by the artist, the context in which it was produced, and the reasons, advantages, and limitations of the chosen medium and technique. As D. Bayles and T. Orland write: "Your tools do more than just influence the appearance of the resulting art – they basically set limits upon what you *can* say with an art piece. . . . And likewise when new tools appear, new artistic possibilities arise."[31]

The Shivah provides new ways and trajectories of being Jewish that move beyond other stereotypes and is based on the practice of Jewish faith. *The Shivah* in its finished form and with the affordances of a point-and-click adventure/serious game is especially geared at merging disparate entities; crossing and realigning the boundaries between diverse discourses (both on a metalevel of fun and the ludic, and on particular themes from the real world in general), social activities, and domains; and constantly relocating and recontextualizing agents and objects that we expect to find in one setting or category into others.

What the multimodal method shows is that, much like the idea of religion itself, the experience of play does not really exist, even though it has been predesigned; rather, it is assembled from a computer program and only comes into existence through the actions of the player, which brings up the complex issue of authorship. This soft coupling makes a multimodal corpus-based analysis particularly desirable both in terms of replicability and as a historical record for games and technologies that change very quickly, which makes studies that rely on memory virtually impossible to use shortly after their publication. Systematization, and especially documentation, of the ways we look at video games is then essential, not only in terms of preserving the usefulness of studies in a field that moves very fast, but also in order to facilitate interdisciplinary collaboration in the study of games in general and of religion in them in particular. A well-documented approach, such as the one proposed here, would facilitate the application of critical tools for their study, and would remove barriers of engagement for scholars in theology and other religion studies. Perhaps the way forward is not only to continue to study the representation and performance of Judaism as the Other but, crucially, to examine the performance of, and the playing with, different "Judaisms," from a Jewish perspective.

NOTES

1. Šisler, "Digital Arabs." Furthermore, although there has been some research into religion in games, little has been written on the portrayal of Judaism, especially in games that deal with epistemological questions on the nature of religion itself. See, for example, Love, "Not-So-Sacred Quests"; Piskorowski-Adams, "Films, Frames and Videogames."

2. L. D. Friedman, *Hollywood's Image of the Jew* (New York: Ungar, 1982); P. Erens, *The Jew in American Cinema* (Bloomington: Indiana University Press, 1984); and N. Gabler, *An Empire of Their Own: How the Jews Invented Hollywood* (London: Allen, 1988).

3. Shamah, "Pokemon and the Jewish Question."

4. A "multimodal corpus" is a collection of texts, in the wide sense of the word, in different media formats. A "project-specific" corpus is one that is made for a particular project, to answer a specific question, as opposed to a reference corpus, such as the Bank of English.

5. Quoted in Lando, "A Rabbi as Superhero."

6. Johnson and Ensslin, "Language in the Media."

7. We use this term to distinguish religious from ethnic Jewishness.

8. *Haredi* (pl. *Haredim*) literally means "one who trembles," deriving from Isaiah 66:5, in which the prophet admonishes his people to "Hear the word of the Lord, you who tremble [haredim] at His word." It is often confused with the much more common term, in American English at least, Hasidic. "Haredi" is translated as "ultra-Orthodox," a definition that does not do justice to this extensive and nuanced term, which covers a range of Jews, not all of whom are "Orthodox" in the strictest definition of that term. See Abrams, *The New Jew in Film*, 215.

9. Elber, "Putting Faith in Film."

10. The prime example of this would be some of the characters in the long-running television series *Friends* (1994–2004).

11. See Abrams, *The New Jew in Film*, esp. ch. 6.

12. Ibid.

13. Rosenthal, "What's in a Name?"

14. Kelman and Schoenberg, *Legwork, Framework, Artwork*, 12.

15. Ibid.

16. Graham, "European Jewish Identity at the Dawn of the 21st Century," 22.

17. See Abrams's *The New Jew in Film* for a detailed treatment of these changes.

18. Festivals such as Purim and Rosh Hashanah are now appearing in film. See ibid.

19. Rosenberg, "Jewish Experience on Film," 44.

20. Dovey and Kennedy, *Game Cultures*, 86–101.

21. Labanotation is a system for dance and movement notation that allows, say, choreography or factory work to be written down and performed according to the written system. See Hutchinson Guest, *Labanotation*.

22. Carrillo Masso, "Mapping the Magic Circle."

23. Kress and Van Leeuwen, *Reading Images*.

24. Baldry and Thibault, *Multimodal Transcription and Text Analysis*, 143.

25. Dovey and Kennedy, *Game Cultures*, 101, emphasis added.

26. "The Hottest Websites in the Whole Wide World."

27. D. Gilbert, "The Shivah," http://www.davelgil.com/wordpress/?page_id=128 (accessed July 2010).

28. Quoted in Lando, "A Rabbi as Superhero."

29. Atkins, *More than a Game*, 57.

30. Carrillo Masso, "Developing a Methodology."

31. Bayles and Orland, *Art and Fear*, 18–19.

REFERENCES

Abrams, N. *The New Jew in Film: Exploring Jewishness and Judaism in Contemporary Cinema*. New Brunswick, N.J.: Rutgers University Press, 2012.

Atkins, B. *More than a Game*. London: Continuum, 2003.

Baldry, A., and Thibault, P. *Multimodal Transcription and Text Analysis*. London: Equinox, 2005.

Bayles, D., and Orland, T. *Art and Fear: Observations on the Perils (and Rewards) of Artmaking*. London: Continuum, 2001.

Carrillo Masso, I. "Developing a Methodology for Corpus-Based Computer Game Studies." *Journal of Gaming and Virtual Worlds* 1, no. 2 (2009):143–169.

———. "The Grips of Fantasy: The Construction of Female Characters in and beyond Virtual Worlds." In *Creating Second Lives: Community, Identity and Spatiality as Constructions of the Virtual.* Edited by A. Ensslin and E. Muse. London: Routledge, 2011.

———. "Mapping the Magic Circle: Towards a Corpus-Based Multimodal Approach to the Study of Videogames." Paper presented at Under the Mask: Perspectives on the Player conference, Luton, England, June 2, 2010.

Chabon, M. *The Secret Yiddish Policemen's Union.* New York: HarperCollins, 2007.

Dovey, J., and Kennedy, H. *Game Cultures.* Maidenhead, England: Open University Press, 2006.

Elber, Lynn. "Putting Faith in Film: Hollywood Takes Back-Door Approach to Religion." 1997. http://www.s-t.com/daily/04-97/04-23-97/c04ae124.htm (accessed July 2007).

Graham, D. "European Jewish Identity at the Dawn of the 21st Century: A Working Paper (Report)." Budapest, May 20–23, 2004. http://www.jpr.org.uk/downloads/European_Jewish_Identity_in_21st_Century.pdf (accessed July 2013).

"The Hottest Websites in the Whole Wide World." *Irish Independent,* January 16, 2007. http://www.independent.ie/unsorted/features/the-hottest-websites-in-the-whole-wide-world-59689.html (accessed October 2012).

Hutchinson Guest, A. *Labanotation: The System of Analyzing and Recording Movement.* London: Routledge, 1987.

Johnson, S., and Ensslin, A. "Language in the Media: Theory and Practice." In *Language in the Media: Representations, Identities, Ideologies.* Edited by S. Johnson and A. Ensslin. London: Continuum, 2007.

Kelman, A., and Schoenberg, E. *Legwork, Framework, Artwork: Engaging the Next Generation of Jews.* Denver, Colo.: Rose Community Foundation, 2008.

Kress, G., and Van Leeuwen, T. *Reading Images: The Grammar of Visual Design.* London: Routledge, 1996.

Lando, M. "A Rabbi as Superhero – The Wacky Premise of a Hit Video Game." *Jerusalem Post,* January 5, 2007.

Love, M. C. "Not-So-Sacred Quests: Religion, Intertextuality, and Ethics in Video Games." *Religious Studies and Theology* 29, no. 2 (2010):191–213.

Piskorowski-Adams, A. "Films, Frames and Videogames: Religious Insights into Media." *Religious Studies and Theology* 29, no. 2 (2010):139–142.

Rosenberg, J. "Jewish Experience on Film – An American Overview." In *American Jewish Year Book, 1996.* Edited by D. Singer. New York: American Jewish Committee, 1996.

Rosenthal, R. "What's in a Name?: The Future of Post-Denominational Judaism." *Kedma* 1 (2006):20–32.

Shamah, D. "Pokemon and the Jewish Question." *Jerusalem Post,* February 3, 2006. http://www.jpost.com/HealthAndSci-Tech/SoftwareReview/Article.aspx?id=12023 (accessed October 2012).

Šisler, V. "Digital Arabs: Representation in Video Games." *European Journal of Cultural Studies* 11, no. 2 (2008):203–220.

THREE

The Global Mediatization
of Hinduism through Digital Games

REPRESENTATION VERSUS SIMULATION
IN *HANUMAN: BOY WARRIOR*

Xenia Zeiler

RESEARCH ON DIGITAL GAMES AND RELIGION HAS PRIMARILY concentrated on European and U.S. settings. Asian developments, except the Muslim Middle Eastern contexts of Syria and Palestine, have long been nearly completely overlooked.[1] This is even truer when it comes to digital games that are related to Hindu and Buddhist traditions, regions, and audiences. Though in the first decade of the twenty-first century, several aspects of Hindu and Buddhist religions and digital media, namely the internet, began to be increasingly researched, so far this research has not extended to digital games.[2] This is surprising since surveys, statistics, and projections on the role and importance of digital games in Asia or for audiences with Asian Hindu or Buddhist backgrounds regularly describe an ever larger percentage of users, as well as rapidly growing markets in the near future.

In this chapter I analyze Hindu deities and narratives in Indian-produced digital games and focus on disclosing negotiations of Hindu authority and identity in gaming contexts. I do so by discussing the first entirely India-developed digital game based on Hindu mythology, *Hanuman: Boy Warrior* (Aurona Technologies Hyderbad for Sony Computer Entertainment Europe, 2009), a console game produced for PlayStation 2. This game has caused heated debate on the appropriateness of incorporating Hindu deities in gaming environments. The debate surrounding the game has focused on the concepts of simulation and performance as opposed to the (pure) representation of Hindu deities, such as Hanuman, who is a major character in the Indian epic *Ramayana* and is mentioned in other important Hindu scriptures.

I first discuss the game's narrative and representations of Hanuman, which stay very close to highly popular and revered Hindu texts and narratives. I discuss theoretical arguments on digital gaming and narrative structures by Gonzalo Frasca, Jonas Carlquist, and Scott Brendan Cassidy and highlight the distinction of representation (as characteristic of narrative structures) versus simulation (as characteristic for gaming environments). Second, I analyze the intense debate on the game, which was initiated by the diaspora-based organization Universal Society of Hinduism, which criticized an alleged disrespect of Hindu deities in gaming environments. This analysis uncovers the debate's underlying processes of negotiating religious identity and authority in global, diaspora Hindu contexts. I argue that diaspora-based religious organizations and communities require and often utilize out-of-the-ordinary means for self-representation and authority negotiation and to generally position or sustain themselves in diaspora environments. In this case, a debate on a digital game with a high amount of media attention in primarily the United States was employed to (1) negotiate Hindu authority, (2) establish a characteristic identity marker for one particular Hindu organization, and (3) construct and present a particular picture of "Hindu-ness" as approved by the Universal Society of Hinduism, a group that clearly represents and promotes an interpretation of Hinduism as defined in classical Hindu texts. The Nevada-based, self-declared "nondenominational religious-philosophical-cultural-educational organization," officially established in 2011 but operating for many years before that, aspires "to provide worldwide Hindu identity, [to] enhance understanding of Hinduism, and to foster interreligious dialogue" and denotes its mission as "motivating, educating and empowering people through Hinduism to make positive social, personal and environmental changes."[3] The group's activities in the United States mainly target a mainstream (Hindu and non-Hindu) public and primarily aims at promoting a rather conventional or even orthodox view of the Hindu religion.

I conclude with a discussion of digital gaming and Hindu settings. By analyzing *Hanuman: Boy Warrior* and considering more recent developments in Indian games, such as *Ra.One: The Game* (Trine Games Mumbai for Sony Computer Entertainment Europe, 2011), this chapter points to key questions in the new field of research on religion and digital gaming which deal specifically with how games are interpreted in global and diaspora settings. Understanding *Hanuman: Boy Warrior* is significant because, in a rather open and easily decipherable way, general Hindu issues and values, and thus Hindu identity, were brought to the attention of an American audience.

BACKGROUND: DIGITAL GAMING IN THE ASIAN AND INDIAN MARKETS

Reports on digital gaming audiences demonstrate growing markets in Asia, moving beyond the traditional Japanese market. For instance, market analysts estimate an increase of the worth of the Asia Pacific digital games market from $US11.2 billion in 2010 to $US30.3 billion in 2016.[4] Starting in the early twenty-first century, game expos have been regularly organized in several Asian regions; the biggest Asian expo, China-Joy, is among the top three game expos in the world. Another influential expo is the Global Gaming Expo Asia (G2E Asia), which promotes digital gaming in Asia and connects Asians to Western markets. Significant games conventions, such as the World Cyber Games in Malaysia; games festivals, such as the Clementi Game Festival in Singapore; and games conferences, such as the Social Gaming Asia Summit in Macao,[5] are the order of the day in many Asian regions as much as they are in the West.

While as yet South Asia has not seen a high rate of growth, India has to be included in the list of Asian countries in which digital games are an influential media genre. Digital gaming is a relevant factor in negotiating and shaping culture, society, and religion in South Asia. Market studies predicted a growth rate of 32 percent for the Indian gaming industry from 2012 to 2014, reaching a height of $US560 million in 2014.[6] The current market share of India in the global gaming industry is still below 1 percent (0.6 percent in 2012), but the estimated growth rate implies that India is on a fast track to gain a significant market share in the global gaming industry soon. India increasingly hosts large and well-visited games expos and conventions, such as the India Gaming Carnival in Noida/Delhi, and games conferences, such as Gaming Conference India in Bangalore.[7]

These changes are rooted in two developments in India since the late 1990s: rapid national economic expansion and the new extensive mediatization in urban regions. For Western contexts, mediatization is an established concept, which has been defined as a process with immense influence on society and culture: "Today, we can say that mediatization means at least the following: a) Changing media environments, . . . b) An increase of different media, . . . c) The changing functions of old media, . . .d) New and increasing functions of digital media for the people and a growth of media in general, . . . e) Changing communication forms."[8]

Since these media changes are increasingly discernible also in South Asia and since they most certainly and massively influence society, culture, and religion in the area, the concept of mediatization, so far described and analyzed for settings in the West,[9] to me seems highly applicable for South Asia as well. Economic growth has resulted in the rise of a relatively broad well-earning middle class in urban India (in addition to a very wealthy, but less broad upper class). Especially in India's megacities, interest in novel leisure activities has expanded along with growing incomes.[10] Mediatized activities based on new technologies, such as digital games, increasingly serve as status markers in the realigning middle class, a factor that again amplifies the rising popularity of such technologies.[11] The spread of especially online gaming is additionally related to another innovation, namely the rapidly evolving broadband internet coverage in Indian cities.[12] Taking all these developments into account, it is important to note that digital gaming in India is still largely a phenomenon of urban and middle- to upper-class contexts and that it is a domain of younger males: "According to an estimate, the typical Indian gamer is a male from the top eight metros, has an average age of 26 and belongs to the affluent section. The average gamer has been playing on an average since 18 months now. The average person plays games three times a week and his usual gaming sessions last an hour in length."[13]

There are four reasons for the very high market growth expectations for digital gaming in India despite the relatively exclusive audience actively involved at present.[14] First, the audience in question belongs to the fastest growing demographic group in India: about 70 percent of the inhabitants are below the age of thirty-five. Second, the targeted group for digital gaming belongs to the most affluent sector of the society, which is showing increasing consumerism. Third, India is actively making efforts to speed broadband coverage in the country. Last, the organization, distribution, and advertising patterns for digital gaming have been extensively restructured in India since about 2010. In order to consolidate and intensify market strategies and to battle piracy, new distribution channels for digital gaming in India were introduced.[15] The restructured chains and networks also initiated extensive mainstream advertising for digital gaming. And a strong pioneering spirit in India's game-developing companies has been noted: "I'm absolutely sure that India is the next frontier for many gaming companies. India as well as Brazil. But Brazil has had a lot of interest and done very well in the last few years. India is still untapped."[16]

Digital gaming is thus increasingly important in India. Additionally, there is a large gaming audience among the so-called NRI (lit. "non-residential Indians," i.e., Indians living outside India, mainly in the United States and in Europe). As digital games are such an increasingly important mass media genre for a rapidly growing part of South Asian society, they have to be taken into account when researching negotiations of culture, society, and religion. As much as they influence cultural and social transformations in general, they also (re)shape and (de)construct details of religious symbols, ideas, and beliefs. They may also contribute to the negotiation of cultural and religious identity.

DIGITAL GAMES IN HINDU CONTEXTS: THE NARRATIVE OF *HANUMAN: BOY WARRIOR*

The majority of digital games sold, played, and produced in India are globally distributed. Globally successful games are also well received in India, and the average player shows no significant cultural or region-based preferences. At present, the Indian digital gaming market is clearly dominated by games produced in the West with almost no references to the South Asian context. This is not at all surprising considering the social – overall Western or globally oriented – background of average Indian gamers. Still, the nearly complete absence of digital games designed and produced especially for an audience with Hindu roots is astonishing. Few attempts have been made to produce elaborate (i.e., expensive) games focusing on Hindu themes, mythologies, or concepts, and there is a limited number of console games or online games on these topics. But this has nothing to do with religious or ideological issues. The fact that a fair number of basic online games on Hindu mythology and deities are freely available and remain without criticism clearly points at market reasons for this absence.[17] To invest in expensive game development and production targeting Hindu gamers *only* seems to still be considered unprofitable. This applies to both the online games and console games markets. For elaborate online games, the internet coverage in many regions of India is still insufficient and only a relatively small audience could be targeted. Console games, on the other hand, require additional costs for hardware, which again limits the potential audience.

Nevertheless, the first elaborate digital game entirely based on Hindu mythology and produced in India was released on March 25, 2009. The console game *Hanuman: Boy Warrior* was developed in the Hyderabad studio of Aurona Technologies Limited and was published by Sony Computer Entertainment Europe. The game was touted in advertisements as being the first Indian game to be released for PlayStation 2 and clearly targeted a Hindu audience.[18] The game is based on the adventures of the Bal Hanuman (lit. "Boy Hanuman"). For the player, the ultimate objective in *Hanuman: Boy Warrior* is to free the sun god and to kill as many demons as possible or banish them back to the underworld:

> This game is a growing up story of Lord Hanuman, where he starts as a powerless being and regains his powers through the game. Throughout the game Hanuman (Player) meets Sadhus (Sages) and learns more about Hanuman and his powers. One day, he realizes that he (Bal Hanuman) himself is Hanuman. From there on he starts regaining his powers, one by one. He finally gets his Gadhaa (mace) which is his primary weapon. Through his Gadhaa he gains the ability to fight the Asuras (Demons) & for every Asura he kills he can accumulate their life force into his Gadhaa.[19]

The game's narrative thus closely follows Hindu mythology as presented in highly popular and revered texts. There, the male deity Hanuman is constantly depicted as a loyal companion of Rama, assisting him and his army in the search for Rama's abducted wife, Sita, and in the battle against evil. The texts indeed frequently speak of Hanuman actively fighting evil Asuras in battle and having a mace as his weapon. The prominent position given in the game to the sun god, Surya, is based on textually transmitted Hindu mythology as well. Several texts refer to Hanuman choosing the sun god as his teacher and describe the process of this teaching.

Hanuman rose to prominence from the second century BCE to the second century CE epic *Ramayana* to become one of Hinduism's most popular deities.[20] In Hinduism, he is strongly associated with virtue and with unquestioning, everlasting love for god. This perception is based on the mythological background of the *Ramayana,* which depicts Hanuman as an extremely devoted but nevertheless vigorously acting attendant to the royal deity Rama. Hanuman's true-to-life depiction in the texts and his attributed warm but powerful character are probably the main reasons for the deity's extraordinary popularity. His manifold mythological adventures have been firmly incorporated into Hindu religions and culture for about two thousand years and they are extensively retold in texts as well as restaged beyond texts, for instance in theatrical performances.[21] Also, modern mass media such as film productions for cinema or television, television series, and comics have repeatedly taken up Hanuman and represented him in various contexts as a heroic divine figure righteously battling evil.[22]

The game's straight storyline would seem to make it a good example supporting the theoretical idea of understanding digital games as a narrative genre, as for instance Carlquist and, partly, Cassidy do.[23] Carlquist clearly defines computer games as narrative genre and, more explicitly, as a hero's journey.[24] This narrative structure is clearly detectable in *Hanuman: Boy Warrior.* Cassidy argues that we should understand digital games as "a form of narrative, albeit a unique one" and stresses the distinct interaction in the genre.[25] This, as well, is applicable to *Hanuman: Boy Warrior,* which clearly displays a narrative pattern very much resembling South Asian textual or filmic storytelling, which is widespread and thus familiar to the gaming audience. For instance, the branching of the storyline by gamers may be easily connected to a characteristic way of storytelling in South Asia, which has a long and elaborate textual tradition of narrative interpolation techniques where branches deriving from the main storyline are incorporated into the frame narrative.[26] The game, then, does not shake the established narrative (or aesthetic) habits of an Indian audience. The specific new elements in *Hanuman: Boy Warrior* (and, as we shall see, the main reasons for the hefty critique of the game) do not concern the way the story is presented. Rather, they are genre specific: what is new is the interactive element. The narrative when transformed into a digital game becomes hypertext and has to be understood and analyzed as such. In this, I follow Frasca, who contradicts the framing of simulation versus narrative (and representation), and Cassidy, who argues that digital games should be conceptualized and analyzed drawing on narratological, as well as ludological, approaches and that "interacting with a videogame text is in fact an act of narration in 'real-time,' in the 'present'" and who sees digital games as narratives created by the player's interaction.[27]

The tradition of representing Hanuman and of actively reenacting his mythology is of long standing and deeply rooted in Hinduism. For this reason and because of the deity's high popularity and "action-oriented" mythological background, it seemed consistent to feature Hanuman in the new emerging media genre of digital gaming. Additionally, Hanuman showed some "media experience" already: he had been successfully incorporated into other genres of modern mass media before digital games, including films, such as *Hanuman* (2005); print comics, such as *Bheema and Hanuman* (1980); and television series, such as *Ramayan* (1987–1988). And Hanuman had been successfully incorporated into gaming genres other than console games before. In all basic arcade and platform online games with an explicitly Hindu background, Hanuman is staged as the main hero more often than any other deity.[28] For all of these reasons, success was expected for the innovative move of the Indian gaming industry to produce a console game incorporating the deity Hanuman as Boy Warrior.

REPRESENTATION AND SIMULATION
IN *HANUMAN: BOY WARRIOR*

Taking the established and popular tradition of representing and staging Hanuman beyond the classical texts of Hinduism into account, choosing the deity as the hero in the first entirely India-developed digital game made perfect sense, and nothing signaled trouble ahead for the game's release. But immediately after its release, *Hanuman: Boy Warrior* drew significant negative attention from two different sides. On one hand, the gaming community reacted with intense critiques of technical aspects of the game. In reviews and reports from journalists and gamers alike, the character modeling was constantly described as bad and the character animations were labeled as stiff. The critique was obviously shared even by reviewers with outspoken sympathy for the Indian gaming industry:

> I've seen better character modelling done by animation students; so to have this kind of quality pour into what the guys at Sony claim to be India's maiden voyage into PlayStation 2 game development, is undeniably shameful.... Come on Aurona! If you're trying to capture a part of Indian Mythology through the gaming medium, at least try to do it justice.[29] I've tried really hard to look for something positive in this game, but it just isn't there.... This is, without a doubt, the worst console game I've ever played, and I'm pretty sure the worst game ever to be published by Sony Computer Entertainment.... It just makes you wonder if they have different quality standards for India and the West.... Studios need to realize that Indians will not settle for garbage just because they're new to gaming.[30]

On the other hand, the game's release immediately kindled a heated debate on the appropriateness of including Hindu deities in digital gaming. *Hanuman: Boy Warrior* was massively attacked by a number of Hindu groups and organizations, mainly based in the United States and Australia, demanding the withdrawal of the game.[31] The debate was headed by the Nevada-based Universal Society of Hinduism, which accused the game of trivializing the Hindu deity Hanuman. But the arguments focused on one specific point of this alleged trivialization, namely that the player could "control and manipulate" the deity in the game. The spokesman for the Universal Society of Hinduism, Rajan Zed, argued that players would control the destiny of Hanuman in the game while in reality believers put their destinies in the deity's hands. His statement was widely taken up in the internet news coverage worldwide: "Controlling and manipulating Lord Hanuman with a joystick/button/ keyboard/mouse is denigration. Lord Hanuman was not meant to be reduced to just a 'character' in a video game to solidify company/products base in the growing economy of India."[32]

This line of argument touches on a number of the most characteristic features of digital gaming. While gaming surely may be discussed by referring to theoretical ideas about ludology, playfulness, or immersion, what seems most clearly referred to here are the concepts of simulation and performance as opposed to (pure) representation. When Zed critiques *Hanuman: Boy Warrior*, he does not focus on the potential to construct ideas, concepts, or values in the game. Nor does he argue against a general inclusion of Hindu topics in digital games or against generally representing Hindu deities in digital media or even in digital gaming. On the contrary, in an open letter to Sony demanding the withdrawal of the game, he welcomes a "serious and respectful" incorporation of Hinduism into new media, as long as the representations stay in line with his interpretation of Hinduism: "Video game makers should be more sensitive while handling faith related subjects, as these games left lasting impact on the minds of highly impressionable children, teens and other young people. Hindus welcomed entertainment industry to immerse in Hinduism but taking it seriously and respectfully. . . . Hindus would gladly provide genuine entertainment industry seekers the resources they needed for their study and research regarding Hinduism."[33]

The focal point of the whole debate, then, is the player's ability to allegedly "control and manipulate" a deity's representation through the technical means of the gaming genre. To proceed from a deity's sole representation in textual or visual narrative frames to the new genre-specific mode of being actively able/obliged to modify – that is, play – the narrative seems to make all the difference for the Universal Society of Hinduism. Even though the practice of staging Hanuman in theatrical performances is widespread in Hinduism, this praxis is restricted to the staging of a textually accurate, predetermined, and sanctified mythological narrative and deity representation. When Hanuman is represented in media genres other than digital games, for instance in film or in television series, this representation remains consistent with textual prescriptions and does *not* include the possibility of alterations in the narrative, for instance to maybe lose a battle.

This way of contrasting representation (as characteristic of narrative structures) versus simulation (as characteristic of gaming environments) has been discussed in game theory before. Frasca clearly stated that "traditional media are representational, not simulational" and sees traditional media, such as photos and films, as restricted to narrative structures. They are characterized by "producing both descriptions of traits and sequences of events (narrative)," and they lack the possibility of manipulation.[34] Drawing on Aarseth, Frasca develops his argument that semiotic sequences of film, for instance, and simulation might be identical, but that this analogy is not sufficient to characterize simulation as a whole. To him, the potential of digital games is not to tell a story, but to create an environment for experimentation.[35] In the context of the debate on *Hanuman: Boy Warrior,* exactly this potential proved to be the offending object: the simulation in the game opened up room for experimenting with an established narrative and representation. This posed a threat to fundamental Hindu objectives *and* to the authority of Hindu organizations – such as the Universal Society of Hinduism – resting upon such objectives.

Consequently, the Universal Society of Hinduism and a number of like-minded organizations in the Hindu diaspora, such as the Forum for Hindu Awakening (United States) and Sanatan Sanstha (Australia), joined by some India-based organizations, such as the Hindu Janajagruti Samiti, Hindu Alliance of India, and Shri Ramayan Pracharini Sabha, demanded the complete withdrawal of the game.[36] When Sony did not react, the debate's tone got less friendly. In an ultimatum that drew vast attention in internet news coverage, Rajan Zed threatened Sony with a general boycott of all its products by Hindus worldwide if the game were not recalled. This was not the first time that he had fiercely demanded censorship when Hindu deities were incorporated into mainstream mass media, attracting both public and media attention.[37]

MEDIATIZED NEGOTIATIONS OF HINDU AUTHORITY AND
IDENTITY IN GLOBAL DIASPORA SETTINGS: SUBTEXTS
IN THE MEDIA DEBATE ON *HANUMAN: BOY WARRIOR*

The dominant arguments brought up by the Universal Society of Hinduism criticize the game's potential to control or manipulate the deity Hanuman, that is, they criticize the potential for simulation, and as such they are applicable only to the genre of digital gaming. But even if the line of argument in this case focuses on a genre-specific detail, the main objective in the debate, namely the wish to ban unapproved incorporations of Hindu deities into modern mass media, has to be understood and analyzed in context. For this, it is important to note the history of the Universal Society of Hinduism's media activity. The protests basically stand on the same ground as criticisms of the alleged disrespectful representation of Hindu deities and concepts in Western films, for instance, *Avatar* (2009) and *The Love Guru* (2008), or in the television series *Xena: Warrior Princess* (1995–2001). Some of these debates drew large media attention and resulted in concessions from the producing companies. The public debate on *Xena: Warrior Princess*, for instance, resulted in a temporarily imposed production code: the episode in question was withdrawn from airing for several months.[38] What essentially distinguishes these earlier media debates from the one on *Hanuman: Boy Warrior* is the shift from criticizing *representations* of Hindu deities to criticizing manipulable *simulations* of Hindu deities. With the emerging genre of digital games, the major objective – to ban the unwanted incorporation of Hindu deities into modern mass media – was adjusted according to the new technological capabilities.

Though other Hindu organizations publicly protest against similar issues, the Universal Society of Hinduism, to the best of my knowledge, is the most active of its type worldwide. And it surely is no coincidence that an organization based in the Hindu diaspora, instead of South Asia, holds this position. Though, occasionally, media protests also occur in India, the majority of intense media protests as discussed here occur outside South Asia.[39] Also, the protest against *Hanuman: Boy Warrior* was almost exclusively restricted to the West. Although some Indian organizations joined the debate once it was opened by Rajan Zed, only diaspora-based Hindu organizations criticized the embedding of Hanuman in a game setting. In India, nobody seemed to care about this issue much. In fact, a large internet audience applauded the inclusion of Hindu mythology and deities in digital gaming, a step obviously understood as a respectful sign honoring the growing number of Hindu Indian gamers.

There are, of course, reasons for such a focusing of media protests in diaspora contexts. Diaspora-based groups and communities, and religious groups or communities in particular, require and apply different identity markers and authority negotiation platforms than do similar groups in non-diaspora settings. In addition to the complex of factors that contribute to the shaping, construction, and negotiation of a religious organization's authority and identity in the homeland, diaspora contexts also must take into account the particularities of the country of residence. One particularity in Western diaspora settings surely is the advanced mediatization of society and religion, which also affects the authority negotiations of religious organizations and their leaders.[40] It is not surprising that diaspora organizations increasingly employ modern mass media for authority and identity negotiations. But such public negotiations are only seldom straightforward in calling the agenda by its name. Rather, they may be interwoven into more general debates on religion, in which case much attention is given to the media news coverage of the debate in question.[41]

There are two general ways that religious authority and identity are publicly negotiated and promoted in the diaspora so as to draw appropriate media attention. Compared to non-diaspora negotiations, first there is a shift in the topics picked up as the initiators for authority and identity negotiations. They are often selected with consideration of the current discourses and debates in the country of residence. Second, there is a shift in the platforms primarily chosen for these negotiations. Digital media and especially the internet are intensively employed.

These points are also true for the Hindu diaspora, and the debate on *Hanuman: Boy Warrior* is a perfect example. By initiating a media debate on the game, the Universal Society of Hinduism created for itself a remarkable platform, drawing much public attention for promoting (1) "Hindu-ness" as approved by the organization and thus Hindu identity in the United States, and (2) its own authority as a powerful defender of "real" Hindu values and thus Hindu authority in the United States. Though religious authority is always constructed and perceived in multiple layers, here, leaning on Weber, "authority" mainly refers to hierarchy (including the leadership of Rajan Zed) and structure (of the Universal Society of Hinduism).[42]

In the debate, in a rather open and easily decipherable way, general Hindu issues and values and thus Hindu identity (as approved by the organization) were brought to the awareness of an American audience. Hindu deities like Hanuman and Hinduism's ancient textual traditions were lauded, Hinduism's global importance was referred to, and so on. But in a more concealed manner, the supremacy of the Universal Society of Hinduism and the authority of its leader were promoted and negotiated. By positioning himself as a true defender of Hinduism not afraid to oppose even giant companies like Sony, Raja Zed staged himself as *the one* Hindu authority before both the American public and the Hindu community in the United States. He claimed the Universal Society of Hinduism's authoritarian supremacy over other Hindu organizations and groups in the United States. The media debate thus brought much-wanted attention to the organization, enforcing its acceptance and status in its own community as well as beyond it.

CONCLUSION AND FUTURE OUTLOOK

Digital gaming is still a relatively new phenomenon in India. It is maybe not surprising, then, that the first elaborate digital game developed in India leaned on Hindu mythology and caused such intense debates. Both the narrative and the deity in the game were based on established and revered religious texts, but the incorporation of Hindu deities and their alleged utilization for commercial purposes was strongly opposed by several Hindu organizations, especially the Universal Society of Hinduism based in the United States. More recent developments in Indian games, on the other hand, show a more open and playful approach to religion. Released in 2011, *Ra.One: The Game,* based on the Bollywood science fiction blockbuster, incorporates Hindu themes in a much more general manner than does *Hanuman: Boy Warrior.* For the first time in Indian history, a number of game versions were released along with the film, and like contemporary Indian cinema (Bollywood), the game seems to confirm a trend in Indian media to increasingly cater to both NRI diaspora and Western audiences. In both the film and the game *Ra.One* are references to Hindu mythology; these are easily and immediately decipherable for the Hindu audience without, at the same time, being overemphasized, so as not to alienate the Western audience. The clearest example of this is the name and character of the film's and game's protagonist, Ra.One. Shorthand for "Random Access Version One," both the name and the character also toy with the mythological figure Ravan, who in Hindu mythology is perhaps the most well-known demonic character. The trend to include references to Hindu mythology without overemphasizing them seems to point to the Indian gaming industry's increasing ambition to catch up with the global market without completely losing its own identity. The result has been a shift from rather conventional, text-conforming representations of Hinduism to new, emerging, playful, and even experimental representations. I label these representations in both digital games and films "global or transcultural representations of Hinduism," since they target a global audience and arise for obviously economic reasons.

This chapter has attempted to provide some groundwork for studying the emerging field of digital games with Indian and Hindu backgrounds, which to date has been understudied. The central issues that are currently being negotiated in digital games with Hindu contexts and that raise public debate include (1) the Hindu religious symbol system (for instance, concerning deities, mythology, and iconography), (2) Hindu religious and cultural identity in global or transcultural diaspora as well as in Indian contexts (for instance, concerning diaspora communities), and (3) social realities with regard to Hinduism (for instance, concerning issues of caste or purity in contemporary, predominantly urban Hindu society). Negotiations on these issues and topics previously dominated the debates on film with Hindu contexts, and they currently also dominate the debates on South Asian digital games. What is clear even at this early stage of research is that digital games are perceived as an adequate media genre, just as for instance film, allowing for (de)constructions and negotiations of Hindu religious issues – more so when relevant for a globalized South Asian audience.

Though this chapter has focused on a Hindu-based digital game, it raises a number of general research issues regarding religiously themed digital games and potential controversies related to them. Protests against the alleged disrespectful or even blasphemous utilization of deities or religious narratives, concepts, and symbols in games are not limited to Hindu contexts. In fact, the concerns of religious groups and organizations around such issues may be so similar that they join hands in their protests, as some did in the case of the multiplayer online battle arena game *Smite* (Hi-Rez Studios for Microsoft Windows, 2012).[43] Here, Catholic, Buddhist, and Jewish organizations supported the Universal Society of Hinduism in protesting the incorporation of the goddess Kali in an online game out of "respect for religious practice and beliefs."[44] Obviously, religious narratives, concepts, or symbols in digital games (as much as in other media genres before) are regularly contested, no matter what religious tradition is involved. But such public debates often carry complex subtexts of implicit negotiations, for instance, around religious authority, identity, or community. These are significant underlying issues to be deciphered, and they are some of the most important topics for further research on religion in digital gaming.

NOTES

1. A number of studies by Vít Šisler have researched digital games and religion in the area, focusing on the Arab-Israeli conflict. See, for instance, Šisler, "Palestine in Pixels"; Šisler, "Digital Arabs."

2. For Buddhist traditions, see, for instance, Cheong, Huang, and Poon, "Cultivating Online and Offline Pathways to Enlightenment"; Connelly, "Virtual Buddhism"; Grieve, "Virtually Embodying the Field"; Grieve, *Digital Zen*. For Hindu traditions, see, for instance, Helland, "(Virtually) Been There, (Virtually) Done That"; Karapanagiotis, "Vaishnava Cyber-Puja"; Scheifinger, "Hindu Embodiment and the Internet"; Scheifinger, "Hinduism and Cyberspace."

3. See Rajan Zed, Official Website; and Universal Society of Hinduism, Official Website.

4. Ovum, *Digital Gaming Market in Asia-Pacific*.

5. For more details on all of these, see ChinaJoy, Official Website; G2E Asia, Official Website; World Cyber Games Malaysia, Official Website;

Clementi Game Festival Singapore, Facebook Event Page; Social Gaming Asia Summit, Official Website.

6. Results of a study by the market research firm Market Xcel, January 2012. For more details and for expected numbers in the different gaming genres, see Exchange4media News Service, "Indian Gaming Industry to Reach Rs. 3,100 cr. by 2014."

7. For more details, see India Gaming Carnival, Official Website; Gaming Conference India, Official Website.

8. Krotz, "Media Connectivity," 24.

9. See, for instance, Couldry, "Mediatization or Mediation?"; Hepp, *Cultures of Mediatization*; Hjarvard, *The Mediatization of Culture and Society*.

10. Brosius, *India's Middle Class*.

11. Zeiler, "Ethno-Indology in Times of Modern Mass Media."

12. Vaidyanathan, "Is 2012 the Year for India's Internet?"

13. Exchange4media News Service, "Indian Gaming Industry to Reach Rs. 3,100 cr. by 2014."

XENIA ZEILER

14. The market research study by Market Xcel in 2012 identified five factors as key growth drivers: "heavy advertising, games with relevant content, innovative distribution models, increasing broadband speeds and [a] large potential [audience] segment." See Exchange4media News Service, "Indian Gaming Industry to Reach Rs. 3,100 cr. by 2014."

15. For this, large companies operating in the media sector basically bundled their digital media distribution and included the advertisement of digital games in their new networks. For one example, see Desai, "Review: *Hanuman: Boy Warrior.*"

16. Robin Alter of Kreeda Games, quoted in Handrahan, "Emerging Markets: India."

17. Online games featuring the deity Hanuman that are freely available include action games, such as *Ravan Dahan Game*; dress-up games, such as *Hanuman Dress Up*; quiz games, such as *Hindu Gods and Goddesses Quiz*; and platform games, such as *Little Hanuman.*

18. For an interview with the Indian producer Santosh Pillai, see Makwana, "*Hanuman: Boy Warrior* Maker Speaks."

19. Official game introduction by Sony, quoted in Prashar, "Sony Way of Denegrating [*sic*] Lord Hanuman."

20. For details on the *Ramayana*, see, for instance, Brockington, *Righteous Rāma.* For Hanuman's development in textual Hindu traditions, see, for instance, Ludvik, *Hanumān in the Rāmāyaṇa of Vālmīki.* For his representations and worship in popular, lived Hinduism, see, for instance, Keul, *Hanumān, der Gott in Affengestalt;* and Lutgendorf, *Hanuman's Tale.*

21. See, for instance, Lutgendorf, *The Life of a Text;* and van der Veer, "Life as Theatre."

22. For examples of Hanuman's representations in modern mass media, see Lutgendorf, "Evolving a Monkey"; Lutgendorf, "All in the (Raghu) Family."

23. Carlquist, "Playing the Story"; Cassidy, "The Videogame as Narrative." For detailed discussions of digital games as narrative genre, see Jenkins, "Game Design as Narrative Architecture"; and Juul, "Gaming Telling Stories."

24. Carlquist, "Playing the Story."

25. Cassidy, "The Videogame as Narrative."

26. For a detailed discussion of the structure and narrative of a Hanuman interpolation in the *Ramayana,* see Lutgendorf, "Hanumān's Adventures Underground." This popular textual practice was also taken up by filmic media.

27. See Frasca, "Simulation versus Narrative"; Frasca, "Play the Message"; Cassidy, "The Videogame as Narrative," 297.

28. As examples, see *Hanuman: Journey to Lanka* and *Little Hanuman.*

29. See Singh, "Review: *Hanuman – Boy Warrior.*"

30. Desai, "Review: *Hanuman: Boy Warrior.*"

31. The leading organization in the debate, the U.S.-based Universal Society of Hinduism, was joined by, for instance, the Forum for Hindu Awakening (United States) and Sanatan Sanstha (Australia). For a list of the protesting groups and the names of their speakers in the debate, see "The Worldwide Hindu Boycott of Sony Is Officially On."

32. Gibson, "Hindu Society Asks Sony to Withdraw Game."

33. Nunneley, "Universal Society of Hinduism Wants Sony to Pull *Hanuman: Boy Warrior.*"

34. Frasca, "Simulation versus Narrative," 223.

35. Frasca, "Simulation versus Narrative"; Aarseth, *Cybertext.* For a discussion of the subject in educational contexts, see Squire, "From Content to Context."

36. For all protesting groups and for the names of their speakers in the debate, see "The Worldwide Hindu Boycott of Sony Is Officially On."

37. A detailed list of Rajan Zed's activities in the press, including his history of protests against incorporating Hindu deities into mainstream mass media mainly in the West, is available at Hindu American Foundation, Official Website.

38. For a discussion and analysis of the debate about representing the Hindu deity Krishna in *Xena: Warrior Princess* and the resulting production code, see Zeiler, "Universal's Religious Bigotry against Hinduism."

39. In India, such protests were brought about nearly exclusively by Hindu nationalist groups. For an example, see Hindujagruti, "Protest: Denigration of Hindu Gods."

40. For detailed theoretical discussions and some case studies, see Campbell, *When Religion Meets New Media*; Campbell, "Religious Authority and the Blogosphere"; Campbell, "Who's Got the Power?"; Cheong, Huang, and Poon, "Cultivating Online and Offline Pathways to Enlightenment"; Cheong, Huang, and Poon, "Religious Communication and Epistemic Authority."

41. See Zeiler, "Universal's Religious Bigotry against Hinduism," for analysis of one example from a Hindu setting.

42. For a typology of religious authority related to the internet, mainly based on Weber, see Campbell, "Who's Got the Power?" For the classical typology of authority, see Max Weber, *Theory of Social and Economic Organization.*

43. van der Byl, "Catholics, Jews, Buddhists Team Up."

44. Ibid.

REFERENCES

Aarseth, Espen. *Cybertext: Perspectives on Ergodic Literature.* Baltimore, Md.: Johns Hopkins University Press, 1997.

Brockington, John L. *Righteous Rāma: The Evolution of an Epic.* Delhi: Oxford University Press, 1985.

Brosius, Christiane. *India's Middle Class: New Forms of Urban Leisure, Consumption and Prosperity.* London: Routledge, 2010.

Campbell, Heidi. "Religious Authority and the Blogosphere." *Journal of Computer-Mediated Communication* 15, no. 2 (2010):251–276. http://onlinelibrary.wiley.com/doi/10.1111/j.1083-6101.2010.01519.x/pdf.

———. *When Religion Meets New Media.* New York: Routledge, 2010.

———. "Who's Got the Power?: Religious Authority and the Internet." *Journal of Computer-Mediated Communication* 12, no. 3 (2007). http://jcmc.indiana.edu/vo112/issue3/campbell.html (accessed September 10, 2012).

Carlquist, Jonas. "Playing the Story: Computer Games as a Narrative Genre." *Human IT* 6, no. 3 (2002): 7–53. http://etjanst.hb.se/bhs/ith/3-02/jc.pdf.

Cassidy, Scott Brendan. "The Videogame as Narrative." *Quarterly Review of Film and Video* 28, no. 4 (2011):292–306. http://dx.doi.org/10.1080/10509200902820266.

Cheong, Pauline Hope, Huang, Shirlena, and Poon, Jessie P. H. "Cultivating Online and Offline Pathways to Enlightenment: Religious Authority and Strategic Arbitration in Wired Buddhist Organizations." *Information, Communication and Society* 14, no. 8 (2011):1160–1180. http://paulinehopecheong.com/media/f64d0095e158f468ffff830affffe41e.pdf.

———. "Religious Communication and Epistemic Authority of Leaders in Wired Faith Organizations." *Journal of Communication* 61 (2011):938–958. http://onlinelibrary.wiley.com/doi/10.1111/j.1460-2466.2011.01579.x/pdf.

ChinaJoy. Official Website. http://www.chinaexhibition.com (accessed September 10, 2012).

Clementi Game Festival Singapore. Facebook Event Page. 2012. https://www.facebook.com/events/391090594264586 (accessed September 10, 2012).

Connelly, Louise. "Virtual Buddhism: An Analysis of Aesthetics in Relation to Religious Practice within *Second Life*." *Heidelberg Journal of Religions on the Internet* 4, no. 1 (2010):12–34. http://archiv.ub.uni-heidelberg.de/volltextserver/volltexte/2010/11296/pdf/03.pdf.

Couldry, Nick. "Mediatization or Mediation?: Alternative Understandings of the Emergent Space of Digital Storytelling." *New Media & Society* 10, no. 3 (2008):373–391. http://nms.sagepub.com/content/10/3/373.full.pdf+html.

Desai, Sameer. "Review: *Hanuman: Boy Warrior*." *IndianVideoGamer*. http://www.indianvideogamer.com/reviews/review-hanuman-boy-warrior (accessed September 10, 2012).

Exchange4media News Service. "Indian Gaming Industry to Reach Rs. 3,100 cr. by 2014." http://www.exchange4media.com/44996_indian-gaming-industry-to-reach-rs-3100-cr-by-2014.html (accessed January 16, 2012).

Frasca, Gonzalo. "Play the Message." Ph.D. diss., 2007, University of Copenhagen. http://www.powerfulrobot.com/Frasca_Play_the_Message_PhD.pdf (accessed September 10, 2012).

———. "Simulation versus Narrative." In *The Video Game Theory Reader*. Edited by Mark J. P. Wolf and Bernard Perron, 221–236. London: Routledge, 2003.

G2E Asia. Official Website. http://www.g2easia.com/en/home (accessed September 10, 2012).

Gaming Conference India. Official Website. http://www.siliconindia.com/events-overview/game-animation-conference-Bangalore-Gaming_AnimationBang.html (accessed September 10, 2012).

Gibson, Ellie. "Hindu Society Asks Sony to Withdraw Game: Says *Hanuman: Boy Warrior* Is Offensive." *Eurogamer*. http://www.eurogamer.net/articles/hindu-society-asks-sony-to-withdraw-game (accessed April 20, 2009).

Grieve, Gregory P. *Digital Zen: Buddhism, Virtual Worlds, and the New Economy*. Forthcoming.

———. "Virtually Embodying the Field: Silent Online Buddhist Meditation, Immersion, and the Cardean Ethnographic Method." *Heidelberg Journal of Religions on the Internet* 4, no.1 (2010): 35–62. http://archiv.ub.uni-heidelberg.de/volltextserver/volltexte/2010/11296/pdf/03.pdf.

Handrahan, Matthew. "Emerging Markets: India." *Gamesindustry International.* http://www.gamesindustry.biz/articles/2012-03-05-emerging-markets-india (accessed March 5, 2012).

Hanuman: Boy Warrior. Aurona Technologies Hyderabad for Sony Computer Entertainment Europe, 2009.

Hanuman: Journey to Lanka. Obsession Games.co.in. http://www.fupa.com/game/Action-flash-games/hanuman-jouney-to-lanka_v444658.html.

Helland, Christopher. "(Virtually) Been There, (Virtually) Done That: Examining the Online Religious Practices of the Hindu Tradition: Introduction." *Heidelberg Journal of Religions on the Internet* 4, no. 1 (2010):148–150. http://archiv.ub.uni-heidelberg.de/volltextserver/volltexte/2010/11302/pdf/08.pdf.

Hepp, Andreas. *Cultures of Mediatization.* Cambridge: Polity, 2012.

Hindu American Foundation. Official Website. http://www.hinducurrents.com/topic/profile/rajan-zed/?page=1 (accessed September 10, 2012).

Hindu Gods and Goddesses Quiz. http://www.funtrivia.com/playquiz/quiz535466240b8.htm.

Hindujagruti. "Protest: Denigration of Hindu Gods in 'Comedy Circus' on SONY TV." http://www.hindujagruti.org/news/11469.html (accessed March 2, 2011).

Hjarvard, Stig. *The Mediatization of Culture and Society.* New York: Routledge, 2013.

India Gaming Carnival. Official Website. http://www.wtf-igc.com (accessed September 10, 2012).

Jenkins, Henry. "Game Design as Narrative Architecture." In *First Person: New Media as Story, Performance, and Game.* Edited by Noah Wardrip-Fruin and Pat Harrigan, 118–130. Cambridge, Mass.: MIT Press, 2004. http://web.mit.edu/cms/People/henry3/games&narrative.html.

Juul, Jesper. "Gaming Telling Stories: A Brief Note on Games and Narratives." *Game Studies* 1, no. 1 (2001). http://www.gamestudies.org/0101/juul-gts (accessed September 10, 2012).

Karapanagiotis, Nicole. "Vaishnava Cyber-Puja: Problems of Purity and Novel Ritual Solutions." *Heidelberg Journal of Religions on the Internet* 4, no. 1 (2010):179–195. http://archiv.ub.uni-heidelberg.de/volltextserver/volltexte/2010/11304/pdf/10.pdf.

Keul, István. *Hanumān, der Gott in Affengestalt: Entwicklung und Erscheinungsformen seiner Verehrung.* Berlin: de Gruyter, 2002.

Krotz, Friedrich. "Media Connectivity: Concepts, Conditions, and Consequences." In *Connectivity, Networks and Flows: Conceptualizing Contemporary Communications.* Edited by Andreas Hepp, Friedrich Krotz, A. Moores, and C. Winter, 13–32. New York: Hampton, 2008.

Little Hanuman. http://www.kongregate.com/games/regniraj/little-hanuman.

Ludvik, Catherine. *Hanumān in the Rāmāyaṇa of Vālmīki and the Rāmacaritamānasa of Tulasī Dāsa.* Delhi: Motilal Banarsidass, 1994.

Lutgendorf, Philip A. "All in the (Raghu) Family: A Video Epic in Cultural Context." In *Media and the Transformation of Religions in South Asia.* Edited by Lawrence A. Babb and Susan S. Wadley, 217–253. Philadelphia: University of Pennsylvania Press, 1995.

———. "Evolving a Monkey: Hanuman, Poster Art, and Postcolonial Anxiety." *Contributions to Indian Sociology* 36, nos. 1–2 (2002):71–112.

———. "Hanumān's Adventures Underground: The Narrative Logic of a Rāmāyaṇa 'Interpolation.'" In *The Rāmāyaṇa Revisited.* Edited by Mandakranta Bose, 149–163. New York: Oxford University Press, 2004.

———. *Hanuman's Tale: The Messages of a Divine Monkey.* New York: Oxford University Press, 2007.

———. *The Life of a Text: Performing the Rāmacaritamānas of Tulsidas.* Berkeley: University of California Press, 1991.

Makwana, Samir. *"Hanuman: Boy Warrior* Maker Speaks." *Techtree.* http:// archive.techtree.com/techtree/jsp /article.jsp?article_id=100483&cat_ id=585 (accessed March 26, 2009).

Nunneley, Stephany. "Universal Society of Hinduism Wants Sony to Pull *Hanuman: Boy Warrior.*" *VG* 24/7. http:// www.vg247.com/2009/04/18/universal -society-of-hinduism-wants-sony-to -pull-hanuman-boy-warrior (accessed April 18, 2009).

Ovum. *Digital Gaming Market in Asia-Pacific to More than Double to US$30.3bn.* Press Release, March 29, 2012. http://ovum.com/press_releases /digital-gaming-market-in-asia-pacific -to-more-than-double-to-us30-3bn (accessed September 10, 2012).

Prashar, A. "Sony Way of Denegrating [*sic*] Lord Hanuman: Review on *Hanuman: Boy Warrior,* Sony Computer Entertainment India." *VivekaJyoti.* http://vivekajyoti.blogspot.de/2009 /08/sony-way-of-denegrating-lord -hanuman.html (accessed August 16, 2009).

Ra.One: The Game. Trine Games Mumbai for Sony Computer Entertainment Europe, 2011.

Rajan Zed. Official Website. http:// rajanzed.com/rajan (accessed January 4, 2013).

The Rāmāyaṇa of Vālmīki: An Epic of Ancient India, vols. 1–5. Translated and edited by Robert P. Goldman. New York: New York University Press, 1990–1996.

Ravan Dahan Game. http://games.web dunia.com/playgame/18/1/action -games/ravan-dahan-game.html.

Samant, V. G., and Ukey, M., dirs. *Hanuman.* 2005.

Scheifinger, Heinz. "Hindu Embodiment and the Internet." *Heidelberg Journal of Religions on the Internet* 4, no. 1 (2010):196–219. http://archiv .ub.uni-heidelberg.de/volltextserver /volltexte/2010/11305/pdf/11.pdf.

———. "Hinduism and Cyberspace." *Religion* 38, no. 3 (2008):233–249. http://www.tandfonline.com/doi /pdf/10.1016/j.religion.2008.01.008.

Singh, Nikhil. "Review: *Hanuman – Boy Warrior.*" *Tech2.* http://m.tech2.com /reviews/console/hanuman-boy -warrior/63912 (accessed April 13, 2009).

Šisler, Vít. "Digital Arabs: Representation in Video Games." *European Journal of Cultural Studies* 11, no. 2 (2008):203– 220. http://ecs.sagepub.com/content /11/2/203.full.pdf+html.

————. "Palestine in Pixels: The Holy
Land, Arab-Israeli Conflict, and Reality Construction in Video Games."
*Middle East Journal of Culture and
Communication* 2, no. 2 (2009):275–292.
http://www.digitalislam.eu/article
.do?articleId=2515.

Smite. Hi-Rez Studios for Microsoft
Windows, 2012.

Social Gaming Asia Summit. Official
Website. http://www.beaconevents
.com/2012/SocialGamingCongress
2012/en/Home/index.jsp (accessed
September 10, 2012).

Squire, Kurt. "From Content to Context:
Videogames as Designed Experience." *Educational Researcher* 35, no. 8
(2006):19–29. http://www.jstor.org
/stable/4124789.

Universal Society of Hinduism. Official
Website. http://www.universalsociety
ofhinduism.org/usoh (accessed January 4, 2013).

Vaidyanathan, Rajini. "Is 2012 the Year
for India's Internet?" *BBC News Business.* http://www.bbc.co.uk/news
/business-16354076 (accessed January 3, 2012).

van der Byl, Tarryn. "Catholics, Jews,
Buddhists Team Up with Hindus to
Protest Hi-Rez Studios' *Smite.*" *Myg-
aming.* http://mygaming.co.za/news
/news/42324-catholics-jews-buddhists
-team-up-with-hindus-to-protest
-hi-rez-studios-smite.html (accessed
August 2, 2012).

van der Veer, Peter. "Life as Theatre: Performing the Rāmāyaṇa in Ayodhya."
In *Rāmāyaṇa and Rāmāyaṇas.* Edited
by Monika Thiel-Horstmann, 169–
184. Wiesbaden, Germany: Harras-
sowitz, 1991.

Weber, Max. *Theory of Social and Eco-
nomic Organization.* Translated by
A. Henderson and T. Parsons. New
York: Oxford University Press, 1947.

World Cyber Games Malysia. Official
Website. http://my.wcg.com (accessed
September 10, 2012).

"The Worldwide Hindu Boycott of Sony
Is Officially On." Allaboutthegames.
http://www.allaboutthegames.co.uk
/feature_story.php?headline=The
-worldwide-Hindu-boycott-of-Sony
-is-officially-on&article_id=9206 (accessed September 10, 2012).

Zeiler, Xenia. "Ethno-Indology in Times
of Modern Mass Media: Researching
Mediatized Religions in South Asia."
In *Banāras Revisited.* Edited by István
Keul. Wiesbaden, Germany: Harras-
sowitz, 2013.

————. "Universal's Religious Bigotry
against Hinduism: Gender Norms
and Hindu Authority in the Global
Media Debate on Representing the
Hindu God Krishna in *Xena: Warrior
Princess.*" In *Ancient Worlds in Film
and Television: Gender and Politics.*
Edited by Almut-Barbara Renger and
Jon Solomon, 229–245. Leiden: Brill,
2013.

FOUR

Silent Hill and *Fatal Frame*

FINDING TRANSCENDENT HORROR IN AND
BEYOND THE HAUNTED MAGIC CIRCLE

Brenda S. Gardenour Walter

ON A RAINY AFTERNOON IN A SLEEPY, MIDDLE-CLASS AMERICAN
town, seventeen-year-old Heather Mason visits an aging shopping mall
on an errand for her father. Walking through the main entrance, Heather
is transported to the horrifying town of Silent Hill, where the mall has
become a monster-infested and blood-soaked nightmare. Descending
through the strange worlds of Silent Hill, Heather crosses through several haunted circles, including a derelict hospital with a filthy, mirrored
storeroom where she sees herself invaded by bloody tendrils and consumed by decomposing walls. Her consciousness raw from terror, she
finally reaches Silent Hill's rotten core where she must master the per-
verse rituals of a religious cult called "the Order" and use them in battle
against their unholy and half-formed god. Thousands of miles away, a
young woman named Miku Hinasaki searches for her brother in the
fabled Himuro mansion high in the hills above Tokyo. Stepping across
its decrepit threshold, she enters a haunted sphere, a foggy realm ruled by
the angry dead, ancient curses, and long-forgotten Shinto rituals for the
binding and loosening of hell. As a horrified Miku performs each arcane
rite, she descends to Himuro's most sacred circle, that of the Strangling
Ritual. There, she not only witnesses the dismembering of the Shrine
Maiden, but also faces the maiden's vengeful ghost in a battle for her sanity and her brother's freedom. In this chapter, I will explore supernatural
horror in the ritualistic game worlds of *Silent Hill* and *Fatal Frame* and
argue that by entering these horrific magic circles, both Western and
Japanese players experience terror, abjection, and ultimately, religious
transcendence.

The formalized religions and rituals constructed within the survival horror game worlds of Konami's *Silent Hill* and Tecmo's *Fatal Frame* are quite distinct from each other. The religion of *Silent Hill* is a mélange of purposely distorted elements, or simulacra, drawn from Western and "non-Japanese" religions embedded in a strict pseudo-Christian hierarchical model.[1] In *Silent Hill,* the rules and rituals of the Order, the game's primary cult, are vital for the deciphering of the plot and the survival of the main character and therefore the player. Even with a good ending, however, the Order is never defeated; instead, it persists as a primary structure that haunts, in ever more elaborate detail, each subsequent installment of the game. In contrast to *Silent Hill,* the formal religion of *Fatal Frame* is constructed from signifiers drawn primarily from Japanese Shintoism and Buddhism. In *Fatal Frame,* the player journeys to sacred sites, such as Shinto shrines and Buddhist temples, and uses ritual objects, such as sacred mirrors, masks, and plaited ropes, in the performance of conflated and scrambled Shinto and Buddhist rituals. The religious hardscape of *Fatal Frame* is for the most part composed of signifiers that accurately reflect religious structures and objects in the material world of Shinto and Buddhism; the religious rituals embedded in the game, however, are secondary simulacra, distortions of traditional practices that exist somewhere between the physical and digital worlds and reflect abstract truths in both.

While the religious structures within the digital game worlds of *Silent Hill* and *Fatal Frame* are dissimilar, both use transcendent horror in and beyond what I call the "haunted magic circle." In *Rules of Play,* Salen and Zimmerman suggest that the ritual sphere of play might be imagined as Johan Huizinga's "magic circle," which he describes in his classic *Homo Ludens: A Study of the Play-Element in Culture* as a "playground marked off beforehand either materially or ideally, deliberately or as a matter of course," a temporary "world within the ordinary world, dedicated to the performance of an act apart."[2] Salen and Zimmerman's use of the open and closed magic circle to describe the realm of digital gameplay has sparked controversy, particularly among those scholars and gamers concerned with the inflexibility of an imaginary bounded circle that divides the virtual and the real into a false binary.[3] While I admit that Salen and Zimmerman's model has limitations, as any model must, it is my belief that the simplicity of Huizinga's magic circle remains a particularly useful tool for the examination of religion and ritual in (and of) digital gaming.

As magic circles, digital game worlds are ritual spaces, "forbidden spots, isolated, hedged round, hallowed, within which special rules obtain."[4] According to Juul, play within gaming spaces is governed by "a rule-based system with a variable and quantifiable outcome, where different outcomes are assigned different values";[5] a digital game's paraludic interface, therefore, is primarily ritualistic, concerned with proper action within a prescribed or, as Salen and Zimmerman would argue, closed circle of rules. If we follow scholars such as Lehrich and Mackay in conceiving of game space as ritual space, then the experience of the player within this space can be imagined as not merely ritualistic but spiritual, concerned with the performance of ritual not only as a means of achieving outcomes in gameplay, but also for a higher purpose within and beyond the game's frame.[6] For Huizinga, not only is there "no formal difference between play and ritual," but also the very act of playing can elevate the player-pilgrim into "the realm of the beautiful and the sacred."[7]

In the game worlds of *Silent Hill* and *Fatal Frame*, the magic circle becomes haunted. The player experiences not only formalized religious structures and rituals, but also spiritual transcendence through the experience of horror.[8] The terrifying loss of self and its absorption into an uncanny and yet wholly divine Other are at the core of both religious transcendence and transcendent horror. Rudolf Otto described this experience as "numinous," the confrontation of an unknowable and omnipotent Other (*mysterium*) with a mixture of terror, dread, and awe (*tremens*) that is at once both horrible and desirable.[9] For H. P. Lovecraft, supernatural horror is not only a part of transcendence, but is itself a religious experience, a primal and maddening confrontation with the nonhuman Other that permeates a false quotidian reality.[10] In *Powers of Horror: An Essay on Abjection,* Julia Kristeva likewise argues that intense fear and horror can lead to transcendence through a process she calls "abjection," in which an individual loses all sense of self while gazing upon something horrific, becomes one with it, and returns to the experience repeatedly out of desire (*jouissance*). Terror, loss of self, communion with the abject Other, and desire, therefore, are key elements of transcendent horror, and all of them are experienced during digital gameplay in *Silent Hill* and *Fatal Frame.*

In both *Silent Hill* and *Fatal Frame,* transcendent horror takes two forms, the first of which is the horror of religion itself, its connections to history, and its power to both define and blur the boundaries between self and other. For example, the Western religion of *Silent Hill* and the Eastern religion of *Fatal Frame* speak very different but powerful languages of horror to the Japanese audiences for which they were first developed. *Silent Hill* presents the horrific nature of Western religion, and specifically fundamentalist Christianity, which insists that there is only one path to truth beyond which lies heresy and fiery damnation, a single-path viewpoint that is both foreign and antithetical to Japanese religious culture. Perhaps even more horrifying to the Japanese player is the sense of abjection, the breakdown between self and other that results from forced participation in the Order's rituals, an experience within the magic circle that ripples outward, echoing deep cultural memories of the American occupation and of self-loathing at attempted assimilation. If *Silent Hill* forces its Japanese audience to become, if only briefly, the dreaded Christian Other, *Fatal Frame* offers a journey into the hidden self to explore Japan's own alienated religious past, in which vengeful and sorrowful ghosts haunt the living, demanding the performance of violent and forgotten religious rituals in order to liberate the present. For Western audiences, the horror of religion in these games is just as potent, but reversed; *Silent Hill* reveals the horror of the self and the Western obsession with hierarchy and orthodoxy, while *Fatal Frame* fuels a fascination with the exotic and non-Christian Other as well as a fear of foreign supernatural beings lurking in the half-light.

The second form in which transcendent horror manifests in *Silent Hill* and *Fatal Frame* is through contact with the supernatural. Intentionally enfeebled, plunged with insufficient weapons into these nightmarish worlds pervaded by seen and unseen forces, the ever-vigilant player wanders through the fog and grapples with unholy beings, relying on her own internal resources in an attempt to survive. Through such "emotionally compelling experiences connected to spirituality and the supernatural," the player transcends the game's religious structures and enters into its horrifying spiritual dimensions.[11] For the religiously minded, then, horrifying digital gameplay might become in and of itself a spiritual action, a sacred conduit to transcendence and communion with the divine. Such transcendent experiences do not remain locked within the ritual sphere of the game, however, but reside in the mind of the player-pilgrim, tracing the memory of and facilitating connections between the sacred virtual world and profane reality until each is imbued with elements of the other. Through online forums, fan fiction, role-playing, and conventions, the magic circle of the game opens wider and is multiplied into a spinning fractal of sacred sites morphing in response to their new environments yet echoing, if imperfectly, the ritual world of the game.

Silent Hill and Fatal Frame move beyond the magic circle because, for some, the very act of playing these games becomes a religious ritual, an act geared toward a horrifying transcendence beyond the material and the mundane. This religious and spiritual experience extends far beyond individual gameplay in the digital worlds of Silent Hill and Fatal Frame, moving into the greater gaming community through what Henry Jenkins calls "transmedia storytelling."[12] The fictional town of Silent Hill and the religion at its core, for example, exist not only within the magic circle of the game, but also in the cinema (Silent Hill [2006], Silent Hill Revelation 3D [2012]), in comic books, in online forums, and at Cosplay conventions and Comic-Con. Devout followers of Silent Hill go on pilgrimage to these virtual and physical magic circles to commune with other believers and to reinforce their spiritual experiences. The religious transcendence experienced by the once-isolated player thereby becomes a communal event, with the signs and signifiers of the ethereal religious gaming world reinforced in real time and in physical forms. Through transmedia storytelling, the magic circle is unbound, allowing the player-pilgrim to find individual and communal alternative religious experiences, identities, and narratives beyond traditional formal religion in the digital gaming multiverses of Silent Hill and Fatal Frame – in short, to find religion in digital gaming.

FINDING RELIGION IN SILENT HILL: OCCULT AND ORTHODOX OTHER

Frédérick Raynal's critically acclaimed Alone in the Dark (Bonnell, 1992), the first three-dimensional horror survival digital game, inspired other

SILENT HILL AND FATAL FRAME

developers to design games in which the protagonist must investigate and survive a supernatural space, or haunted magic circle, with minimal defenses. In an effort to develop its own horror survival game, Konami gathered together a group of developers, including Keiichiro Toyama, *Silent Hill*'s creator and director of the first game in the series, Masahiro Ito, Hiroyuki Owaku, Masashi Tsuboyama, and Akira Yamaoka.[13] Ultimately known as Team Silent, they would go on to design the game worlds of *Silent Hill* (Kitao, 1999), *Silent Hill 2* (Imamura, 2001), *Silent Hill 3* (Yamaoka, 2003), and *Silent Hill 4: The Room* (Yamaoka, 2004). Subsequent installments in the series included *Origins* (Oertel, 2007) and *Shattered Memories* (Hulett, 2009), both of which were developed by Climax Studios; *Homecoming* (Oertel, 2008), developed by Double Helix Games; *Downpour* (Shatsky, Hulett, and Airey, 2010), developed by Vatra Games; and the much-anticipated spin-off *Silent Hill: Book of Memories* for PlayStation Vita (Hulett, 2012). The transmedia multiverse of *Silent Hill* exists not only within the magic circle of gameplay but also at a multitude of sacred sites, including the original guide, *Book of Lost Memories* (Konami, 2003), a series of short stories by Ciencin and others called *The Silent Hill Omnibus* (IDW, 2008), Tom Waltz's comic books *Sinner's Reward* (IDW, 2008) and *Past Life* (IDW, 2011), and two film adaptations, *Silent Hill* (Christophe Gans, 2006) and *Silent Hill Revelation 3D* (Michael J. Bassett, 2012). Myriad online forums provide devotees with yet other sites of pilgrimage at which to commune with their fellow believers and experience the supernatural world of *Silent Hill.*

The Lovecraftian supernatural town of Silent Hill provides the backdrop for the formalized religious structures and rituals that dictate the rules of gameplay, the closed element of the magic circle.[14] In all of its permutations, Silent Hill is dominated by the Order, a dark religious sect whose secret rites and rituals shape the half-living nightmares of the character-players who are drawn there. The structure of the Order is shrouded in a dense fog that occasionally lifts, if only for a moment, allowing the player to see into its tangled web. Like an initiate into a Gnostic sect, the player moves through levels of secret knowledge, gathering clues about the religious rituals and symbols that are the key to survival. While minor aspects of the Order are an amalgam of non-Japanese traditions, such as Native American animism and Aztec sun worship, its foundational hierarchical and trinitarian structure is rooted in Judeo-Christianity as imagined through a Japanese lens. The divine pantheon of the Order is a hierarchy of pseudo-Christian trinities, at the center of which is the God, a female entity created from the tears of man and woman and represented by the sun.[15] Emanating from the God are Xuchilbara, a male symbolized by the red of sacrificial blood, and Lobsel Vith, a female entity represented by the yellow of cleansing fire.[16] From these secondary deities emanate two tertiary entities, Samael, the fallen angel or seducer, and Metatron, the angel charged with protecting the God and aiding in her rebirth. Samael and Metatron, whose names are taken from Hebrew texts such as the Tanakh and midrashim, are often at war as they manipulate the player into fulfilling the Order's prophecies. Between these two angels sits Valtiel, a being who serves the God alone. In the form of Pyramid Head, a monster with a butcher's apron and an impossibly large sword, Valtiel executes all who interfere with the God's return.

The Order itself, like its pantheon, is hierarchical and trinitarian in structure, containing three subsects, each of which has as its primary goal the rebirth of the God. The most powerful sect is the Cult of the Holy Woman, which follows the teachings of a prophet named Dahlia Gillespie, who burned her daughter, Alessa, believing that the child's agonizing pain would make her a perfect vessel for the God's birth. The second sect in the trinity is the Cult of the Holy Mother, which holds that only a chosen conjurer can bring the God to earth through a Mother Stone held sacred by the group. In order to find this conjurer, the cult runs an orphanage called Wish House where violent atrocities are committed against the children in the name of ritual and rebirth. The third group, the Cult of Valtiel, is dedicated to the angel of punishment and the preservation of order through execution; in imitation of Pyramid Head, members of the sect don pointed red hoods in their rituals. Within each of these sects, as in the Order as a whole, there are three levels of initiation: novitiates enter the Servant Circle, move through the Daughter Circle, and ultimately enter the Circle of the Mother.

Like an unwitting insect that creeps along a spider's web toward the horrific revelation at its center, the player-pilgrim descends through the Order's levels, each of which corresponds with one of Silent Hill's triadic expressions. The seemingly placid town of Silent Hill represents the knowledge of the novitiate; Fog World signifies the acquisition of deeper wisdom; while Nightmare World indicates the player's achievement in exposing the hidden and horrifying truths at the rotten core of the Order. By using triads as the foundation of the Order's religious structure, Team Silent emphasized the cult's obsession with hierarchical power and its fanaticism for orthodoxy and the persecution of heretics. With unwavering devotion, members of the Order must be willing to torture and murder those who do not comply with its unbending system of beliefs and violent rituals. The twisted and authoritarian nature of religion in *Silent Hill* causes much of the sorrow, violence, and horror that hangs over the town like a fog. From the Japanese perspective, these same characteristics tie the Order symbolically and ideologically to Christianity and the West.

The Order, with all of its rules and rituals, exists only within the bounded haunted magic circle of *Silent Hill;* the player's response to the Order, however, exists in both the game world and the mind of the player, an example of how, following Salen and Zimmerman, a magic circle might be simultaneously closed and open. A player's experience of religion in *Silent Hill* is shaped by his or her own cultural and historical lenses. The Japanese player's experience with the Order, for example, might echo Japanese perceptions of Western Christianity as a strange and ancient faith founded on the death of a man-god who promises to return and remake the world for his faithful as long as they remain orthodox and either convert or persecute wrong-believers. From this perspective, one of the most terrifying tenets of the Order as a simulacrum of Christianity is the insistence that there is but a single path to truth, beyond which there is only evil. In Japan, religious syncretism prevails; Shinto birth rituals are followed by Western wedding rituals and funerary customs from Japanese Buddhism. To demand that an individual only follow one religious tradition is seen as abhorrent; nevertheless, within the magic circle of *Silent Hill,* the Japanese player is drawn into the fanatic beliefs of a strange and distant Other that demands conformity or death. In the digital skin of the character, the player must master the structure of the Order, learn its history and its hierarchies, and perform its sacred rites and rituals, all while trying to preserve some sense of sanity and self. This experience of abjection, or becoming the Other, echoes the horror of Japanese historical and cultural memory: fervent evangelical ministers preached brimstone sermons and attempted to lure the Japanese into the Christian faith before, during, and after the U.S. occupation. In the cultural and historical context of Japan, then, surviving and eventually escaping *from* religion in *Silent Hill* is a digital signifier for abstract realities in the physical world beyond the haunted magic circle.

Japanese perceptions of Christianity as tyrannical are borne out in Western responses to religion in *Silent Hill*. Unlike their Japanese counterparts, Anglo American gamers revel in the Order, obsessing over every detail of its history and hierarchical structure, its pantheon, its rituals, and their meanings. One of the most popular topics of discussion in online forums, such as *Silent Hill Wiki* and *Silent Hill Heaven*, is the structure and function of the Order in *Silent Hill*.[17] Posts in the forums often become heated as players discuss the "true" beliefs of the Order, their "real" history, and the "official" pantheon of the demongods. Is Metatron really an angel from the Hebrew Bible, or is he a version of Enoch? Where in the hierarchy are we to put Valtiel? Which sect is valid, and why? And which of the post–Team Silent game versions is truly canonical, and which heretical?[18] Reading the threads, it becomes clear that for Anglo players orthodoxy is a major concern – that right belief matters in *Silent Hill*, both within the magic circle and in the many permutations beyond it. Some of this is undoubtedly due to the hypertextual nature of the *Silent Hill* experience, which includes piecemeal revelations and disconnected signifiers laden with deep religious meanings that are difficult to articulate. A player alone within the magic circle encounters these religious signifiers and imbues them with individual meaning; but in an online forum, a world both in and out of the magic circle, such individual interpretations must be fleshed out and, according to the binary Christian theological paradigm, either accepted as orthodox truth or rejected as heretical falsehood.[19] Once the most respected leader on the boards pronounces dogma, his followers accept his word as law and correct (sometimes harshly) others who come to the boards with ideas deemed noncanonical.[20] The Western response to the Order is informed by the deep structures and dark history of Christianity itself, an ancient religion (like the Order) that continues to haunt the foggy

Western mind (*Silent Hill*).[21] Perhaps it should not be surprising, then, that for the Western gamer the experience of *Silent Hill* has itself become both transcendent and religious, strangely familiar yet wholly Other, its various horrifying sites the focus of endless pilgrimage, a gaming cult worthy of devotion to the point of persecution.

RELIGION IN *FATAL FRAME:* OCCULT FAILURES AND MODERN SACRIFICES

As in *Silent Hill*, the structure and experience of religion and ritual both within and beyond the haunted magic circle are central to *Fatal Frame*, a horror survival game released by Tecmo in 2001 and known in Japan as 零 (*Zero*). While working on Tecmo's *Deception* series, Keisuke Kikuchi, *Fatal Frame*'s designer, was inspired to create a game in which a young girl explores a haunted mansion and has to defend herself from ghosts through purely supernatural means.[22] The idea for *Fatal Frame* came not only from games such as *Alone in the Dark* but also from *Otogirisō*, a popular sound novel released by ChunSoft in 1992, which tells the tale of a young couple, Kohei and Nami, who become stranded in a forest and spend the night in a haunted mansion.[23] Along with his partner, Makoto Shibata, and a team of designers that would come to be known as Project Zero, Kikuchi wove the haunted house theme from *Otogirisō* with religious imagery and rituals drawn from Shinto and Japanese Buddhism, elements culled from ancient folklore, and tales of the supernatural from Mutsu Province in northeastern Japan.[24] The fog-enshrouded and haunted magic circle created in *Fatal Frame* is echoed throughout its sequels, *Fatal Frame II: Crimson Butterfly* (Mayama, 2003), *Fatal Frame III: The Tormented* (Kikuchi, 2005), and *Fatal Frame IV: The Mask of the Lunar Eclipse* (Kikuchi, 2008), and through spin-offs such as *Spirit Camera: The Cursed Memoir* (Kikuchi, 2012) for the Nintendo 3DS.[25] The basic premise of each of these games is the same: the enfeebled player-character, armed only with the mythical ghost-capturing Camera Obscura, enters into a supernatural realm and must master complex religious systems and archaic rituals in order to destroy ancient curses, liberate the spirits of the past, and return to the present. The futility of this attempt to separate hungry past and haunted present is one of the primary tenets

of the game; no matter how the player tries to abandon the past, it forever calls her back in sequel after sequel, demanding sacrifice and ritual
performances within and beyond the magic circle.

Religious themes, ritual spaces, and ritual actions dominate the
narrative and gameplay in the digital world of *Fatal Frame*. In the first
installment of the series, a young girl named Miku Hinasaki goes in
search of her older brother, Mafuyu, who has disappeared in the haunted
Himuro Mansion while following his mentor, the renowned folklorist Junsei Takamine. While there, Miku progresses through a series of
twisted religious rituals, including the Blinding Ritual, in which a priest
wearing the Mask of Reflection places the Blinding Mask, which has two
inward-facing spikes at the eyes, on a young girl's face, thereby literally
and figuratively transforming her into the Blinded Maiden. The bloodied mask then serves as a key to the ritual caves beneath Himuro, access
to which is gained via the Demon Mouth, a room where the Demon
Tag Ritual is performed. During this ritual, the Blinded Maiden chases
several girls in a seemingly harmless game of tag;[26] the first girl caught,
however, will be the next one blinded, and the last girl caught will be the
next Rope Maiden and sacrificed in the Strangling Ritual.

After four nights of ghost-haunted rituals, Miku realizes that Kirie,
the entity that stalks her most viciously, is not a demon but a failed Rope
Maiden. Like all previous Rope Maidens, Kirie was expected to live a
life of celibacy and isolation in anticipation of her sacrifice. Despite this,
Kirie secretly met and fell in love with a folklorist conducting research
at the mansion. The young man was killed for this transgression, and at
the appointed time, a mourning Kirie was forced to walk across the Hell
Bridge to the Rope Altar, where she was tied between five pillars, also
known as the Five Buddhas, and slowly strangled and dismembered. The
bloodied ropes from the ritual were then tied across the chasm beneath
Himuro, where they were meant to seal the Hell Gate and protect the
region from the Abyss. Because of her sorrow, however, Kirie remained
tied to the world and the Strangling Ritual failed with horrific results:
Kirie became a vengeful spirit, the Hell Gate remained open, and the
Malice spread over Himuro, killing all who once lived in the mansion
and those who still dare to visit it, trapping their souls within its walls.[27]
One of those lost is Mafuyu, Miku's brother, who resembles Kirie's lover;

willing to make the sacrifice that she is not, Mafuyu offers to remain with Kirie in Hell, thereby closing the gates and redeeming the region. As her brother sinks into the Abyss, Miku sees the spirit legions of Himuro, no longer trapped, rising into the sky and freedom.

The responsibility of the younger generation to complete failed ancient rituals long neglected by their ancestors is the foundation of the entire *Fatal Frame* series. *Fatal Frame II: Crimson Butterfly* tells the tale of Mio and Mayu Amakura, twins who wander through an ancient forest and are spirited away to the ghostly Minakami village, which has fallen under the curse of perpetual night because of a failed ritual called the Crimson Sacrifice. In this ritual, twins are kept apart from the world in twin houses linked by a tunnel that only they can access. At the appointed time, the twins are led by Shinto priests into the caves below the village, to the very edge of the hellish Abyss, where the second-born twin is meant to strangle the first-born, thereby closing the Hell Gate and safeguarding the village. As at Himuro, the most recent attempt at the ritual was a failure. The twins Yae and Sae had not fully committed to sacrificing themselves for the protection of the community. Yae escaped, but Sae was captured and thrown into the Abyss against tradition, causing the Repentance, which had terrifying results: the hellish Abyss was opened, the Darkness was released into the world, and the corrupted spirits of Sae and the Kusabi (a sacrifice of appeasement made in place of the Crimson Sacrifice) killed the inhabitants of the village and continue to kill all those who come near. Ultimately, Mio and Mayu are forced to enact the Crimson Sacrifice themselves, with Mio strangling Mayu and tossing her physical form into the Abyss, releasing her soul along with those of all previous sacrifices as crimson butterflies.

Both *Fatal Frame III: The Tormented* and *Zero 4: The Mask of the Lunar Eclipse* (Keisuke Kikuchi, 2008) continue the themes of failed ancient rituals, the haunted past, and the necessity for sacrifice in the present.[28] In *Fatal Frame III*, Rei Kurosawa, her assistant Miku Hinasaki (the survivor from the original *Fatal Frame*), and Kei, the uncle of Mio Amakura (the survivor of *Fatal Frame II*), are each drawn into a dream version of Himuro Mansion called the Manor of Sleep; there, they must discover the secret behind the Tattooed Priestess who haunts their sleeping and waking visions. As in previous installments of *Fatal Frame,* the

Tattooed Priestess is the victim of several failed religious rites, including the Piercing of the Soul Ritual and the Impaling Ritual, both of which have led to the opening of the Hell Gate. It falls to Rei to complete the Impaling Ritual and seal the passage by which the dead return to haunt the living. Likewise, Ruka Minazuki in *Fatal Frame IV* must return to Rougetsu Island in order to reclaim her own lost memories and complete a failed ritual in order to seal the gates of Hell. Two versions of the ritual were performed in Ruka's childhood: the Kagura, a false ritual designed for tourists in an above-ground temple, and the true Kiraigou, which was held in the caves deep below the town. Because of a young woman named Sakuya's unwillingness to sacrifice herself in the Kiraigou, the ritual failed and the Hell Gate was opened. In order to prevent the spirits from infecting all of Japan, Ruka must reconstruct the Kiraigou Ritual with Sakuya so that she can fulfill her destiny and lead the earth-bound souls of the dead to the Afterlife.

In each installment of *Fatal Frame*, the characters are dragged into a foggy and nearly forgotten past because of the selfishness and naïveté of their ancestors. In their unwillingness to remember their duty and sacrifice themselves for the communal good, Kirie, Yae, Rei, and Sakuya damned not only themselves to a sorrowful existence between life and death, but also their contemporary kindred and future generations.[29] Like tendrils from some poisonous plant, these ancient ritual failures creep into the modern world, destroying the lives of those like Mafuyu and Mayu who are sacrificed and those like Miku and Mio who are left behind, suspended between two worlds.

Suspensions between past failure and present responsibility are made manifest in *Fatal Frame* through Shinto and Buddhist iconography and rituals. Throughout the gameplay, characters encounter sacred ropes and plaited paper suspended from Shinto torii and shrines, doorways and trees, all of which signify transition from the profane to the sacred, from one world to another. Rope and other suspension bridges, such as the Hell Bridge, Whisper Bridge, and Heaven Bridge, perform a similar function. Suspension and liminality are likewise incorporated into each of the failed rituals: the Shrine Maiden is suspended between the Five Buddha pillars with rope, the Kusabi is entwined in ropes and tortured above the Hell Mouth, and the Tattooed Priestess is held in her hanging prison, somewhere between life and death. Similarly, Ruka is suspended between two rituals, the Kagura above, where modern tourists are blissfully ignorant of the true meanings behind what they are witnessing, and the Kiraigou below, where those connected to the dead and to the ancient ways are aware of deeper, more horrible truths and the responsibility that comes with them.

Like a sacred rope bridge, the ritual world of *Fatal Frame* serves as a conduit between past and present, a pilgrimage route by which the Japanese player can journey inward to a long-obscured cultural self. Just as the camera's lens uncovers ghosts, curses, and other supernatural clues within the game, so too does the magic lens of *Fatal Frame* reveal Japan as a supernatural landscape, a spirit-haunted world where traces of the past might bubble up unexpectedly before the eyes of the mindful watcher. The religious signifiers within the game closely resemble those of everyday Shinto and Buddhism, further blurring the boundary of the magic circle. For the Japanese digital gamer, the uncanny experience of religion in *Fatal Frame* is a reflection of very real tensions in twenty-first-century Japan, a place beyond the magic circle where premodern religious rituals or "superstitions" have often served as reminders of a past self, both naïve and monstrous, that must die in order for the new modern and secular self to progress.[30]

Once marginalized as superstition, folkloric and religious traditions such as those in the *Fatal Frame* series found new life with the struggles of the Japanese economy in the 1990s. After generations of unwavering belief in an ever-prosperous and "ever-emerging technical, global, and post-modern Japan," Japanese culture after the crash was left to question what it had left behind, and whether it could – or should – escape from a "return to origins."[31] In response to being trapped between an "undead past" reaching out from beyond the grave and an "unborn future" filled with fear and uncertainty, creators of popular culture used religious horror as a means of navigating the divide.[32] Through the lens of Japanese horror, the struggle for the future would not merely be a battle against the monstrous forces of a distant and fog-enshrouded past, but would require an intimate understanding of a forgotten self, one not only familiar with ancient Shinto and Buddhist rituals but also willing to make the necessary sacrifices to safeguard the future from occult failures.

THE HAUNTED MAGIC CIRCLE UNBOUND: FINDING
HORRIFYING TRANSCENDENCE IN DIGITAL GAMING

Fatal Frame and *Silent Hill* offer both the Japanese and Western player-pilgrim an opportunity to commune with the supernatural realm, which exists both within the magic circle of the game and in the player's own haunted heart. Again and again, through overwhelming horror, the devotee enters the "hallowed" and "sacred ground" of Huizinga's magic circle in order to perform rituals and encounter the divine. Through experiences of fear, horror, and abjection, the player travels beyond the self in order to return and confront it; through this pilgrim's progress, she achieves a grounded self-knowledge and spiritual transcendence similar to that promised by religion. But religious experiences in and of *Silent Hill* and *Fatal Frame* do not reside solely within the player's mind or the game console; they have taken on mediated realities of their own. For example, in 2012 Konami released *Silent Hill: Book of Memories* in which the player must rewrite his history with the help of other players in a pervasive gaming environment, thus making *Silent Hill* a truly communal event. Likewise, in 2012 Tecmo released *Spirit Camera: The Cursed Memoir,* an immersive/augmented reality game for the Nintendo 3DS in which a physical book comes to life under the very real lens of the handheld game. Through the game's camera lens, the player can see *Fatal Frame*'s ghosts haunting her physical environment, blurring the imagined boundaries between the virtual and the real – the mental, metaphysical, and physical.

The multivalent nature of transmedia storytelling has further facilitated the expansion of the magic circle. The religious worlds of *Silent Hill* and *Fatal Frame* exist in novelizations, graphic novels, and live action films, as well as in online forums, which offer communal spaces for discussion and shared experiences, and at Comic-Con and Cosplay conventions, which allow for the congregation of player-pilgrims in physical time and space. In both *Silent Hill* and *Fatal Frame*, religious signifiers and ritual actions within the game and the players' individual and collective emotional responses to them have created a shared religious experience and belief system that exists in the magic circle both bound and unbound, allowing the devoted player to find religion in the multivalent world of digital gaming.

NOTES

1. Baudrillard, "XI. Holograms."
2. See Salen and Zimmerman, *Rules of Play*; Huizinga, *Homo Ludens*, 10.
3. Castronova, *Synthetic Worlds*. See also discussions of pervasive gaming in Nieuwdorp, "Pervasive Gaming."
4. Huizinga, *Homo Ludens*, 10.
5. Juul, *Half-Real*, 36.
6. Mackay, *The Fantasy Role-Playing Game*; Lehrich, "Ritual Discourse in Role-Playing Games."
7. Huizinga, *Homo Ludens*, 19.
8. See Rockett, *Devouring Whirlwind*.
9. Otto, *The Idea of the Holy*.
10. Lovecraft, *Supernatural Horror in Literature*.
11. Bainbridge and Bainbridge, "Electronic Game Research Methodologies," 35.
12. Jenkins, "Transmedia Storytelling."
13. Other members of the original Team Silent include Akihiro Imamura, Suguru Murakoshi, Takayoshi Sato, and Kazuhide Nakazawa. See *Silent Hill Wiki*, "Team Silent," http://silenthill.wikia.com/wiki/Team_Silent (accessed July 1, 2012).
14. See Evans, "A Last Defense against the Dark"; Lovecraft, *Supernatural Horror in Literature*. It is also interesting to note that *Alone in the Dark* is based on the works of Lovecraft.
15. See "Birth Memo" in *Silent Hill 3*: "A man offered a serpent to the sun and prayed for salvation. A woman offered a reed to the sun and asked for joy. Feeling pity for the sadness that had overrun the earth, God was born from those two people."

16. See the "Creation Memo" from *Silent Hill 3*: "God created beings to lead people in obedience to Her. The red god, Xuchilbara; the yellow god, Lobsel Vith; many gods and angels."
17. See http://silenthillheaven.com/main and http://silenthill.wikia.com.
18. See the thread "Canon or No?" at *Silent Hill Heaven*, http://www.silenthillforum.com/viewtopic.php?f=30&t=10765&start=320 (accessed October 23, 2012).
19. See "Valtiel?," *Silent Hill Heaven*, http://www.silenthillforum.com/viewtopic.php?f=4&t=1503 (accessed October 20, 2012).
20. See "Religious Pantheon of *Silent Hill*," *Silent Hill Heaven*, http://www.silenthillforum.com/viewtopic.php?t=10942 (accessed October 20, 2012). The arbiter of truth on this particular thread is an individual called "The Adversary."
21. On Christianity and the creation of a persecuting society, see Moore, *Formation of a Persecuting Society*; Nirenberg, *Communities of Violence*.
22. http://www.cameraslens.com/fatalframewiki/index.php5?title=Fatal_Frame_series.
23. A film version of *Otogirisō*, known also as *Saint John's Wort*, was directed by Ten Shimoyama and released in 2001; in 2007 the original sound novel was ported to Wii's virtual console.
24. Makoto Shibata claims that the team was also inspired by the urban legend of the dreaded Himuro family and their haunted mansion, which is purported to exist somewhere just outside of Tokyo. The legend of the Himuro mansion, however, does not seem to exist outside

of the magic circle of *Fatal Frame.* For a quote from Makoto Shibata on the legend of Himuro, see http://www.paranormala.com/himuro-mansion-haunting. For a vehement discussion between believers, nonbelievers, and those who, like Detective Mulder on *The X-Files* "want to believe," see the threads in http://slug gosghoststories.blogspot.com/2009/07/himuro-mansion-tokyo-japan.html.

25. Also *Fatal Frame: Deep Crimson Butterfly,* as yet unreleased but much anticipated in the community.

26. This is similar to the traditional Japanese children's game Hidden Onigokko, in which one child is blindfolded and must chase and tag the others, and the aquatic game of Marco Polo played in the United States.

27. For more on hell in Japanese religious culture, see Hirasawa, "The Inflatable Collapsible Kingdom of Retribution."

28. *Zero 4* was released only in Japan for the Nintendo Wii. While no Western release is expected, fans have created a language patch that provides a rough translation for English-speaking players.

29. Kirie in her benevolent form constantly reminds the player, "Don't forget your duty."

30. For the Western player, however, the experience is quite different; mastering seemingly bizarre ancient rituals, wandering through dark and foggy shrines, peeking behind the sliding partitions of desolate mansions, and fighting Japanese ghosts all provide a deliciously terrifying but not truly unnerving experience. The topography and architecture in the game are distant, the religious signifiers and ghostly dead completely foreign, and the Western self absent.

31. McRoy, *Nightmare Japan,* 20.

32. Ibid., 77.

REFERENCES

Bainbridge, William S., and Bainbridge, Wilma A. "Electronic Game Research Methodologies: Studying Religious Implications." *Review of Religious Research* 49, no. 1 (2007):35–53.

Baudrillard, Jean. "XI. Holograms." In his *Simulacra and Simulations.* Translated by Sheila Faria Glaser. Ann Arbor: University of Michigan Press, 1994.

Castronova, Edward. *Synthetic Worlds: The Business and Culture of Online Games.* Chicago, Ill.: University of Chicago Press, 2005.

Ciencin, Scott, et al. *The Silent Hill Omnibus.* San Diego, Calif.: IDW, 2008.

Evans, Timothy H. "A Last Defense against the Dark: Folklore, Horror, and the Uses of Tradition in the Works of H. P. Lovecraft." *Journal of Folklore Research* 42, no. 1 (January–April 2005):99–135.

Hirasawa, Caroline. "The Inflatable Collapsible Kingdom of Retribution: A Primer on Japanese Hell Imagery and Imagination." *Monumenta Nipponica* 63, no. 1 (2008):1–50.

Huizinga, Johan. *Homo Ludens: A Study of the Play-Element in Culture.* Boston: Beacon, 1955.

Jenkins, Henry. "Transmedia Storytelling: Moving Characters from Books to Films to Video Games Can Make Them Stronger and More Compelling." *Technology Review.* January 15,

2003. http://www.technologyreview.com/biomedicine/13052.

Juul, Jesper. "The Game, the Player, the World: Looking for a Heart of Gameness." In Level Up: Digital Games Research Conference Proceedings. Edited by Marinka Copier and Joost Raessens, 30–45. Utrecht, Netherlands: Utrecht University Press, 2003.

———. Half-Real: Video Games between Real Rules and Fictional Worlds. Cambridge, Mass.: MIT Press, 2005.

Kristeva, Julia. Powers of Horror: An Essay on Abjection. New York: Columbia University Press, 1982.

Lehrich, Christopher I. "Ritual Discourse in Role-Playing Games." Forge. 2004. http://www.indie-rpgs.com/_articles/ritual_discourse_in_RPGs.html (accessed June 15, 2004).

Lovecraft, H. P. Supernatural Horror in Literature. New York: Dover, 1973.

Mackay, Daniel. The Fantasy Role-Playing Game: A New Performing Art. Jefferson, N.C.: McFarland, 2001.

McRoy, Jay. Nightmare Japan: Contemporary Japanese Horror Cinema. New York: Rodopi, 2008.

Moore, R. I. The Formation of a Persecuting Society: Authority and Deviance in Western Europe 950–1250. London: Blackwell, 2007.

Nieuwdorp, Eva. "Pervasive Gaming: Tracing the Magic Circle." Proceedings of the DiGRA 2005 Conference: Changing Views, Worlds in Play. http://www.digra.org/dl/db/06278.53356.pdf (accessed June 12, 2012).

Nirenberg, David. Communities of Violence: Persecution of Minorities in the Middle Ages. Princeton, N.J.: Princeton University Press, 1998.

Otto, Rudolf. The Idea of the Holy. Eastford, Conn.: Martino, 2012.

Rockett, Will H. Devouring Whirlwind: Terror and Transcendence in the Cinema of Cruelty. Westport, Conn.: Praeger, 1988.

Salen, Katie, and Zimmerman, Eric. Rules of Play: Game Design Fundamentals. Cambridge, Mass.: MIT Press, 2004.

Waltz, Tom. Past Life. San Diego, CA: IDS, 2011.

———. Sinner's Reward. San Diego, CA: IDS, 2008.

PART TWO

Religion in
Mainstream Games

From *Kuma\War* to *Quraish*

REPRESENTATION OF ISLAM IN ARAB
AND AMERICAN VIDEO GAMES

Vít Šisler

VIDEO GAMES INCREASINGLY RECREATE REAL-WORLD EVENTS and spaces, making tangible connections to the outside world. In doing so, they use real people, places, and cultures as their referents, opening new forms of representation.[1] Since 9/11 there has been an increase in video games, mainly first-person shooters, produced in the United States and dealing with the representation of the Middle East, Islam, and Muslims.[2] For example, in the popular *Kuma\War* (Kuma Reality Games, 2004), players can "replay" missions from the real military campaigns in Iraq and Afghanistan. These missions navigate players through Iraqi and Afghani cities, including many Muslim holy sites and mosques. They also feature Sunni and Shia Muslim characters, who are portrayed mostly as enemies in the narrative framework of insurgency, international terrorism, and religious fundamentalism.[3]

Simultaneously, many video game producers in the Muslim world have started to produce their own games dealing directly with the representation of Islam and Muslims. By doing so, they attempt, first, to provide their audiences with more culturally relevant representations and, second, to educate the outside world about Islam and Muslim culture.[4] For example, the Syrian real-time strategy game *Quraish* (Afkar Media, 2007) allows the player to witness the origin of Islam and "replay" key battles from its early history, including the defeats of the Iranian Sassanid Empire and the Byzantine Empire. Although *Quraish* and *Kuma\War* similarly use what Ian Bogost in *Persuasive Games* calls the "expressive power of video game[s]," the images of Islam and Muslims these games offer are significantly different.[5]

In *Cultural Encounters in the Arab World,* Tarik Sabry argues that in the twenty-first century, with the spread and "overabundance" of media technologies and signifiers of the Other, the role of place as a necessary element for encounters has been undermined. According to Sabry, witnessing or encountering other cultures now has little to do with physical space and has become more of a symbolic phenomenon.[6] At the same time, video games have become a sociocultural phenomenon of increasing relevance. They constitute a mainstream leisure activity for broad levels of society and are increasingly becoming spaces where cultural encountering takes place. Today, there is a crucial need to critically understand the symbolic and ideological dimensions of in-game representational politics – particularly in relation to Islam and Muslims.

In this chapter I discuss three American and three Arab video games and analyze the ways in which they (a) construct virtual representations of Islam and Muslims and (b) communicate these representations to their audiences. On a broader theoretical level, I aim to explore how Islam, both as an organized system of belief and as a lived reality, is integrated into the video game medium and what ethical considerations this implies.

THE REPRESENTATION AND SELF-REPRESENTATION
OF ISLAM AND MUSLIMS IN VIDEO GAMES

Existing research on Islam and video games can be divided into three clusters: (a) the representation of Muslims in Western games, (b) the construction of identity in Muslim games, and (c) the communication of Islamic moral and ethical values.

Early research on the representation of Muslims in mainstream Western games was often entangled with research on the representation of Arabs. Ibrahim Marashi in "The Depiction of Arabs in Combat Video Games" has outlined the stereotypical modes of representing Arabs and Muslims in video games focusing on the Arab-Israeli conflict. Philipp Reichmuth and Stephan Werning in "Pixel Pashas, Digital Djinns" have described the exploitation of Oriental topoi in various genres of Western video games.[7] Johan Höglund in "Electronic Empire" has discussed representation of the Middle East and Muslims in U.S. action games in relation to "war on terror" discourse. The results of this research indicate that the dominant mode of representation of Muslim cultures in Western video games (a) exploits stereotypical generalizations and clichés, (b) presents most followers of Islam as a threat, (c) most likely links Islam with terrorism, and (d) marginalizes the representation of "ordinary Muslims."[8]

Sahar Khamis in "The Role of 'New' Arab Satellite Channels in Fostering Intercultural Dialogue" argues that although the distorted images of Arabs and Muslims in the West have existed and have been studied for a long time, new international developments necessitate readdressing this issue.[9] In the post-9/11 world, polarized rhetoric of "us" and "them" has intensified in Western media, reinforcing simplistic ideas of a collective self and its hostile Other. Arab and Muslim identities have become politicized through an ascribed interrelationship between Islam, Arab identity, and terrorism.[10] As a result, most Muslims now find themselves misperceived as an isolated and excluded minority that resists integration with other cultures and faiths, or as a group of "terrorists," who violently attack others and threaten their safety.[11] In turn, since 9/11, many Muslims have made their identities more salient, mainly because they feel the need to educate people about Islam and also to justify being Muslim.[12] Khamis suggests that the introduction of new digital technologies signified the start of a new era of self-definition and self-representation for Arabs and Muslims.[13]

Correspondingly, research on the construction of identity in Muslim games has focused on games produced in the Muslim world and on the issues of self-representation and identity. David Machin and Usama Suleiman in "Arab and American Computer War Games" have compared how two Arab and American games recontextualize and frame real-world events. Helga Tawil-Souri in "The Political Battlefield of Pro-Arab Video Games" has presented an ethnographic account of how Palestinian children play, comment, and make sense of Arab video games. In "Digital Arabs," I have provided exploratory research on how Muslim and other identities are constructed and communicated to players in Arab games. The question of a specific Arab or Muslim identity and its construction in video games seems to be important to the majority of producers I interviewed in Egypt, Lebanon, and Syria.[14] Most Arab games available on the market today deal primarily with the identity of the main hero; they use different concepts and values, including Islam and its ethics, in the construction of that identity.

As a result, research on the communication of Islamic moral and ethical values deals with Islam as an organized system of religion and its relation to video games. Krystina Derrickson in "*Second Life* and the Sacred" has explored how virtual worlds recreate Islamic holy sites and rituals. In "Video Games, Video Clips, and Islam," I have analyzed how video games are appropriated by the emerging Muslim consumer culture. In "Islamogaming," Heidi Campbell discusses how video games are used to teach the basic tenets of Islam and to communicate Islamic moral and ethical values.

All of this research indicates that the appropriation of video games in the Arab world has, from the beginning, been "engaged" in the sense that it focuses on the issues of cultural and religious identity as well as on the educational aspects of video games. This must be kept in mind when exploring the different modes of representation of Islam in American and Arab games. On one hand, we have a mainstream, commercial, American production designed with its consumer base and its tastes and expectations in mind. On the other, we have an emerging, enthusiastic, engaged industry in the Arab world. It is this asymmetrical nature of the frameworks that led Campbell to label Arab and Muslim video games as "alternative storytelling" that counters the dominant cultural narratives about their religious community promoted by the dominant media cultures.[15]

PLAYING WITH RELIGION: METHODOLOGY AND AIMS

The scholarly work done to date on Islam and video games has mostly been written from the perspectives of Middle Eastern or Islamic studies, cultural studies, and communication studies. Despite the importance of the research in these fields (primarily in expanding boundaries and exploring new ethical dimensions), from the perspective of game studies the existing research provides mostly anecdotal evidence on the subject matter and rarely analyzes the content of these games in detail. In this

Table 5.1. Video Games Used for Analysis of Each Layer

LAYER	GENRE	AMERICAN GAME	ARAB GAME	METHODOLOGY
audiovisual	first-person shooter	*Kuma\War* (Kuma Reality Games, 2004)	*Special Force 2* (W3DTEK, 2007)	shot-by-shot analysis
narrative	real-time strategy	*Age of Empires 2* (Ensemble, 1999)	*Quraish* (Afkar Media, 2007)	textual analysis
procedural	turn-based, real-time	*Civilization IV* (Firaxis, 2005) strategy	*Arabian Lords* (BreakAway Games /Quirkat, 2007)	rule-system analysis

chapter I attempt to fill that void (theoretically as well as empirically) by investigating the possible ways in which video games utilize their core representational layers: audiovisual, narrative, and procedural. (By the "procedural layer," I mean how Islam is embedded into the rule systems governing the player's interaction with the game.)

Each of the three following sections analyzes how the virtual representation of Islam is constructed in one of these layers. For content analysis in each section I have used one American and one Arab video game in which the representation of Islam or Muslims is central to the respective layer. Both games for each analysis have been chosen from within the same genre. As Simon Egenfeldt-Nielsen and his colleagues in *Understanding Video Games* note, genres are to a large extent arbitrary. Yet they are useful as analytical constructs imposed on a group of objects in order to discuss the complexity of their individual differences in a meaningful way.[16] Games of the same genre arguably share similar expressive forms and thus a similar method of analysis may be applied to them. For the audiovisual layer, I have chosen the first-person shooter genre and a shot-by-shot analysis; for the narrative layer, the real-time strategy genre and a textual analysis; and for the procedural layer, the turn-based strategy genre and a rule-system analysis (see table 5.1).

Beyond playing the games in question, I have examined related booklets, manuals, and websites and interviewed two Arab game producers. Substantial portions of the materials were gathered during fieldwork trips to Damascus in 2005, Beirut in 2006 and Cairo in 2007. All the American games were played in English; the Arab games were played in Arabic. Interviews with producers were recorded in Arabic.

THE AUDIOVISUAL LAYER: MEETING VIRTUAL
HEROES AND ENEMIES IN FIRST-PERSON SHOOTERS

As Jay Bolter and Richard Grusin argue in *Remediation,* the desire for immediacy leads digital media to borrow from each other as well as from their analog predecessors, such as film, television, and photography.[17] Video games have a long-standing connection to cinema, deploying similar visual syntax, grammar, and vocabulary in introductions, cutscenes, and in-game graphics. As technological capabilities have improved, many video games utilize photorealistic imagery in order to create a believable universe. This applies in particular to the first-person shooter genre with its emphasis on visual realism.[18]

Since 9/11, video games released by the U.S. gaming industry have increasingly sought to mirror real-world conflict scenarios, particularly the U.S. military interventions in Iraq and Afghanistan. One such game is *Kuma\War,* a tactical first- and third-person shooter game with downloadable missions available for free online. *Kuma\War* was developed by Kuma Reality Games, which was set up in 2004 in New York by a group of retired military officers.[19] According to the authors, *Kuma\ War* is "more than just a game; it is an interactive chronicle of the war on terror with real news coverage and an original video news show for each mission."[20] In recreating real-world events, *Kuma\War* uses information culled from Fox News reports, military experts, Department of Defense records, and original research. Each episode consists of a playable mission, extensive background text, satellite photos, and a multimedia library, often including interviews with event participants. The transcript in table 5.2 describes part of the trailer for the *Mission 29: Fallujah: Operation al-Fajr* game (2004), which aims to recreate the coalition forces' ground attack on the Iraqi city of Fallujah in November 2004.

The game closely mimics the visual style of TV news coverage. It provides a "real-world hook" by offering privileged glimpses from the front lines (taken directly from video footage of landscapes in which the U.S. military has been engaged).[21] This gritty realism centers on the authenticity of weapons, sounds, and combat scenarios. Yet the same principles of "realism" are not extended to the enemy as the Other.

Table 5.2. Transcript of Trailer for Kuma\War's "Fallujah: Operation al-Fajr" (excerpt)

Virtual newsroom. We see a female reporter in front and images of a U.S. soldier, a military helicopter, and the U.S. flag in the background. The headline says: "Kuma\War Jacki Schechner."	Jacki: "Hello and welcome. I am Jacki Schechner and this is *Kuma\War*."
Real-world footage from Iraq. U.S. Humvees move on road in a rural landscape.	Dramatic music
Close-up of two Sunni militants in plain clothes, their faces wrapped in *kufiyas*, wielding machine guns and RPGs.	J: "April 6, 2004. U.S. Marines launched a massive offensive campaign in Fallujah in an attempt to suppress the Sunni insurgents."
A group of Iraqi soldiers enters the city. Citizens welcome them and wave Iraqi flags.	J: "By the end of the month, political agreements bring an end to the assault. Marines withdraw, and the Iraqi Fallujah brigade takes over."
Close-up of a masked Sunni militant firing an RPG.	J: "But the Iraqi unit quickly dissolves, leaving this key city under insurgent control."
Black-and-white photo of Zarqawi. Cut. A glimpse of real footage of Berg's beheading.	J: "In May Jordanian militant Abu Moussa Zarqawi, believed to be operating out of Fallujah, beheads American Nick Berg."
Al Jazeera footage. Five masked militants, armed with machine guns and scimitars, read a statement to the camera. In front of them sits a civilian prisoner. His face is blurred. In the background, a black banner with the *shahadah*, the Islamic declaration of faith, in Arabic: "There is no god but God and Muhammad is His messenger."	J: "The terrorist and his followers launched a campaign of beheadings, kidnappings, assassinations, and car bombings throughout Iraq."
Virtual newsroom. Close-up of Schechner.	J: "General Wilkerson, what sort of resistance can U.S. troops expect to encounter?"
Close-up of Wilkerson. A computer screen and a map of Iraq are in the background.	W: "Well, I think all of you gamers have been watching the news . . . and noticed that the innocent civilians and perhaps

	some of the operative insurgents are all streaming out of Fallujah. With that, I suspect when the assault actually begins there might be less resistance than we have expected. And the end result will be not a standoff battle but rather the anticlimactic control of the city passing to coalition forces."
Virtual newsroom. Close-up of Schechner.	J: "Thank you, General. Now, let's talk to Dante Anderson, Kuma's head of product development, about our recreation of the latest offensive in Fallujah."
Close-up of Anderson. A software development studio is in the background.	J: "Events are developing in Fallujah as we speak. What's going to be the most challenging part of this mission for your development team?"
Actual in-game footage. Close-up of a U.S. Marine in desert camo aiming an assault rifle. Cut. Close-up of two masked Sunni militants hiding behind a car and wielding machine guns and RPGs.	A: "We've spent a lot of time trying to figure out what is really real. We've built it, and we spent a lot of time also redoing things that we had done initially because we got better information. Our main challenge is to get it out as quickly as possible when the operation concludes and to make sure that it is as accurate as possible."
Close-up of Schechner.	J: "Thank you, Dante. . . . For Kuma Reality Games, Jacki Schechner."

The enemy is depicted as a set of schematized attributes which refer to Arab Muslims – head cover, loose clothes, dark skin color, and so on. Distinctive clothing and head covers are used when the enemy's Shia or Sunni identity needs to be emphasized in connection with the real-world campaign. The in-game narrative then links these visual signifiers to international terrorism or Islamic extremism. Thus, the player is navigated through "insurgent-infested Fallujah" where "Sunni terrorists hide in mosques" (*Fallujah: Operation al-Fajr*); has to infiltrate Karabilah "where terrorists wage war . . . from homes and stores, mosques and schools – none of which are sacred in the eyes of the insurgents" (*Mission 53: Operation Spear*); and is confronted with "vicious killers" in a "violent urban assault, one that uncovers the resourcefulness, determination, and sheer brutality of the terrorists" (*Operation Spear*).

Marcus Power in "Digital War Games and Post 9/11 Geographies of Militarism" argues that the Arab Muslim culture in *Kuma\War* is portrayed as savage, terroristic, and uncivilized, constructing racialized meanings which in turn provide an ideological sanction for the war on terror.[22] The link between terrorism and Islam is emphasized in particular by the game's audiovisual layer, for example, the appropriated footage of beheadings with Quranic verses played in the background during the game's introduction or the photorealistic reconstructions of Iraqi mosques, which serve as terrorist hideouts in the actual game. As is the case with most Western video games, the representation of ordinary Muslim citizens is marginalized. In the game there is no possibility for civilian casualties caused by the U.S. war effort – because the Iraqi cities are mostly depicted as uninhabited.[23] *Kuma\War* presents a clean, sanitized, and enjoyable version of war for popular consumption, obscuring the realities, contexts, and consequences of actual war.[24]

The existence of such games and the (mis)representation of Islam they promote are of concern to many in the Muslim world. A prime example is the following statement by the Central Internet Bureau of the Lebanese Hezbollah movement: "The problem behind video games is that most of them are foreign made, especially American. Therefore, they bear enormous false understandings and habituate teenagers to violence, hatred and grudges. In addition, some cause humiliation to many of our Islamic and Arab countries, where battles are running in these Arab countries, the dead are Arab soldiers, whereas the hero who kills them is – the player himself – an American."[25] In response, the Hezbollah movement has produced several games based on "Arab and Islamic values" that aim to foster national pride and glorify the movement's struggle with Israeli forces in southern Lebanon. I will examine the first-person shooter game *Special Force 2* (W3DTEK, 2007), aka *Al-wa'd as-sādiq* (*Tale of the Truthful Pledge*), which is a sequel to the Hezbollah game *Special Force* (*Al-quwwa al-khāsa;* Solution, 2003). The new game retells a story from the 2006 war between Israel Defense Forces and Hezbollah (see table 5.3).

Although the video is completely rendered through 3D, in-game computer graphics, it closely approximates the visual style of "real" promotional and propaganda video clips used by the Lebanese Hezbollah

Table 5.3. Transcript of Trailer for Special Force 2

W3DTEK company logo appears on a
green background.

Text (in Arabic): "In the name of   Dramatic music
God, the Most Merciful, the Most
Compassionate. Among the believers
are men who have been true to their
covenant with Allah; of them some have
completed their vow and some wait, but
they have never changed in the least."

Text (in Arabic): "Against them make   Music reaches a climax: drums, male
ready your strength to the utmost of   chorus
your power, including steeds of war,
to strike terror into the hearts of the
enemies of Allah, and your enemies, and
others besides, whom ye may not know,
but whom Allah doth know. Whatever
ye shall spend in the cause of Allah shall
be repaid unto you, and ye shall not be
treated unjustly."
Background changes to red flames.

In the distance, an Israeli military truck   Dramatic music
moves fast on a road in a hilly landscape.
It is followed by a typical Israel Defense
Forces jeep.

Suddenly, the jeep explodes. Close-up   Crescendo. Male chorus repeats:
of its wreckage and the dead bodies of   "Allahu Akbar! Allahu Akbar!"
Israeli soldiers.

The backs of Hezbollah soldiers running   Male voice: "Allahu Akbar! Oh
toward the road. A jeep arrives, and   Invincible Lion! The Truthful Pledge!"
the soldiers get in. The jeep continues
to the site of the explosion and then
disappears.

movement. Correspondingly, the emphasis on Islam is central to the audiovisual layer of the game. The mission starts with *basmala*[26] followed
by verses from the Quran taken from the sūra Al-Anfal ("The Spoils
of War"). The introductory videos are accompanied by *Takbir* (the call
"Allāhu Akbar") or a religious *nashid* (hymn) in the background. Similarly, the Muslim identity of the main hero is emphasized by the visual

signifiers used in the game, for example, the Quran, a prayer rug, posters of the Dome of the Rock and the Al-Aqsa Mosque, and so on.

At the same time, the game borrows from its American counterparts. It simply reverses the polarities of the narrative and visual stereotypes observed, for example, in *Kuma\War*. It substitutes an Arab Muslim hero for the American soldier and substitutes the Israeli forces for the enemies. But unlike the American games, where the hero is usually individualized, *Special Force* 2 promotes a higher obligation to a collective spiritual whole.[27] By situating the player in the immersive simulation of real conflict in Palestine and Lebanon, and by framing this conflict in primarily religious terms, the game contributes to the notion of a global Muslim identity. The focal point is defending Muslim *ummah* against outside aggression, with emphasis on the just and moral cause of the fight and the glorification of the Muslim fighters. By schematizing complex and diverse conflicts into a single, bipolar scheme of good and evil, these games mirror their Western blueprints, including the collectivization and functionalization of enemies, the exclusion of civilians from the virtual battleground, and legitimizing the authors' point of view through highly selective references to real-world events.

Despite their fundamentally different ideological backgrounds, *Kuma\War* and *Special Force* 2 share many similarities in the audiovisual layer. Both games are unrealistic, yet still cinematic. They don't reproduce the real-world experience of war; instead, they theatrically romanticize war. Death and bodily dismemberment have been banished from both games. Both *Kuma\War* and *Special Force* 2 thus reinforce the image of a clean war with clear battle lines; no moral questions are put forward, and no consideration is given to the reality of taking a life.[28] The way Islam as a religion is depicted, however, is significantly different. Whereas *Kuma\War* presents Islam as a threat and schematizes Muslims as religious fanatics and "enemies to democracy and freedom," *Special Force* 2 honors the Muslim identity of the hero and links Islamic values to the heroic and legitimate defense of rights.

Regarding our understanding of religion and digital gaming, analysis of the audiovisual layer shows that both American and Arab games construct their virtual representations of Islam by using signifiers borrowed from their media predecessors, particularly TV news coverage and propaganda video clips. This observation fits with Bolter and Grusin's concept of remediation mentioned earlier. More important, in order to create a believable universe for their audiences, these games appropriate not only the visual imagery, but also the schematizations and clichés surrounding Islam in their respective media cultures. The visual "realism" of these games legitimizes these schematizations, simultaneously recreating the real world and obscuring it.

THE NARRATIVE LAYER: ENCOUNTERING ISLAM IN REAL-TIME STRATEGIES

A number of games, especially those in the adventure genre, contain strong narrative elements. Even in genres where stories are not part of the gameplay, such as strategies or simulations, fictional worlds prompt players to imagine that their actions take place in a meaningful setting.[29] Several real-time strategy games present the player with complex and well-elaborated storylines, which are typically told in the cutscenes between missions and amended through the in-game scripts. The American game I have chosen for my analysis of the narrative layer, *Age of Empires 2* (Ensemble, 1999), goes back to the roots of narrative since it tells the story by framing its campaigns with recorded voiceovers and a few sketched images. The "Saladin Campaign" offers the player the opportunity to "encounter" Islam through the eyes of a Crusader knight imprisoned by the Saracen army. Saladin and his Muslim warriors are depicted in an unusual way in the realm of digital entertainment. As the opening scene states:

> Egypt. A month since I entered the Holy Land. . . . And I was dying. I wandered the cold desert for four nights before the horse archers found me. . . . They were Saracens, the rulers of the Middle East. I had ridden to the Holy Land with the Crusaders from France and Normandy, so I was by all rights these Saracens' enemy. Yet they gave me water and a spindly horse and led me back to their leader. And that was how I met Saladin. The paintings in Europe show Saladin as demonic, barbarian. Yet he is more chivalrous than any knight I'd met before and prefers the palaces of Damascus to slaughtering Normans in the desert. I had not expected hospitality from Saracens – we Normans execute any armed Arab we capture. But Saladin left me free to explore this camp.

In a classic narrative scheme, the main hero becomes attached to his jailers and adopts their culture and manners. The game deliberately incorporates hints of Arab and Muslim cultural heritage and their contribution to world civilization: "Although I am still a prisoner, Saladin and his generals dine with me. Over meals we discuss mathematics and astronomy. I never imagined a race of desert folk could be so wise. Baghdad, the Saracen capital, is the most civilized city in the world, with free hospitals, public baths, a postal service, and banks with branches as far away as China." Nevertheless, as the game progresses and the violence of the war increases, the "once noble Muslim warriors" become cruel and fanatical. Here, for the first time, the game introduces the concept of jihad: "In reaction to European hostility and fanaticism, the Saracens have steadily become more resolute . . . more bloodthirsty. Their love of art is replaced by a love for battle. Now, in answer to the Crusade, they have adapted their principle of Jihad for warfare."

Finally, in a fierce battle over Jerusalem, Saladin subdues the army of his rival, Richard the Lionheart. The game finishes with both adversaries signing a peace treaty and the end of the Third Crusade. Yet, as the narrator predicts, the "war that has been fought over religion and land" is not over.

The narrative of *Age of Empires 2* resembles medieval travelogue and constitutes something of an exception in the dominant representations of Islam in historical and fantastical video games. These games typically construe the "Orient" as an exotic and ahistorical entity and schematize Muslims in the framework of arbitrary cruelty, barbarism, and religious fanaticism.[30] Yet when we examine the story of *Age of Empires 2* closely, as it is presented in both the cutscenes and the gameplay, we see that it remains to a certain extent within the cultural stereotypes that surround the Crusades in European popular culture. Choosing Saladin, often depicted as "the noble prince of Islam," to be the virtual Muslim representative does not in fact contradict Orientalist tendencies. The characterization of Saladin as "far nobler than any competitor" can be easily incorporated into the narrative of European knighthood.[31] Other Muslims in the game remain within the typical scheme, for example, Saladin's Mamluks, who mock the "Franks" as "the infidel dogs of the West," or the "treacherous Egyptians," who betray the player's noble master.

Perhaps it was the unusually positive framing of Islam and the rich-
ness of the story in *Age of Empires 2* that inspired Arab developers (the
Syrian company Afkar Media) to craft *Quraish,* released in 2007. The
latter is a real-time strategy game dealing with pre-Islamic Bedouin wars
and the early Islamic conquests (Al-Futūhāt al-Islāmīya). The game is
clearly inspired by *Age of Empires 2* and it similarly utilizes introductory
sequences, which are narrated in classical Arabic and accompanied by
simple visuals. The first campaign, Al-Jāhilīya ("First Encounter"), can
be played from the perspective of pagan Bedouin chieftains Hani and
Abu Qatada, and narrates a story from a war between two Arab tribes,
the Ghassanids and the Lakhmids. More important, as the name suggests, it revolves around the "encounter" of the pagan Arabs with Islam.
It starts with the young hero, Hani, being appointed by his father as the
new leader of the Shaiban tribe in a time of famine and on the brink
of tribal war:

> My father pointed to me as he clenched the reins of his horse, which had
> been provoked by the running of the other one and begun hitting the ground
> nervously.... The sound of his hooves mixed with my father's voice. "O Hani!
> O people of Shaiban! Keep your promise, your promise!" I have never imag-
> ined being the leader of Shaiban so quickly, and under these circumstances.
> ... Now I am responsible for a thousand mouths to feed and guard during
> a sharp drought where the goats are all dry. Moreover, the Arab tribes are
> fighting each other because of hunger. "O Lord of Mecca, what do you want?
> What's your order? If there is no other choice, so let it happen as you wish."

The narrative style of the game bears a striking resemblance to classical Arab literary genres, including the *Ayyām al-Arab* ("The Days of the
Arabs," stories of the tribal wars) and Muhammad Ibn Ishāq's *Sīrat rasūl
Allāh* ("Life of Allah's Messenger," a biography of the Prophet Muhammad). Through the unusually long and well-developed introduction,
many concepts of pre-Islamic Arab culture and early Islamic history
are communicated to the player, for example, *sharaf* and *'ird* (Bedouin
honor codes), *thar* (retributive justice), and *muruwa* (manliness). The
game navigates the player through many real-world events and historic
places (including the cities of Ukaz, Mecca, and Medina) and recounts
a complicated story designed along the lines of classical Arab oral and
literary heritage, including scenes of poetry contests, blood revenge,
oaths, and tribal alliances.

Finally, in the last mission, the main hero's tribe is asked to fulfill their oath and help the Quraish tribe in their war with a newly emerged power – Muslims led by a prophet called Muhammad. The game models the historical Battle of the Trench (627 CE) in which the outnumbered Muslim forces successfully defended the city of Medina, partly because of the trench they dug around it. The game's main narrative follows these historical events, so after an unsuccessful charge the leaders of the Quraish tribe decide to withdraw from the battle. The player then has the choice to accept Islam and join the Muslim forces of Medina in their victorious battle. If he accepts, the campaign ends and makes way for the second part of the game, based on the history of early Muslim conquest.[32] The final narrative sequence then describes the religious conversion of Abu Qatada to Islam:

> Thank God, the mighty and omnipotent, who let his poor servant, Abu Qatada, live and embrace Islam, and see the Shaiban embracing Islam in huge numbers. The Bedouins who fought for a poem, a date, or a horse saw the revealed message of Allah descended to Man from them. He came to complete their ethics and convert them to believers who didn't prostrate except to one mighty God. They changed from worthless shepherds to great leaders of all nations. At night, they read the holy book Quran and by day they are knights to free mankind from the tyranny and falsehood of other creatures.

Regarding religion and digital gaming, I find it significant that the narrative layers of both the American and the Arab game appropriate traditional literary genres in order to present the concept of Islam to the player. Thus, we have on one hand a European medieval travelogue, and on the other Arab prophetic literature (*sira*). In comparison to the audiovisual layer, the narrative layer offers more space for developing the plot and presenting Islam. It thus arguably provides a more multifaceted image of the latter.

Yet again, the traditional narrative figures and schematized concepts associated with these literary genres are passed to the games deriving therefrom. Despite structural similarities, the two games present Islam in fundamentally different ways. Whereas in *Age of Empires 2* Islam is initially presented as the Other, then humanized through the character of a noble Muslim ruler, and finally problematized again through the acts of violence conducted in its name, in *Quraish* Islam begins as the player's enemy, but in the end the player's avatar embraces Islam.

THE PROCEDURAL LAYER: INCORPORATING
ISLAM INTO GAME RULES

Alexander Galloway in "Social Realism in Gaming" suggests that it is no longer sufficient to talk about the visual or textual representation of meaning in game studies. Instead, computer-enabled simulation and its rules, which both facilitate and limit a player's actions and choices, have to be studied. Similarly, Gonzalo Frasca in "Videogames of the Op-pressed" argues: "Video games not only represent reality, but also model it through simulations. This form of representation is based on rules that mimic the behavior of the simulated systems. However, unlike narrative authors, simulation authors do not represent a particular event, but a set of potential events. Because of this, we have to think about their objects as systems and consider what laws govern their behaviors."[33]

   There exist only a few games that deliberately embed Islam into their game rules. One of the few American games dealing procedurally with Islam is Sid Meier's *Civilization IV.* The *Civilization* series (1991–) consists of turn-based strategy games that allow players to act on the part of various civilizations and engage in building cities, establishing trade routes, and interacting with others on a diplomatic or military basis throughout thousands of years of virtual history. The fourth in the series incorporates seven world religions into its gameplay. It enables players to "found" these religions, build the religions' holy sites, and spread the reli-gions through missionary work. The most important aspect of the game's representation of religion is that all the religious systems available to the player – Buddhism, Hinduism, Judaism, Christianity, Confucianism, Taoism, and Islam – are procedurally equal and generally presented in a "neutral" way. As *Civilization IV's Manual* states: "Through religion, man has sought to make sense of the universe around him and to determine his place in it. Religion has always played a critical part in human history. Religion has inspired, enlightened and ennobled man; in its name men have erected beautiful buildings, written books of great wisdom, and made music of surpassing beauty. In its name men have also murdered and enslaved their fellows."[34]

   Essentially, all religions in the game have the same effects; the only difference is their technological requirements. Thus, Buddhism is founded when the first player invents "meditation," Christianity is similarly linked with "theology," and Islam with "divine rights." Generally speaking, religion is deeply embedded in the game rules and is represented via a complex system of effects and bonuses. Once founded, a religion spreads automatically between cities connected via trade routes. However, players can also spread it actively through the use of missionaries. The player can adopt a particular religion as a state religion, boosting its positive effect on her cities' culture and happiness. The state religion also has further implications for in-game diplomacy. Civilizations that follow the same official religion tend to have friendlier relations. The game also allows for forced conversions since the player can threaten weaker civilizations, coercing them to adopt the religion of her choice.

From the way religion, including Islam, is implemented in the game rules, it is clear that the authors strived to be religiously sensitive, while maintaining challenging and balanced gameplay. As they state: "Given the importance that religions have had in human development, we didn't want to just leave them out of the game altogether; instead we have tried to handle them in as respectful, fair and even-handed [a] manner as possible. . . . We offer no value judgments on religion; we mean no disrespect to anyone's beliefs. We're game designers, not theologians."[35]

As a result, religion as presented in *Civilization IV* is essentially a database of effects, bonuses, and penalties; religion is about relations between quantifiable processes, where everything is a question of the acquisition and allocation of resources and their proper management. As McKenzie Wark argues in *Gamer Theory,* games in the *Civilization* series erase the difference between the everyday and the utopian and embrace all differences by rendering all space and time quantifiable. The *Civilization IV* algorithm can produce every possible combination of resources mapped in the database, dividing everything into manageable chunks of data. Wark suggests that this insistence "on the reality of the possible, on what resides within resources, is the American dream." In other words: "When playing *Civilization . . .* , it doesn't matter if the civilization you choose to play is Babylon or China, Russia or Zululand, France or India. Whoever wins is America, in that the logic of the game itself is America [*sic*]."[36]

It has to be emphasized here that all simulations intrinsically trans-
code historical realities into specific mathematical models, thus making
any axiological judgments problematic. As I argued in "Digital Arabs,"
despite the possible contradictions in the ideological setting of *Civilization IV,* the game is one of the rare exceptions in which Muslims are not
functionalized as enemies nor depicted in an Orientalist manner. Rather,
the game constitutes a possible representation of the player's self.[37] In
this respect, it is crucial to explore the ways in which Islam is embedded
into the game rules of Arab games. As far as I know, the only Arab game
that deals with Islam on the level of game rules is *Arabian Lords.*

Arabian Lords (Sādat as-sahrā') is a PC strategy game inspired by
the Rise of Islam (during the seventh to thirteenth centuries) and developed by the U.S. company BreakAway Games in close collaboration with the Jordanian company Quirkat in 2007. From the beginning
Arabian Lords was intended to be shipped primarily to regions in the
Middle East and is available in Arabic and English. According to the
developers, maintaining appropriate content, historical accuracy, and
cultural sensitivity was crucial for the game's design. As the introduction to the game states:

> Before the birth of Islam, Arabia stood at the crossroads of trade between
> Africa, Asia, and Europe. Its desert was a harsh place but its people knew
> how to navigate caravans between the oases so they benefited from the trade
> that crossed their land. These people were the nomadic Arabs, the merchant
> lords of the desert. During the seventh and eighth centuries Islam grew and
> Muslims spread north into Syria, West to the Atlantic, and East to the river
> Indus. Wherever Muslim armies went traders followed. . . . At its height in
> the ninth century the Islamic world rivaled the great empires of the past.
> Now it is your time to help expand the rule of Islam between the seventh and
> thirteenth centuries. Can you succeed as a merchant lord during this rise
> of wealth and power?

Surprisingly, although the game invites the player to "help expand
the rule of Islam," most of the gameplay revolves around harvesting resources, building, trade, and city management, that is, activities typical for the strategy game genre. Islam is integrated into the game rules
only through the existence of a single building, the Mosque, and a single
unit, the Vizier. The only procedural action a player can perform in-

volving religion is donating money to the Mosque, which increases the player's popularity and her chances of producing a Vizier. The Vizier then provides the player with several bonuses, for example, speeding up the productivity of nearby workers, improving nearby units' statistics, and so on.

When comparing *Arabian Lords* and *Civilization IV* we find that the fundamental difference in the way Islam is included in the game rules evolves primarily from the scale of the model. The procedural role of Islam in *Arabian Lords* is seriously limited. This could be the result of the cultural sensitivity of the game's developers. As they state:

> We knew that culturally religion played a major role during this time span covered in the game, and that it still does today. We wanted to make sure to include this in a way that would honor its significance, while being sensitive to all religious and cultural concerns. At one point in the design we had included an "Imam" unit that players would be able to control. Because this seemed inappropriate to a number of our experts, we made significant changes to the design in order to remove it so as to not offend. In general, we always tried to error on the side of caution when it came to cultural issues.[38]

The cultural and religious sensitivity of the game, manifested in the very limited presence of Islam in the game rules, can thus be perceived both as a token of respect for Islam and as a pragmatic step aiming to ease the acceptance of the product in the more conservative societies of the Arab world. As we have seen, similar caution regarding the representation of religion was expressed by the team behind *Civilization IV*. Yet in both games religion is essentially schematized as a mere system of advantages and bonuses. By forsaking a deeper integration of Islam and its ethics and moral values into the rules, both games deliberately fail to utilize the strength of the medium. In other words, both games miss out on gameplay that would allow the player to experience ethical dilemmas related to religion and draw her own conclusions.[39] It remains an open question whether this is the result of the developers' inner constraints and religious and cultural sensitivities or the inherent limitations of the strategy and simulation game genre. As far as I know, no game today offers players a fully procedural representation of Islam, integrating its ethics and values into the game's rule system.[40]

CONCLUSION: GENRE, REMEDIATION, AND PROCEDURE

This chapter has analyzed how mainstream American and Arab video games construct the virtual representation of Islam and Muslims. I have examined three representational layers of video games and analyzed two different games of a similar genre (one American and one Arab) for each layer.

In the audiovisual layer, examined in two games of the first-shooter genre, the representation of Islam was seen to be schematized and monolithic. It doesn't change throughout the game. While the American game, *Kuma\War*, presents Islam as a threat, the Arab game, *Special Force 2*, links Islamic values with heroism and a legitimate defense of rights. Both games offer racialized representations of enemies and schematize complex, real-world events into a bipolar frame.

In the narrative layer, examined in two games of the real-time strategy genre, the representation of Islam was seen to be more multifaceted and, following the traditions of storytelling, it evolves throughout the game. In the American game, *Age of Empires 2*, Islam is initially portrayed as the Other, then humanized through the character of a noble Muslim ruler. Islam ultimately becomes once again problematic through acts of violence conducted in its name. The Arab game, *Quraish*, presents Islam in the beginning as the enemy, while in the end the player's avatar embraces it.

Finally, in the procedural layer, examined in two games of the strategy genre, Islam was seen to be embedded in the games' rule systems. Yet both in the American game, *Civilization IV*, and in the Arab game, *Arabian Lords*, religion is represented as a mere system of advantages and bonuses. The games' authors abstained from a deeper integration of Islam and its ethics and moral values into the gameplay.

On a more theoretical level, the analysis presented in this chapter can be summarized in the following remarks:

First, a game's genre seems to fundamentally determine the way Islam, and perhaps religion in general, is presented in the game. Since most of the Arab games examined here utilize genres established by their successful American counterparts, their authors had to appropriate the existing patterns of representation and refashion them along the lines of Islamic principles. In other words, although contemporary Arab games vary significantly in their background, aims, and design and offer multifaceted concepts of Islam and of Muslim identity, they do not transcend the patterns established by a global, in most cases American, video game industry.

Second, video games seem to borrow a lot from their media predecessors. The audiovisual layer in the American first-person shooter genre appropriates the cinematic representation of war known from Hollywood movies and the hyperrealism of T V news coverage. Meanwhile, an Arab game of a similar genre appropriates the language of Hezbollah's video clips and martyr videos. In the narrative layer the American and Arab games similarly borrow from their cultures' traditional literary genres, that is, travelogues and prophetic literature.

Third, it seems that the schematized images of Islam associated with the remediated genres are passed on to video games. Erkki Huhtamo in *Media Archaeology* describes how topoi (clichés found in any form of literature) spread to all spheres of life addressed by literature and to which it gives form. As he argues: "No matter how dominant 'media culture' may have become in the contemporary world, it does not constitute an all-encompassing realm. It coexists with and may even be embedded in other cultural formations. One may therefore expect topoi from other realms, including ancient ones, to reappear within [a] media-cultural context."[41]

The quasi-historical representations of Islam found in the narrative structure of *Age of Empires 2* are similar to the Orientalist discourses of European novels and nineteenth-century paintings, whereas the audiovisual representations of Islam and Muslims found in *Kuma\War* follow the hyperrealistic schematizations of the U.S. military-entertainment complex. While the American game presents Islam as a threat, flattens out diverse Muslim identities, and reconstructs them into a series of social stereotypes, the Arab game uses a distinctive Islamic narrative to frame its gameplay and communicate Islamic principles and moral values to the players.

In the games' procedural layer, which is not directly appropriated from other media, Islam as a belief system and an organized religion is transcoded into a mathematical model, seemingly taking into account no ethical considerations. In Huhtamo's terms, there are no topoi associated with Islam in the procedural level. Therefore, arguably, no clichés or schematizations of Islam are communicated to the player in this particular layer. Nevertheless, the very rules of the simulations I have analyzed, which model the world as consisting of quantifiable variables and offer everyone an equal possibility to "win" the game, bear culturally significant meaning. In this respect, Wark poignantly argues that the rule system in *Civilization* stems from the ethics and values of Protestant America.[42]

As Huhtamo suggests, topoi are not limited to literary traditions, but can also manifest as designs.[43] Regarding our understanding of religion and digital gaming, it is of crucial importance to study video games' rule systems and investigate how they are shaped by their developers' cultures and religious traditions. Moreover, rule systems migrate between cultures and significantly influence local production. As we have seen, many Arab game designers have been directly inspired by particular American games and have appropriated their patterns. We can conclude that the way Islam, and perhaps any other religion, is represented in a video game is fundamentally shaped by (a) the power relations in global cultural exchange, (b) local religious and cultural topoi and media traditions, and (c) the video game's rule system, which is used to convey such representations.

NOTES

1. Bogost and Poremba, "Can Games Get Real?," 12–21.
2. Šisler, "Digital Arabs."
3. Ibid.
4. Šisler, "Video Games, Video Clips, and Islam."
5. Bogost, *Persuasive Games,* 45.
6. Sabry, *Cultural Encounters in the Arab World,* 11.
7. Reichmuth and Werning, "Pixel Pashas, Digital Djinns," 46–47.
8. Šisler, "Digital Arabs."
9. Khamis, "The Role of 'New' Arab Satellite Channels," 39.
10. Witteborn, "The Situated Expression of Arab Collective Identities."
11. el-Nawawy and Khamis, *Islam Dot Com,* 3.
12. Witteborn, "The Situated Expression of Arab Collective Identities."
13. Khamis, "The Role of 'New' Arab Satellite Channels," 41.
14. Ibid.; Šisler, "Video Games, Video Clips, and Islam."
15. Campbell, "Islamogaming."
16. Egenfeldt-Nielsen, Smith, and Tosca, *Understanding Video Games,* 41.

17. Bolter and Grusin, *Remediation,* 9.

18. Halter, *From Sun Tzu to Xbox.*

19. Sims, "When Reality Is Just an Illusion."

20. http://www.kumawar.com/about.php (accessed July 30, 2012).

21. Power, "Digital War Games."

22. Ibid., 208.

23. In a few missions, civilians are present as "hostages, whose fate lies in your hands," since they have been "neglected, beaten and left to die" by the insurgents (*Operation Spear*).

24. Power, "Digital War Games."

25. http://web.archive.org/web/20050105091655/www.specialforce.net/english/indexeng.htm.

26. The phrase *bismi-llāhi ar-rahmāni ar-rahīmi* ("In the name of God, Most Gracious, Most Merciful") constitutes the first verse of every sūra (chapter) of the Quran (but one) and is often used as an opening phrase in letters, books, and public speeches.

27. Machin and Suleiman, "Arab and American Computer War Games."

28. Power, "Digital War Games," 210.

29. Egenfeldt-Nielsen, Smith, and Tosca, *Understanding Video Games,* 171.

30. Šisler, "Digital Arabs."

31. Stanley, *Saladin.*

32. Although the player is given the option to reject Islam, it seems the last mission is then impossible to win, and there is no campaign prepared for that case. See Šisler, "Digital Arabs."

33. Frasca, "Videogames of the Oppressed," 21.

34. *Civilization IV's Manual,* 77.

35. Ibid.

36. Wark, *Gamer Theory,* 73.

37. Šisler, "Digital Arabs."

38. http://www.arabianlords.com/Public/public_master.aspx?Site_Id=2&Page_Id=922&Path=66.

39. Newgren, "*Bioshock* to the System," 145.

40. However, a few such games are in development. See Šisler, "Video Games, Video Clips, and Islam."

41. Huhtamo, "Dismantling the Fairy Engine," 35.

42. Wark, *Gamer Theory.*

43. Huhtamo, "Dismantling the Fairy Engine."

REFERENCES

Bogost, Ian. *Persuasive Games: The Expressive Power of Videogames.* Cambridge, Mass.: MIT Press, 2007.

Bogost, Ian, and Poremba, Cindy. "Can Games Get Real?: A Closer Look at 'Documentary' Digital Games." In *Computer Games as a Sociocultural Phenomenon: Games without Frontiers, War without Tears.* Edited by Andreas Jahn-Sudmann and Ralf Stockmann, 12–21. New York: Palgrave Macmillan, 2008.

Bolter, Jay David, and Grusin, Richard. *Remediation: Understanding New Media.* Cambridge, Mass.: MIT Press, 1999.

Campbell, Heidi. "Islamogaming: Digital Dignity via Alternative Storytellers." In *Halos and Avatars: Playing Video Games with God.* Edited by Craig Detweiler, 63–74. Louisville, Ky.: Westminster John Knox, 2010.

Civilization IV's Manual. Firaxis Games, 2005.

Derrickson, Krystina. "*Second Life* and
the Sacred: Islamic Space in a Virtual
World." *Digital Islam.* 2008. http://
www.digitalislam.eu/article.do?article
Id=1877 (accessed November 14, 2010).
Egenfeldt-Nielsen, Simon, Smith, Jonas
Heide, and Tosca, Susana Pajares. *Un-
derstanding Video Games.* New York:
Routledge, 2008.
Frasca, Gonzalo. "Videogames of the
Oppressed: Critical Thinking, Educa-
tion, Tolerance, and Other Trivial
Issues." In *First Person: New Media as
Story, Performance, and Game.* Edited
by Noah Wardrip-Fruin and Pat Har-
rigan, 85–94. Cambridge, Mass.: MIT
Press, 2004.
Galloway, Alexander R. "Social Realism
in Gaming." *Game Studies* 4, no. 1
(2004). http://www.gamestudies.org
/0401/galloway (accessed July 30,
2012).
Halter, Ed. *From Sun Tzu to Xbox: War
and Video Games.* New York: Thun-
der's Mouth, 2006.
Höglund, Johan. "Electronic Empire:
Orientalism Revisited in the Military
Shooter." *Game Studies* 8, no. 1 (2008).
http://gamestudies.org/0801/articles
/hoeglund (accessed July 30, 2012).
Huhtamo, Erkki. "Dismantling the
Fairy Engine: Media Archaeology as
Topos Study." In *Media Archaeology:
Approaches, Applications, and Implica-
tions.* Edited by Erkki Huhtamo and
Jussi Parikka. Berkeley: University
of California Press, 2011.
Khamis, Sahar. "The Role of 'New' Arab
Satellite Channels in Fostering In-
tercultural Dialogue: Can Al Jazeera
English Bridge the Communication
Gap?" In *New Media and the New Mid-
dle East.* Edited by Philip Seib, 39–53.
New York: Palgrave Macmillan, 2007.

Machin, David, and Suleiman, Usama.
"Arab and American Computer War
Games: The Influence of a Global
Technology on Discourse." *Critical
Discourse Studies* 3, no. 1 (2006): 1–22.
Marashi, Ibrahim. "The Depiction
of Arabs in Combat Video Games."
Paper presented at the Beirut Institute
of Media Arts, Lebanese American
University, November 5–9, 2001.
el-Nawawy, Mohammed, and Khamis,
Sahar. *Islam Dot Com: Contemporary
Islamic Discourses in Cyberspace.* New
York: Palgrave Macmillan, 2009.
Newgren, Kevin. "*Bioshock* to the Sys-
tem: Smart Choices in Video Games."
In *Halos and Avatars: Playing Video
Games with God.* Edited by Craig De-
tweiler, 135–145. Louisville, Ky.: West-
minster John Knox, 2010.
Power, Marcus. "Digital War Games and
Post 9/11 Geographies of Militarism."
In *War Isn't Hell, It's Entertainment:
Essays on Visual Media and the Repre-
sentation of Conflict.* Edited by Rikke
Schubart, Fabian Virchow, Debra
White-Stanley, and Tanja Thomas,
198–215. London: McFarland, 2009.
Reichmuth, Philipp, and Werning,
Stephan. "Pixel Pashas, Digital
Djinns." *ISIM Review* 18 (2006):46–47.
Sabry, Tarik. *Cultural Encounters in the
Arab World: On Media, the Modern
and the Everyday.* London: Tauris,
2009.
Sims, Josh. "When Reality Is Just an Illu-
sion." *Independent,* March 29, 2004.
Šisler, Vít. "Digital Arabs: Representa-
tion in Video Games." *European
Journal of Cultural Studies* 11, no. 2
(2008):203–220.
———. "Video Games, Video Clips, and
Islam: New Media and the Communi-
cation of Values." In *Muslim Societies*

in the Age of Mass Consumption. Edited by Johanna Pink, 231–258. Newcastle: Cambridge Scholars, 2009.

Stanley, Diane. *Saladin: Noble Prince of Islam*. New York: HarperCollins, 2002.

Tawil-Souri, Helga. "The Political Battlefield of Pro-Arab Video Games on Palestinian Screens." *Comparative Studies of South Asia, Africa and the Middle East* 27, no. 3 (2007):536–551.

Wark, McKenzie. *Gamer Theory*. Cambridge, Mass.: Harvard University Press, 2007.

Witteborn, Saskia. "The Situated Expression of Arab Collective Identities in the United States." *Journal of Communication* 57 (2007):556–575.

SIX

Citing the Medieval

USING RELIGION AS WORLD-BUILDING
INFRASTRUCTURE IN FANTASY MMORPGS

Rabia Gregory

"A BETRAYAL. A CURSE. THE AGE OF STRIFE BEGINS. . . . WARRIORS, heroes, and adventurers begin the restoration. . . . What role will you play? Join the battle for supremacy or let chaos rule. *Shadowbane.*" This resonant baritone voiceover to the cinematic introduction to Wolfpack's 2003 massively multiplayer online role-playing game (MMORPG) lists dualistic clichés of fantasy role-playing games as the camera pans over scenes of armed three-dimensional male bodies engaged in combat, shooting arrows, casting spells, wielding siege engines, and arguing over strategy at campaign tables. As the only opportunity for cinematic narrative in the game, this opening video informs each new player that the game loading on their screen offers more than the realistic mechanics of premodern warfare. The conflict they are about to join is purposeful, each player a participant in a tragic battle originating in religious violence, which will frame their game experience as part of a war-torn world's history. The cutscene's camera slowly pans over the runes etched on the blade of a bloody sword thrust into the shattered trunk of a dying tree, capturing a moment of tragic betrayal when Cambruin, a mighty human king, was transfixed to the World Tree. As his blood ran down the tree's trunk, the Shadowbane blade petrified the tree, shattering creation.

The runes appear upside down and backward on Shadowbane's blade, in the medieval runic alphabet known as the Elder Futhark. The letters transliterate into the roman alphabet as a meaningless cluster of conso-nants: "h-d-z-p-t-th-s," but the director of this video certainly did not ex-pect that its subscribers would be able to read early Germanic languages.

Rather, those familiar with the game's lore are expected to recognize the seven "runes of power," whose meaning supersedes any linguistic purpose. The camera's slow pan over their angular forms on the bloody blade identify the sword as the legendary Shadowbane, transporting the viewer to the instant after the sword pierced and shattered the World Tree. This event irrevocably altered the cycle of life and death for the world of Aerynth. The cinematic trailer then dissolves to login and character creation screens, allowing players to mark the bodies of their own avatars with runes that determine race, dexterity, strength, and other character statistics, along with any special attributes. Fully integrated into the mythography of the game they are about to play, players then enter the game world at the base of the Tree of Life, grown from the seeds of the shattered World Tree.

This blending of historical medieval elements, such as Germanic runes and the World Tree, into the mechanics of contemporary computer gaming conventions, such as character attributes of strength, dexterity, and stamina, is often described by gamers and scholars of gaming as "medieval fantasy." It is more precisely what Umberto Eco has termed "neomedievalism," a repurposing of medieval imagery to represent contemporary values and problems and to engage contemporary audiences. Eco's neomedievalism distinguishes the invention of modern narratives that remake and reimagine medieval history from "medievalism," depictions of the historical medieval in post-medieval media.[1] Rather than exactly recreating the medieval past, these games blend the costumes, weaponry, and cultural traditions of different places and times to create different, yet still recognizably human worlds. Game designers incorporate katanas, battle bishops, flamberges, leather jerkins, lace-up bustiers, synthesized plainchant, cartoonish wattle-and-daub houses, vaguely Gothic cathedrals, woods filled with rats and spiders, and spear-wielding amazons in plate-mail miniskirts into their worlds as narrative elements that make the superhuman and magical feats of players' characters plausible.

Eco's notion of neomedievalism is essential to understanding the experience of realism elicited by religion in video games. *Get Medieval* (Monolith, 1998), an overhead, two-dimensional, shooter-spoofing fantasy adventure game, is driven by the witty lines mocking serious medieval heroism from the Barbarian, Sorceress, Thief, and Amazon players rather than by the challenges posed by its dungeons or the innovation of its gameplay, which closely copied Atari's 1986 arcade game *Gauntlet*. Electronic Arts' 2010 take on Dante's *Inferno* embellishes a fourteenth-century storyline with exaggerated violence. The spirit of Dante transforms from an exiled political dissident and father into a muscular Templar, amusing players with the audacity of the adaptation rather than novel gameplay. And MMORPGs, which often use the same layouts for graphical user interfaces, offer similar if not identical commands and emoticons, and design combat encounters for the same tactics, are distinguished by their social and role-playing opportunities. Neomedieval religious systems and cosmologies invented for video games are not just replicas of historical religions; they reflect contemporary values, resonate with modern audiences, and guide players into and through gaming worlds.

Neomedievalism is widespread in fantasy role-playing games, whether played in elaborate server-based worlds, on java consoles through websites like Facebook, on tabletops, or free-form in chat rooms and on websites. In *Shadowbane* (Ubisoft, 2003) and other MMORPGs, citations of medieval culture, and particularly of the imagery and vocabulary of medieval religions, encompass everything from character creation to the landscape of the game world and the names of items of clothing, spells, or special attacks. These game worlds are creations of pure fiction, virtual alternative realities that might have been designed without any religion at all, or with religious symbols unrelated to medieval Europe. In games with elaborate quest narratives or player-versus-environment combat scenarios, such as *Everquest* (Sony Online Entertainment, 1999), neomedieval religion embellishes scripted fantasy. Citations of medieval religion in less structured games, like *Shadowbane, Guild Wars* (NCSoft, 2005), *Darkfall* (Audiovisual Enterprises, 2009), and *War of the Roses* (Paradox Interactive, 2012), which are driven by player-versus-player combat, suggest that these elements are not simply recycled fantasy narratives. In less structured MMORPGs like *Shadowbane*, these neomedieval citations embed players into the world's narrative and guide players' social interactions.

These are fictive worlds, built for entertainment, in which contemporary games represent the historical religious practices of the medieval past. In this chapter, I offer a reading of religion as a narrative technique in neomedieval gaming worlds that argues that these citations of medieval religion have many of the same effects as their historical medieval analogues. By considering the relationship between religion, play, and media in contemporary gaming worlds through comparisons to devotional media of the fifteenth century, I offer a model for conceptualizing the virtual realities and complex identities of contemporary gaming. I propose that game designers continue to incorporate elements of medieval religion into their products because neomedieval religious elements can narrate a game world's story without direct involvement from game masters or lengthy scripted dialogues from non-player characters. These citations addressed a real design problem that was introduced when the fantasy role-playing game migrated to immersive multiserver multiplayer platforms by teaching new players how to behave and play within a game world without requiring them to read a manual explaining the game's backstory while simultaneously transitioning experienced gamers who were intimately familiar with other virtual worlds into a new environment.

My analysis focuses on the development of second-generation MMORPGs in the early twenty-first century, a period during which game developers began differentiating the genre from other forms of fantasy role-playing games with novel server architectures, in-game communication technologies, and unscripted narration. Drawing from the late Dutch scholar Johan Huizinga's work on gaming and late medieval culture, I argue that borrowed imagery from historical medieval religions, which have become familiar tropes of fantasy MMORPGs, act as world-building infrastructure. By "world-building infrastructure," I mean to describe the mediated technologies that enable users to perceive stepping into virtual realms. For instance, when encountering a walking skeleton or a horned, fork-tailed imp, both modeled on late medieval images of death and the devil, even the least experienced gamer will recognize a hostile opponent. Similarly, architectural elements borrowed from Gothic cathedrals – stained-glass windows, vaulted ceilings, naves dedicated to a virtual world's deities, chanting, and flickering candles – connote "religious" space.

The overlap between play and religious devotion in the medieval past and neomedieval gaming universes is often overlooked as a fantasy trope. As I show, these citations of medieval religion are neither accidental nor inconsequential. In the specific context of combat-oriented fantasy MMORPGs, neomedieval religion serves the dual purpose of guiding players as they participate in a world's narrative and making plausible the exaggerated violence and gender performativity typical of MMORPGs. These references do more than make a virtual world feel "real." They act as axes or icons connecting the "reality" of the game world to the gamer's real life, helping to form communities that continue to use those religious symbols even after a game world is deactivated. Because the religions created by game designers are modeled on historical artifacts and devotional practices, they can be studied in much the same way as their medieval prototypes. Thus even if gamers are only "playing" at religion – or ignoring it entirely – player actions in neomedieval games are framed by and are related to the medieval devotions that they mimic.

The medieval in-game religions effect a plausible and comprehensible sense of realism for players. In addition to establishing complex world histories (or lore), usually published on the game's home page during the development and advertisement phase preceding a release date, game architecture, items, player classes, and many attacks and spells subtly draw players into participating in a game as if their character were affiliated with the religious traditions of that fictive world. This holds true even for those players who elect not to role-play, or who overlay contemporary gaming language onto a game's neomedieval elements by, for instance, describing deity-referencing enhancement prayers as "buffs" or offensive spells citing the names of demons or gods as "nukes"; using voiceover-internet-protocol chat programs like Ventrilo or Teamspeak to coordinate combat while role-playing in-game; or generically identifying player classes as "tanks" or "healers" rather than using the neomedieval categories designated by game designers.[2] Whether or not players participate in the religious systems invented for MMORPGs, citations of medieval religion give meaning to activities that might otherwise seem to be tedious time sinks, by framing the repetitive killing of identical creatures to earn experience points, acquire wealth, and develop combat skills as part of a heroic quest or by transforming the enormous number of hours players invest to acquire rare items through raiding or crafting into an important part of that game world's history.

If finding "religion" in video games is a contestable and slippery concept because the religious actions performed in games are not always viewed as religion by their performers, identifying the "medieval" in video games is a simple matter: citations either accurately recreate the culture of Europe between the fifth and fifteenth centuries, or they do not. Though the basic categories of player-controlled healers and fighters and non-player shopkeepers and townsfolk parallel the tripartite feudal classes of *oratores* (those who pray), *bellatores* (those who fight), and *laboratores* (those who labor), the items they wear, the worlds they inhabit, and the products of their labor are not as tangible as the dateable objects and actual social categories of the historical past. Rather, these elements have been remade to reflect our own cultural memory of the medieval past as a time of exceptional piety and brutality. The medieval in gaming also, crucially, justifies the violence of gameplay. As Carolyn Dinshaw has shown, modern artists imagine the medieval to be "brutal private vengeance in a triumphal and unregulated bloodbath . . . [or] turning from an impure identity to some solidity guaranteed by God."[3] Dinshaw writes to challenge this brutal medievalism, advocating bringing an awareness of modernity to medieval scholarship, but she describes what game designers and players do when they cite the medieval – using ideas from the past to relate to present communities. This is as true when "medieval" is used to express barbarism or religious piety as it is when "medieval" becomes a comic farce. Neither the religion nor the feudalism of MMORPGs is an exact replica of their real-world counterparts; they are meant to be, at most, plausible elements of a work of entertainment, and are thus something entirely new.

Despite the enduring influence of Huizinga and Eco as theorists of gaming, and despite the fact that the Oxford medievalists C. S. Lewis and J. R. R. Tolkien, progenitors of the fantasy genre, already inform the scholarship of video games, scholars of contemporary gaming culture rarely consider the nuances of medieval history, which informed their writings.[4] Johan Huizinga's two seminal works of history, *Homo Ludens* and the *Herfsttij,* are rarely put into dialogue.[5] The Sanskritist Huizinga introduced the enduring language of playing cards and their table as one of the ways that gamers inscribe a "magic circle," differentiating between the real world and the alternative reality of the game. This magic circle continues to frame conversations about contemporary gaming culture, as revisionists update his model for new generations of games. But Huizinga also wrote extensively about gaming in the *Herfsttij,* his magisterial history of Burgundian court culture and fifteenth-century devotion.[6] Huizinga's social observations about the role of image and word in medieval society in the *Herfsttij* provide an important addendum to his theories of play and ritual in *Homo Ludens.*

   In *Homo Ludens,* Huizinga wrote that medieval cities were a space for glorious ideas about play (*luisterrijke spel-ideeën*). Drawing from *Homo Ludens,* scholars of gaming often posit that play, like religious ritual, creates alternative worlds into which the individual might step. Game theorist Vili Lehdonvirta suggests that the dichotomous relationships between the two realities of virtual and real worlds are perpetuated by the gamer's own use of the distinction between "in game" and "in real life," a verbal trick that obscures what this particular medium is actually doing.[7] Following Huizinga and Lehdonvirta, religion becomes one of the tricks that erases the perception of the medium. If religion and virtual reality offer, as Rachel Wagner suggests, many "of the same benefits, and by implication, some of the same risks," then spiritual and virtual worlds are close cousins, equally isolated from the material world's play and prayer.[8] For gaming scholars reading *Homo Ludens,* it may seem a straightforward conclusion that the game world is not an alternative reality, even if it continues to change and exist when the gamer logs out. Like the magic circle, the game world exists within and as a reflection of the real world, acting as a medium to bring individual players into a new community and a new way of understanding the real world by interacting with images and words. But Huizinga's work in the *Herfsttij* and subsequent discoveries about art, devotion, and media in the late fifteenth century suggest that the magic circle does not simply divide the real world from the game world. The apparatus and actions of gaming also create communities, regulate social hierarchies, and mediate perceptions of reality.

Huizinga's *Herfsttij* returned to the late medieval city at a time of excess, luxury, violence, and social dissolution, where gaming is secondary to art and devotion. He insisted that representations, both visual and verbal, composed the "infrastructure" of late medieval society. The *Herfsttij* was unusually interested in the images and forms of human life, depending on literary sources, panel paintings, religious texts, and accounts of the lives of nobles. Huizinga described a culture of devotion driven by images of blood and torture and held together by the relationship between image and word, themes mirrored in the art exhibitions, commemorative jousts, and other public medievalisms that first drew his interest to the fifteenth century. Huizinga noted the persistence with which the fifteenth-century nobility treated life, love, war, and chess as games of equal import. Though each "game" had rules and boundaries, they shared many of the same symbols and their play often spilled into "real" life.

Homo Ludens's magic circle cannot satisfactorily mark the boundary between game and reality in contemporary MMORPGs. Rather, like the games of the Burgundian court, the apparatus of the gaming device inscribes a circle that links different social and cultural activities that otherwise have no apparent relation. Modern gaming devices are platforms capable of simultaneous tasks, and the software of a game can only partially inscribe a magic circle. Huizinga explained his concept of the magic circle, a space set aside for the purpose of play, by using a series of images, including a table on which players deal cards. Once elaborate hand-painted objects available only to the wealthiest patrons, playing cards became cheap portable tools for personal amusement through print technology, and facsimiles of playing cards are now installed on most digital devices. Situating Huizinga's playing cards and their table from *Homo Ludens* in medieval and modern iterations shows how the medium of play changes the meaning of a game.

Devotional woodcuts and playing cards were two of the first and most often reproduced items during the earliest phase of the so-called printing revolution. Both could be produced with relatively little cost or skill: a design was outlined on a block of wood, the background cut away to leave a raised outline of the image, and then impressions were made by inking the block, placing a sheet of paper on top, and applying pressure with rubbing until the ink transferred from wood to paper. These easily produced images enabled the personal ownership of objects – cards and icons – once available only to the very wealthy, and made into something personal and private forms of devotion and play that had previously been available only in public spaces.[9] The proliferation of these items also created new communities of strangers, each of whom could own a distinct copy of an image, speak its prayers, or shuffle their own playing cards. Some printed devotional images invited play; for instance, prints of the rosary sometimes showed the beads as if in motion, allowing devotees to move the beads in their mind as they recited prayers. Impressions from woodcuts were often decorated by their owners with paint or embroidery, cut up, pasted into other books, exchanged as gifts, and mailed as letters. Print also supported the establishment of prayer confraternities, loose brotherhoods whose only requirement for membership was the utterance of set prayers, which were often distributed on woodcut broadsheets.[10] Owners of the same print were part of a virtual community even though they might never meet one another.

Medieval art historians have shown that devotional images acted as technologies of salvation, which invited the practitioner into an alternative space composed of words and images seen physically but experienced spiritually.[11] With the introduction of printmaking, multiple devotees could simultaneously enter the same virtual space. Kathryn Rudy has argued that the use of images and narratives of journeys to Rome and Jerusalem by the fifteenth and sixteenth century enabled enclosed nuns to create a "virtual" reality of the pilgrimage. With carefully designed prayers, guidebooks, and paintings, sisters could travel and earn indulgences without ever leaving their convent.[12] These medieval virtual realities closely resemble what Wagner terms the "virtually religious communities" of game worlds.[13] Because the virtual worlds of the fifteenth century are already well studied, the ways that late medieval people encountered novel media can guide our understanding of contemporary virtual religious communities.

In the late twentieth century, with the introduction of the personal computer and its portable kin, play and prayer were again remade for new media. To use an example related to Huizinga's concept of the magic circle, the software infrastructure for Windows 3.0 (ca. 1990) included a digital version of cards for playing solitaire. Printed decks of cards can be used for any number of games, played honestly or dishonestly, with a full deck or missing cards, as well as for magic tricks, psychic and memory testing, and prognostication. But digitized playing cards deal a single game with a single standardized number of cards in standardized suits, and they eliminate players' freedom to cheat or switch from one game to another. They can, however, be used in games against strangers, and the game can be played within one of many windows on a screen that might include work, pornography, or other gaming programs. Huizinga's magic circle could be initiated by shuffling playing cards on a gaming table, whether the cards were deluxe hand-painted status symbols or mass-produced pocket toys, but the parameters of play and community changed when cards migrated to software. Similarly, when fantasy role-play migrated from tabletop to internet, players exchanged control of their intellectual property for access to a graphically mediated community. After agreeing to rules governing social interactions in end-user license agreements, consigning the rolls of their dice to computer algorithms, and submitting to the game publisher's terms, players create a community, co-writing narratives through play. Violating the terms of use leads to banned accounts, even though an individual has already purchased a copy of the game and access to its server. Whether characters bring their personal real-world faith into a game or not, by accepting a game's rules, they have entered that virtual world's religious system.

Like playing cards' migration from manuscript to print to computer screen, medieval religious technologies take on new meanings through time and translation. For instance, the medieval Cathedral of Chartres was initially designed to educate and to enhance contemplative devotion, and the twenty-first-century Chartres marks both virtual and physical spaces as medieval and sacred.[14] From the complex visual narratives in the stained glass to the exterior stone sculptures, every aspect of the building was designed to link the present to the biblical past, and draw the individual closer to heaven, yet cathedrals were also vibrant public gathering places, sites of feasts, brawls, and theatrical performances. The modern building remains a place of worship but has become a tourist attraction. Architectural elements of Chartres were incorporated into *Assassin's Creed* (Ubisoft, 2007), enhancing the in-game challenge of climbing with explicitly sacred medieval architecture.

Images painted on a late medieval altarpiece made comprehensible the mysteries of the mass and could transport skilled viewers to the experience of another place and time interiorly while their physical bodies engaged in subtle gestures to enhance that experience. In much the same way, citations of medieval religion in computer games, combined with keystrokes, conversation, music, and narrative elements, transport players into an alterity that they experience privately and communally when their eyes look at the images on the screen. In *Godwired*, Rachel Wagner elaborately demonstrates a strong resemblance between gaming and religion and briefly discusses the idea that late medieval devotion might be a form of premodern "hybrid identity akin in some ways to today's virtual experimentation."[15] Citing a blog post by Ruth Evans, a specialist in fifteenth-century English literature, Wagner writes that a medieval devotee's interactions with Christ through portable images might be analogous to the contemporary experience of engaging with the nonphysical through modern communication devices. Following Evans, Wagner has linked the modern gamer to a medieval devotee possessing a diptych, an expensive, two-panel, hinged devotional image, which opened and closed like a book. Holding the diptych, a devotee would step into the scene with the aid of prayers and the realism of the painted image until she drew near to the real Christ beyond the painted image. Wagner concludes that game worlds are "always perceived as play... [while] for medieval Christians, there was only one other world, ... [and] Jesus was both the figure with which they identified, and the unachievable desire that drove their love of him."[16] But medieval readers used a range of devotional tools, which allowed their souls to visit virtual pleasure gardens, hellscapes, and foreign lands; Jesus was not the only figure with whom they identified. Some medieval manuscripts even explicitly link prayer and play by providing rules and illustrations to dice games meant to help a devotee meditate on the passion.[17] Neither Wagner nor Evans considers how the medieval devotional practice they consider analogous to modern gaming was also revolutionized by mass media technologies. This private experience was mass-produced through printmaking technologies, just as the availability of high-speed internet access and personal computers has changed gaming.

That new technology would be used simultaneously for religious devotion and personal entertainment both in the first decades of printing and in the first decades of personal computing may be either an accident of survival or a reflection of commercialism. It is also an invitation to consider the similarities between the technology-driven religious changes of the medieval period and the relationship between play, devotion, and technology in contemporary gaming. There is a difference between the transposition of old media into new, more communal formats, and the adaptation of a single fixed narrative to new media: Tolkien's *Lord of the Rings* creates the same world whether as an e-book, a paperback novel, an original manuscript, a video game, or a film. MMORPGs, which have neither a fixed narrative nor a pre-internet counterpart, have taken the radical but necessary step of incorporating narrative elements into the world environment itself, and neomedieval religion is an essential part of that project.

COMPREHENSIBLE VIOLENCE AND MEANINGFUL PLAY

Before developing mastery of the abbreviations and unique terms that make up gaming vocabulary and before discovering how to step forward, engage in combat, or equip items, a new player may still recognize priests, mages, and warriors on sight; be able to distinguish a dwarf from an elf; or understand why a bard's "magic" manifests through song. This has been of particular importance in MMORPGs, which offer original worlds rather than expanding on existing literary or gaming universes, but this also allows gaming franchises to attract larger audiences. For instance, in the market-dominating *World of Warcraft* (Blizzard, 2004), player races, cityscapes, non-player characters, and even player quests for both Horde and Alliance derive from medieval earth analogues. Thus players who have no familiarity with the three real-time strategy *Warcraft* games nonetheless recognize their own characters' relationships with other characters and the world environment. *Warcraft*'s races are

modeled on medieval folklore and romance, and it is set in a facsimile
of medieval England. Players participate in conflicts between the Alliance and the Horde, and between player races and the many supernatural and monstrous creatures of Azeroth. Similar character classes and
models also populate Korean MMORPGs, allowing non-Korean players
to step in and participate in a gaming world whose language they cannot understand – as I did playing the imperfectly translated *Lineage 2*
(NCSoft, 2003) and *SilkRoad Online* (Joymax, 2005) alongside Korean
nationals who spoke no English, just as Asian players can enjoy *World
of Warcraft*.

Neomedieval religion also cloaks the technological infrastructure
behind games when servers are named after deities (*Everquest* [Sony
Online Entertainment, 1999]) or heroes (*World of Warcraft*), or called
shards of a shattered world (*Shadowbane* [Ubisoft, 2003]), and when
customer service representatives appear as gods or other supernatural
beings. These citations are modern and localized, reflecting the aesthetic
tastes and cultural preferences of the game designers and their target
audiences. Korean and Japanese games are more likely to cite medieval
Buddhism or the Three Kingdoms period, with characters modeled after
anime, while European and American games cite medieval Christianity
and Germanic mythology, with characters modeled on comic books. Localized medievalisms sometimes create dissonance: American players
of the Korean-designed *Lineage 2* were disturbed that male dwarves were
burly, muscular, bearded fellows, while female dwarves were petite girls
in miniskirts. The "cute" female dwarves, however, were easily marketed
to Korean players.

Fantasy novelist R. A. Salvatore described the world building for
the single-player role-playing game *Kingdom of Amalur* (Electronic Arts,
2012) as "an exercise in philosophy and logic" that drew on and twisted
the history, myths, and religions of our real world into a creation-de-
struction myth whose history approximates our own. For Salvatore, the
point of world building is to view "our own human history through a . . .
prism [turned] just a bit to the side," to create a system that can stand
alongside our own in perfect symmetry.[18] Decisions made during world
building reveal that game designers think their products need narratives
to explain violence and give meaning to play. When players appear in

urban environments surrounded by animals like rats and wolves, even without scripted dialogues with non-player characters, most quickly intuit that their first task is to kill these animals, just as most recognize that cruciform symbols identify healing objects. Dragon slaying is celebrated across server populations in raid-oriented games by players who do not know a virtual dragon's history but have internalized the iconography of dragon-slaying knights. These narratives give purpose to the repetitive actions of gaming, and are often packaged as neomedieval religious histories.

NEOMEDIEVAL RELIGION AND PLAUSIBLE

REALISM IN *SHADOWBANE*

More elaborate uses of neomedieval religion for narrative occur in MMORPGs deemphasizing player-versus-environment challenges (narrated by non-player characters) in favor of player-versus-player conflict. *Shadowbane* used its religious lore to explain "free-for-all player v. player combat," the idea that each player is free to kill anyone else he or she encounters. Instead of simply explaining these rules in the manual or in an in-game tutorial, *Shadowbane* used a complex religious narrative introduced online and in IRC chat to make the game rules and technological limitations part of the game world's own history.[19] These intricate in-game design elements connected gamers directly to the world whose story their play was co-writing.

Two moments from *Shadowbane*'s lore crystallize how neomedieval religion was woven into every layer of the game's mechanics. The first explains kill-and-be-killed unending war (free-for-all player-versus-player combat); the second explains the game's cycle of death and rebirth. In a struggle to conquer the world and even the gods, an elf king by the name of Sillestor draws the mighty sword Shadowbane and slays Loromir, Archon of Peace, initiating unending violence (archons are "emanations" of the All-Father, thus a blend of Scandinavian and Gnostic origin stories). According to the lore, "all of the strife, pain, and war that has troubled our broken World was born in that instant, and . . . since Loromir's death true peace is impossible." This confrontation explicitly sets *Shadowbane* in a world of eternal war; peace is *literally* dead. The lore goes on to explain the historical origins of religiously motivated rivalries among the available player races, each linked to the death of Loromir.

Through both the detailed religious rivalries between different player groups and the death of Loromir, Archon of Peace, *Shadowbane*'s lore requires players to resolve disputes through violence rather than peaceful negotiation. Players are not just *allowed* to kill each other in any circumstance, for any reason; they have no alternative but to do so. From its earliest iteration as a web portal hosting a teaser trailer, *Shadowbane* promoted the lore authored by Meridian, the game company's official "sage." Because Meridian's history was available several years before the game's release, it also served as advertisement. The lore wove medieval Christian and Nordic religious systems into its virtual landscape. For instance, permanent death was no longer possible after the sword Shadowbane shattered the world into shards (game servers) and disrupted the cycle of death. Instead, players immediately "respawned" at two possible locations, Soul Stones and Trees of Life. Some players took the game up without studying the lore, and others formed guilds that wrote their own centuries of historical involvement into the backstory. Guilds that strictly adhered to the lore were at a disadvantage in combat due to imbalances between races and classes. Some guilds thus formed alliances of necessity with those who should, by the logic of the lore, be their bitterest enemies.

Though game imbalances meant that ARAC (all-race, all-class) guilds dominated the server maps, with each action players continued to participate in the game's neomedieval religions. Cities could only be built with the assistance of a druid who had acquired the necessary runes to plant the seed of a Tree of Life. Acts of war – placing of a "bane stone" on a Tree of Life, and the subsequent destruction of that tree – and basic combat also depended on lore. For instance, the control of siege weaponry required a player to possess the commander rune, an item acquired by defeating an elven blademaster. Consequently, *Shadowbane*'s players participated in that world's religion just by playing the game, no matter how they perceived their own play. Without this elaborate infrastructure, *Shadowbane*'s software could have partitioned the computer for play, but could not have created a realistic world.

CONCLUSION

In this chapter I have shown that MMORPGs use neomedieval religious symbols as a world-building infrastructure that enables users to step easily into virtual realms. As other scholars of religion and gaming have recognized, there is a two-sidedness to the interpenetration of game world and real world that characterizes the immersive experience of gaming in general and the practice of role-playing religion in particular. The interplay between player, virtual world, and game community, which is now being read as religious by some gaming scholars, is also essentially neomedieval. As an individual loads and begins to play a game, the actions of the body in the real world are nearly irrelevant to experiences in the game world, while the events and encounters within the game often extend back into the real world. The axes of this in many MMORPGs are replicas of medieval religion. Medieval images and neomedieval replicas both link the devotee-player to material and virtual worlds. The relationship between religion, play, and media enabled by the development of immersive three-dimensional gaming worlds closely resembles the virtual devotional techniques introduced in fifteenth-century Europe. In contemporary games, immersive details of architecture, attire, and world culture reproduce the two-sidedness of hyperrealistic perspectival art and the mass media technologies of printing and woodcut production.

Through the medieval devotional technologies they emulate, neomedieval MMORPGs elicit an experience that is entirely personal yet simultaneously places each gamer within a virtual community. Medieval people used hyperrealistic images to trigger virtual realities and formed communities of strangers, but also used gaming as a means of communication and an infrastructure for society. The virtual worlds created by historical medieval religions also offer a useful way to reconcile the seeming dichotomies between "prayer" and "play," "real" and "virtual," "self" and "avatar," which continue to vex scholars of religion and gaming. Religions designed for video games can be studied like the medieval devotional technologies they mimic. Both medieval and contemporary gaming and devotion became communal and virtual following the introduction of multidimensional multimedia narratives powered by three-dimensional images. The fifteenth-century examples suggest that modern gaming worlds may also affect interior experiences and create virtual communities through visual narratives that allow players to enter into and participate in the represented narratives they pay to consume.

Technological advances introduced the social elements that distinguish massively multiplayer and online role-playing games from their single-player and tabletop cousins, just as print technologies altered interactions with devotional images and playing cards. Both medieval devotional media and neomedieval role-playing games create a sense of realism and an interior experience of entering a virtual world, an experience altered, replicated, and magnified by the adaptation of these forms of narrative to new media (print and internet, respectively). In both the print and computer ages, migrating to new media platforms created new communities united through experiences related to a virtual world. For contemporary MMORPGs, this community construction has had real financial implications: players often start new games with groups of friends, or resubscribe to an older game for social purposes even after exhausting the game's content. In both the old and the new media revolutions, playing and praying are twin profit makers, which are transformed by the imposition of new rules and restrictions introduced by a shift in media.

For MMORPGs, neomedieval religion cues players to interact with one another and game elements in ways appropriate to the world narrative they are collectively building. Whether embedded in MMORPGs by world builders or imported by players, neomedieval religion mediates between the gamer, the gaming apparatus, and the experience of gaming. The narrative use of neomedieval religion originated in two-dimensional single-player RPGs, such as *The Bard's Tale* (Electronic Arts, 1985), and has remained integral to both plot and landscape in three-dimensional RPGs, such as *Heretic* (Raven Software, 1994), *Diablo* (Blizzard, 1996), and *Assassin's Creed* (Ubisoft, 2007). In MMORPGs such as *Shadowbane*, which expect players to interact with other players and to alter the landscape of the gaming world, neomedievalism also guides the social behavior of virtual communities. By blending historical religions into contemporary virtual combat simulators, MMORPGs harness a medieval religious culture that permeates modern society. The effect of these culturally familiar religious citations cannot be replaced by higher-quality graphic realism or elaborate scripts. From a marketing perspective, the realism introduced by neomedieval religion creates an addiction to an alternative reality. These intentional citations draw links between the real world and the game world to make that alterity relevant and intelligible and to help link the community of the game to the community of the gamer. Neomedievalism also makes players into participants in fictive religious systems designed not for worship but for narration.

The fragmentary evidence from medieval and contemporary virtual gaming worlds is productively complementary. Rather than simply asking "what is religion in gaming worlds?" or "what is being reconstructed out of medieval history in these faux medieval worlds?," I hope others will join me in considering the coincidental similarities between body and avatar and body and soul, between ascending the spiritual ladder and grinding the gaming treadmill, between achieving salvation and leveling up, between meditating on a hand-painted woodcut while spinning and playing an MMORPG while making dinner. Like fifteenth-century games, contemporary gaming connects disparate social and cultural activities and creates communities of strangers united only by shared narratives. Just as print created new communities linked through virtual worlds and just as computers disrupted the functions of playing cards, MMORPGs are devising new modes of storytelling and communal play, including using neomedieval artifacts to guide players through virtual realities. We should continue studying these two analogous worlds for what each can reveal about the other.

NOTES

1. Eco, *Travels in Hyperreality*, 61–72; Shippey and Arnold, *Appropriating the Middle Ages*.

2. Alex Golub's examination of the makeup, social hierarchies, and communication practices of a *World of Warcraft* raiding guild demonstrates how these practical gaming shorthands override a game world's idioms. Golub, "Being in the World (of Warcraft)."

3. Dinshaw, *Getting Medieval*, 206.

4. Aarseth, *Cybertext*, 6; Chance, *Tolkien and the Invention of Myth*; Shippey, *Road to Middle-Earth*; Wagner, *Godwired*, 5–8. Wagner also cites the discussion of Huizinga in Suits, *Grasshopper*.

5. The title of the *Herfsttij* in English translations has been the subject of considerable controversy. Initially translated as "Waning," then as "Twilight," the

book is now known more literally as "Autumn of the Middle Ages." I have given my own translations from the Dutch original and used the Dutch title rather than any of the English versions to avoid these possible confusions. All citations are from the 1949 Dutch edition, which is more comprehensive than any of the English translations: Johan Huizinga, *Verzamelde Werken* (Haarlem: Tjeenk Willink, 1948–1953), 3:3–345, http://www.dbnl.org/tekst/huiz003herf01_01. For Huizinga's influence on medieval studies in the late twentieth century, see Courtenay, "Huizinga's Heirs"; Tollebeek, "At the Crossroads of Nationalism."

6. As Peters and Simons note, the *Herfsttij* may give the earliest scholarly citation of William James's *Varieties of Religious Experience* and also engaged with Tylor's *Primitive Culture*. Huizinga was also an early supporter of Malinowski. Peters and Simons, "The New Huizinga and the Old Middle Ages," 611.

7. Lehdonvirta, "Virtual Worlds Don't Exist."

8. Wagner, *Godwired*, 4.

9. On the relationship between printing cards and printing devotional images, see Parshall and Schoch, *Origins of European Printmaking*, 23–24.

10. Marcus and van der Lee, *Der Spiegel Hochloblicher Bruderschaft*.

11. John R. Decker, *The Technology of Salvation and the Art of Geertgen tot Sint Jans* (Farnham, England: Ashgate, 2009).

12. Rudy, *Virtual Pilgrimages in the Convent*.

13. Wagner, *Godwired*, 126.

14. An accessible introduction to the construction of sacred space and the secular uses of medieval cathedrals can be found in Richard Kieckhefer, "The Impact of Architecture," in *Medieval Christianity: A People's History*, ed. Daniel Bornstein (Minneapolis, Minn.: Fortress, 2010), 109–146.

15. Wagner, *Godwired*, 123.

16. Ibid., 123–124.

17. Two copies of the "Spiritual Dice Game [Geistliche Würfelspiel]" survive in manuscript form, another in print. Wolfgang Stammler, Karl Langosch, Kurt Ruh, and Gundolf Keil, *Die deutsche Literatur des Mittelalters: Verfasserlexikon* (Berlin: de Gruyter, 1978), 11:510–511.

18. R. A. Salvatore, "R. A. Salvatore on Building the World of Amalur," *3 News: New Zealand*, http://www.3news.co.nz/R-A-Salvatore-on-building-the-world-of-Amalur/tabid/418/articleID/240341/Default.aspx (accessed January 24, 2012).

19. All references to *Shadowbane* lore come from the now-defunct official website, *Shadowbane: Chronicle of Strife*, http://chronicle.ubi.com (accessed October 6, 2007).

REFERENCES

Aarseth, Espen J. *Cybertext: Perspectives on Ergodic Literature.* Baltimore, Md.: Johns Hopkins University Press, 1997.

Chance, Jane. *Tolkien and the Invention of Myth: A Reader.* Lexington: University Press of Kentucky, 2004.

Courtenay, William J. "Huizinga's Heirs:
Interpreting the Late Middle Ages."
In *Herbst Des Mittelalters?: Fragen zur
Bewertung des 14. und 15. Jahrhunderts*.
Edited by Jan A. Aertsen and Martin
Pickavé, 25–36. Berlin: de Gruyter,
2004.

Dinshaw, Carolyn. *Getting Medieval:
Sexualities and Communities, Pre- and
Postmodern*. Durham N.C.: Duke University Press, 1999.

Eco, Umberto. *Travels in Hyperreality:
Essays*. Translated and edited by William Weaver. San Diego, Calif.: Harcourt, 2002.

Golub, Alex. "Being in the World
(of Warcraft): Raiding, Realism, and
Knowledge Production in a Massively
Multiplayer Online Game." *Anthropological Quarterly* 83, no. 1 (2010):17–45.

Huizinga, Johan. *Homo Ludens: Proeve
Eener Bepaling Van Het Spel-Element
der Cultuur*. Edited by L. Brummel
et al. Haarlem: Tjeenk Willink and
Zoon, 1950. http://www.dbnl.org
/tekst/huiz003homo001_01 (accessed
March 30, 2012).

Lehdonvirta, Vili. "Virtual Worlds Don't
Exist: Questioning the Dichotomous
Approach in MMO Studies." *Game
Studies: The International Journal
of Computer Game Research* 10, no. 1
(2010). http://gamestudies.org/1001
/articles/lehdonvirta (accessed
March 30, 2012).

Von Weida, Marcus. *Der Spiegel Hochloblicher Bruderschaft des Rosenkrantz
Marie*. 1515. Facsimile edited by
Anthony van der Lee. Amsterdam:
Rodopi, 1978.

Parshall, Peter, and Schoch, Rainer.
*Origins of European Printmaking:
Fifteenth-Century Woodcuts and Their
Public*. New Haven, Conn.: Yale University Press, 2005.

Peters, Edward, and Walter, Simons.
"The New Huizinga and the Old Middle Ages." *Speculum: A Journal of Medieval Studies* 74, no. 3 (1999):587–620.

Rudy, Kathryn M. *Virtual Pilgrimages in
the Convent: Imagining Jerusalem in the
Late Middle Ages*. Turnhout, Belgium:
Brepols, 2011.

Shippey, T. A. *The Road to Middle-Earth*.
London: Allen and Unwin, 1982.

Shippey, T. A., and Arnold, Martin. *Appropriating the Middle Ages: Scholarship, Politics, Fraud*. Rochester, N.Y.:
Brewer, 2001.

Suits, Bernard. *The Grasshopper: Games,
Life and Utopia*. Toronto: University
of Toronto Press, 1978.

Tollebeek, Jo. "At the Crossroads of Nationalism: Huizinga, Pirenne, and the
Low Countries in Europe." *European
Review of History/Revue Européenne
d'Histoire* 17, no. 2 (2010):187–215.

Wagner, Rachel. *Godwired: Religion,
Ritual and Virtual Reality*. London:
Routledge, 2012.

SEVEN

Hardcore Christian Gamers

HOW RELIGION SHAPES EVANGELICAL PLAY

Shanny Luft

ON THE WEBSITE *HARDCORE CHRISTIAN GAMER* (HCG), EVAN-
gelicals share their faith as they deliberate over their favorite video
games.[1] Their religiosity is overt. Members engage in online Bible study,
post prayer requests, and share spiritual testimonies with one another.
For example, in a discussion forum designated for sharing spiritual tes-
timony, someone wrote of contemplating suicide before finding spiritual
and community support in a church. Someone else shared witnessing
a church member's broken leg healed through prayer, and yet another
described his spiritual struggle upon learning his brother was gay. Alongside these sincere and personal testimonies of faith, members of HCG
converse about their favorite video games, including action games like
Assassin's Creed (Ubisoft, 2007–), role-playing games like *Elder Scrolls*
(Bethesda Softworks, 1994), and first-person military shooters like *Halo*
(Bungie, 2001–2010; 343 Industries, 2011–) and *Call of Duty* (Activision,
2003–). What many, although not all, of the games discussed on these
forums have in common is their overt depictions of violence. In *Assassin's Creed II*, for example, the player controls an assassin slaughtering
his way through sixteenth-century Italy, dispatching enemies by thrust-
ing swords into their backs, plunging knives through heads, burying
axes in skulls, slitting throats, and jamming spears into the spines of his
adversaries.

Since these may not be the games that immediately come to mind
when imagining a Christian gamer, it is necessary to appreciate that
for the community of HCG, "hardcore" modifies both "Christian" and
"gamer." In the first sense, they are "hardcore Christians" who are vocal

about their experience of God working in their lives every day, who seek opportunities to share their faith with others, and who study the Bible as God's revealed word. In the second sense, they are "hardcore gamers," a term used in the video game industry to describe a prominent share of the market. Hardcore gamers are typically (though not exclusively) young men in their twenties and thirties who invest the most time and money gaming on consoles and personal computers, often organize into competitive communities, and generally embrace violent action games. HCG caters to a community that is hardcore in both senses, a community seeking to share its members' enthusiasm for gaming in an environment of like-minded Christians. As HCG's mission statement explains, "We have taken a passion that we have for gaming and intertwined it with the passion we have for God."[2]

In this chapter I consider how these evangelicals intertwine religion and gaming, and I elucidate some of the ways in which evangelicalism impacts their experience playing and interpreting video games. In the next section, "Christians as Gamers," I compare Christian gamers to the broader gaming community, identifying several ways in which these evangelical gamers emulate the broader gaming community. The following section, "Gamers as Christians," considers the traits that make these evangelicals a distinct community of gamers. I argue that religion is a determining factor in how evangelicals experience the video game medium, in at least three ways: first, with regard to their self-identification; second, with regard to the choices and behaviors they exhibit during the course of gameplay; and third, with regard to how they interpret the contents of their games. I do not assert that these three criteria constitute the only ways in which religion shapes evangelical gaming; nevertheless, expounding on each offers insight into how religion shapes evangelical play.

TERMS AND METHODS

Before going further, I should clarify my use of three terms central to this chapter: evangelical, Christian gamer, and religion. "Evangelicalism" describes a movement within Protestantism defined in part by a set of beliefs that include the doctrinal authority of the Bible, the pros-

pect of salvation, eternal life through Jesus Christ, and the importance
of spreading one's faith to others.[3] Back in the 1970s, as the home video
game market first emerged, evangelicals often identified as "born-again
Christians." Today, though, they more commonly identify as "Christians"; therefore, this chapter uses the terms "evangelical" and "Christian" interchangeably. Second, I offer the term "Christian gamer" to
identify the subculture of gamers who are the focus of this chapter.
What makes Christian gamers distinct as gamers is that they mediate
their video gameplay through the lens of religion. To put it another way,
to be a Christian gamer is to continually adjust one's gaming practices
so that they are in accord with one's religion. The body of this chapter
explicates that process of adjustment. The final key term, "religion," has
been defined in countless ways. One definition that resonates with this
project was provided by historian of religion Jonathan Z. Smith, who
wrote that "religion is the quest, within the bounds of the human, historical condition, for the power to manipulate and negotiate one's 'situation' so as to have 'space' in which to meaningfully dwell."[4] The value
of this definition, in the present context, is the emphasis on ceaseless
effort ("questing") and on the negotiation that is necessary to construct
a "meaningful space." Smith's characterization of religion aligns with
my depiction of Christian gamers as engaged in a process of making
gameplay into a religiously meaningful experience.

In order to shed light on the Christian gaming community, my research drew from six Christian gaming websites and an online survey.
I located the Christian gaming websites by conducting web searches
with variations on the terms "Christian" and "video games," ultimately
focusing on four websites, *Hardcore Christian Gamer, GameChurch, The
Cross and the Controller,* and *Christian Gamers Online,* all of which provided active community forums, up-to-date editorial content, industry
news, blogs, podcasts, and game reviews.[5] My engagement with these
sites connected me to two others that influenced my analysis. *Christ
and Pop Culture* began as a podcast in 2007 and developed into an online
magazine with commentary that evaluates films, television, music, video
games, and literature from an evangelical world view.[6] And *Follow and
Engage* is a blog by Jordan Ekeroth that reflects on issues of Christianity

and video games.[7] All of these websites provided valuable material on evangelical gaming culture.

My research involved the critical reading of these websites, where I became a public member and engaged in conversation about my project in online discussion forums. These conversations led me to develop an online questionnaire, which I advertised in the gaming discussion forums on the websites.[8] The survey invited participants to describe their religious identity and how they apply their faith in their lives, to list their favorite games and games that they avoid, to explain how religion has influenced their gaming, and to identify differences between Christian and non-Christian gamers, if they perceived such a difference. In total, seventy-four participants completed the survey.

Given these methods, my investigation cannot be taken as an exhaustive depiction of all Christian gamers. Nevertheless, the data gleaned offer insight into how some Christian gamers seek to harmonize their gaming with their religion.

CHRISTIANS AS GAMERS

There has been a great deal of scholarship since the 1990s on evangelical media and popular culture, most of which has scrutinized the variety of music, fiction, T-shirts, jewelry, movies, theme parks, mouse pads, and every other imaginable consumer product and experience that has been explicitly rebaptized for evangelical consumers.[9] Clearly, modern American evangelicals have had a strong appetite for products produced by and marketed to their community. However, the weight of scholarship on Christian consumer culture has reinforced the perception that evangelicals exist in a consumer society outside of the mainstream. For example, Colleen McDannell in *Material Christianity* describes Christian retail as an "attempt to create a parallel religious culture to that of secular America."[10] This framing presents evangelical culture as independent and distinct from secular culture, a perspective that obscures the significant overlaps and interactions between evangelical and secular cultures. My research on Christian gamers, however, asserts that Christian gaming is not wholly distinct from secular gaming; rather, there are significant areas of overlap between evangelical and mainstream gamers. Thinking about Christians as gamers invites consideration of ways that evangelical video game enthusiasts reflect the practices and tastes of the broader gaming community.

Consider the following data from a 2010 market study of avid mainstream PC and console gamers, which found that men were more likely than women (21 percent compared to 5 percent) to play games in the genre of first-person shooters (FPS), a genre of military-style games where the primary objective is to kill opponents on a battlefield.[11] The same study found that men were more likely than women (39 percent to 24 percent) to play video games more than ten hours per week, and 22 percent of male gamers self-identified as "hardcore" gamers, whereas only 9 percent of female gamers identified with that term. Age was also correlated with the types of games that appeal to mainstream gamers, so that gamers between eighteen and thirty-four years old were more likely to have played shooters and role-playing games within the past six months.

These findings about mainstream gamers provide useful points of comparison with the seventy-four Christian gamers who completed my survey. For example, sixty-nine of my survey participants were male and five were female. While the mainstream gaming market also tends to skew toward males, my survey of Christian gamers was even more unbalanced in favor of men. Perhaps my results reflect an oversampling of Christian men because the websites on which I advertised skewed heavily toward men. On the other hand, it is possible that Christian gaming is severely split along gender lines. Future scholarship on evangelical gamers might delve more specifically into the issue of gender.

Other results of my survey of Christian gamers tracked more closely with the 2010 market research on mainstream gaming. For example, the average age of my survey participant was twenty-seven, and the average number of hours he or she devoted to gaming per week was fourteen and a half, findings comparable to those of mainstream gamers. Another area of overlap between mainstream gamers and evangelical gamers is in consumer habits. With few exceptions, evangelical and mainstream gamers play many of the same video games. For example, the most popular game series among the Christian gamers I surveyed was *Call of Duty,* identified as a favorite by twenty-nine gamers. Second was the *Battlefield* series with twenty-six votes. Third was the *Elder Scrolls* series with twenty-two votes. Fourth was the *Halo* series with nineteen votes. And *Assassin's Creed* tied with *Final Fantasy* (Square Enix, 1987) with sixteen votes, the fifth most popular series among Christian gamers in my survey.[12] The video games evangelicals identified as favorites correlated closely with mainstream gaming tastes. According to video game industry sales data, *Call of Duty: Modern Warfare 2* (Activision, 2009) and *Call of Duty: Black Ops* (Activision, 2010) were the two top-selling console games of 2010. *Halo: Reach* (Microsoft Studios, 2010) was the third best-selling game of that year, and *Assassin's Creed: Brotherhood* (Ubisoft, 2010) was ninth.[13] In fact, nearly all of the games that evangelicals cited as favorites were among the best-selling titles in the console gaming market, reinforcing my argument that the consumer tastes of Christian gamers overlap in key areas with the mainstream gaming market.

One final point about the intersection between evangelical and mainstream console gamers: the video games mentioned above indicate that Christian gamers do not recoil from brutal depictions of violence in games. In most of their favorite games, the player's primary mission is to kill opponents, and the depictions of bloodshed can be unflinchingly graphic. For example, *Call of Duty: Modern Warfare 2* received worldwide scrutiny in 2009 for its depictions of graphic violence.[14] In the level of the game that received the most media attention, the player goes undercover with Russian terrorists and must participate with them in a terrorist attack against civilians in a Russian airport. Because the game is a first-person shooter, the player gets a first-person perspective of civilians weeping, scrambling to find cover, and attempting to drag bodies to safety even as they are gunned down in a ceaseless spray of bullets. With an unlimited arsenal of automatic weapons and grenades, the terrorists transform the airport into a horror show of shattered glass, shredded suitcases, and bloody corpses. To be clear, none of the other popular games identified in my research present scenes of graphic violence comparable to this scene in *Modern Warfare 2*, but all of the top five games identified by my survey participants (except for *Final Fantasy*) were rated M by the video game industry ratings board, a rating for games that "may contain intense violence, blood and gore, sexual content and/or strong language."[15]

Obviously, not all Christian gamers play violent video games like *Modern Warfare*, and my research indicated that even among Christian gamers who enjoy military shooters, some refused to play *Modern Warfare 2* specifically because of the airport sequence. But others defended *Modern Warfare 2*, such as one evangelical writer on *Christ and Pop Culture* who maintained that the game was a commentary on violence, challenging players to reflect on the nature of terrorism.[16]

Thus far, I have noted some ways in which Christian gamers reflect some of the characteristics of mainstream gamers. Areas of intersection include a gender imbalance in favor of men, the average age of the gamer, the amount of time spent playing per week, and attraction to the same popular gaming titles. However, Christian gamers also exhibit traits that distinguish them as a distinct subculture. How this works, particularly in light of their penchant for highly violent games, is the topic of the remainder of the chapter.

GAMERS AS CHRISTIANS

Christian gamers are an identifiable subculture of gamers, I argue, because of their effort to bring their gaming interests into harmony with their religion. For example, in negotiating their gaming interests to suit their religious values, Christian gamers place a premium on sportsmanship within their community. Also, when Christian gamers play mainstream, violent games, they often make choices within those games that avoid content they feel compromises their religious values, particularly having to do with vulgar language and sexually suggestive content. At the same time, it is important to keep in mind that Christian gamers are not a uniform body. Their forum conversations and questionnaire responses reveal variations in religious beliefs, practices, and gaming habits. Below, I identify patterns of similarity and difference among Christian gamers in order to better understand the role religion plays in their gaming experience.

One of the distinguishing characteristics of Christian gamers is their perception that they are dissimilar from most gamers. When asked in the questionnaire whether they perceived a difference between Christian and other gamers, only sixteen out of seventy-four participants did not think so.[17] The examples they cited most often revolved around player behaviors in multiplayer games. (In multiplayer first-person shooters, such as the *Call of Duty* or *Halo* series, players form teams online and play mock military exercises, with a typical goal to kill enemy players before they kill you.) In describing how they differed from other gamers, evangelicals often cited their online conduct, and their responses also indicated that many of them give careful thought to their online persona, such as one survey participant who wrote:

> In . . . *Call of Duty, Battlefield* or other multiplayer games, you are interacting with real people. Now, this is the part that matters. How you interact with them. Yes, you are trying to kill them in the game, or work together to accomplish the quest, but in either case, how do you treat them? Do you curse them out when they kill you, or tell them how that was a good shot? Do you freak out if they mess up during a team fight, or do you help them out and try to uplift them. This has nothing to do with the objectives of the game but how you interact with the others playing it. This would fall under the "loving other people" that I mentioned before.[18]

This quotation is illustrative of the majority of Christian gamers surveyed who pointed to their conduct online as what distinguished them from non-Christian gamers. They repeatedly described Christian gamers as "more respectful," "kind," "nice," and "positive" in comparison to non-Christian gamers. Moreover, they felt that Christian gamers were less likely to use profane language, less critical of the mistakes of others, more welcoming to new players, and more encouraging of teammates. As one put it, "I feel Christians tend to be more prone towards civility in discourse and cooperation."[19] To be sure, not all of them agreed that Christian gamers lived up to the highest moral standards. Some described playing with non-Christians who exhibited more commendable conduct than their Christian colleagues did. Yet most Christian gamers felt that their tendency to be more supportive and considerate in online gaming distinguished them from non-Christian gamers.

Without further research, it is not possible to assert as fact that Christian gamers are genuinely more courteous than other gamers, but I suspect that these perceptions have some basis in truth. In my personal experience, it is common in playing online shooters to experience unpleasant, discourteous, and uncooperative behavior – even among players ostensibly on the same team. Anonymity in gaming, like anonymity generally on the internet, seems to facilitate incivility. Therefore, it is quite possible that Christian gamers evince more civility toward team-mates and opponents in online gaming. But whether there is a measur-able difference is immaterial at this point. What makes this issue signifi-cant is that the Christian gamers themselves perceive their community's online conduct to be different. This perception of difference, I argue, is a significant factor driving Christian gamers to seek out online forums where they can meet and interact with like-minded gamers. Christian gaming websites have been instrumental in establishing communities of evangelical video game enthusiasts. Their feeling that Christian gam-ers place a premium on supportive and pleasant behavior drives them to develop online communities where they can play with one another and perhaps avoid playing with outsiders altogether. What's more, these stan-dards of conduct become self-perpetuating as Christian gaming web-sites reinforce expectations of mutual cooperation and civility.

Online Christian gaming forums also exert influence on the behav-iors of Christian gamers. One survey participant reported: "I regret to say I used to be like most gamers, and would sometimes insult or curse at other players who were acting in a way I did not appreciate."[20] He then explained that after discovering and playing with fellow evangelicals at *Christian Gamers Online*, "I now try to steer conversations away from insults and into friendly chats." This comment suggests how standards of conduct are reinforced. Evangelicals are drawn to gaming forums to seek out gamers with shared religious identities, and by spending time together in forums and gaming, Christian gamers begin to adopt the behaviors valued by this community.

While many evangelicals identified their online conduct as a key dis-tinguishing trait of their community, my research identified other dis-tinct qualities of Christian gamers as well, such as using their religious values to guide their gaming behaviors in role-playing games. RPGs take their inspiration from the *Dungeons and Dragons* pen-and-paper games popularized in the 1970s. Like those pen-and-paper counterparts, video RPGs allow players to construct avatars to interact in a rich and complex world. Some contemporary RPGs, like *World of Warcraft* (Blizzard Enter-tainment, 2004–), are designed to be played online, in an environment where gamers interact with other players in real time. Other RPGs, like *Dragon Age* (Electronic Arts, 2009–) and the *Fable* series (Microsoft Studios, 2004–), are single-player games where players engage with characters controlled by the game's software.

Christian gamers often put a great deal of thought into how to play RPGs in ways that conform to their religious values. One example arose in a discussion on *Hardcore Christian Gamer*, when a community member solicited advice about whether to purchase the RPG *Fable 2*. As he explained, "I was thinking about getting it but wanted to know what was in it that I should know about as a Christian. Is most of the bad stuff avoidable?" His phrasing is revealing. This gamer did not inquire whether offensive material dictated that he reject *Fable 2* altogether. Rather, he wanted to know if it would be possible to avoid content he deemed offensive *while playing the game*. His decision to play the RPG hinged on whether the game allowed the player a degree of control over narrative elements that he considered anathema to his religion. Several community members responded to his initial query, reporting that they had played *Fable 2* in such a way as to avoid content they found problematic and, in fact, that the game allowed the player to make morally exemplary choices. As one explained: "It is really up to you how bad [*Fable 2*] is. You are free to marry multiple people (of the same or opposite sex), have casual sex, or follow Christian morals (marry one person of the opposite sex, and only have sex with that person). As long as you ignore the 'bad' parts, it isn't bad at all [in my opinion]."[21]

My survey further confirmed that many Christian gamers direct their avatars in ways that comport with their religious values. For example, when my survey asked whether they had made "Christian choices" when playing video games (without defining what constituted a Christian choice), many indicated that they had. One explained: "There was a point where I had the choice of killing or freeing a blood mage who had done some bad stuff. I chose to forgive him and let him go."[22] Another survey participant explained: "The player is often given the choice of taking violent action (often unprovoked) against an opponent or trying to talk out the disagreement. I almost always chose the latter option. I also chose options to forgive companions who had wronged me or had done something terrible and to speak kindly, not forcefully, to others."[23] Though this was not true of all Christian gamers, the majority of participants in the survey cited examples where they felt that their religion drove their decisions about how they directed their avatar within games.

Many of their anecdotes of applying religion to video game choices arose in discussions of RPGS, a game genre that often encourages players to make moral choices in the game and then explore the consequences of those choices. Yet even in other gaming genres, I found that Christian gamers negotiated gameplay strategies in order to satisfy their religious values. For example, some Christian gamers mentioned that they edited gaming software in order to adjust their experience, a practice known as "modding." One survey participant modified a game in order to remove the profanity.[24] For gamers without the expertise to edit software code, some games provide options to disable content that gamers might find offensive. For example, in *Gears of War 3* (Epic Games, 2011), the player has the option to disable profanity within the game, as well as reduce the level of gore depicted in the fight sequences. Although only a few video games currently provide such options in games, evangelicals in online forums were quick to identify such games and expressed a desire to see more games provide options to disable undesired features.

Even when games do not allow the player to modify the content, some Christian gamers found other ways to avoid content they found offensive. For example, some who played *Modern Warfare 2* skipped the portion of the game that depicted the airport sequence described above. And one survey participant found a novel approach to minimize his view of violence in the game. He had his avatar turn his back on the scene in order to avoid viewing the sequence when the terrorists open fire on a large crowd of civilians. When it was necessary to face forward in order to progress through the level, he "let the AI shoot all the people." In other words, he did not fire his gun, but merely walked through the airport as a passive observer while computer-controlled terrorists slaughtered computer-controlled civilians.[25]

My research revealed numerous techniques evangelicals employed in order to bring mainstream video games in line with the standards of their community, including modifying game content, making choices within games that correspond with their real-world values, and directing their avatar away from undesirable content. But I also found some Christian gamers who insisted that religion had no impact on their gaming at all. A minority of survey participants indicated that they viewed video games as an escape from reality and they rejected suggestions that their religion has any relevance to their gaming interests. However, even among such evangelicals, I occasionally found that when they provided more detailed descriptions of their gameplay, they exposed, perhaps unconsciously, ways in which they too sought to harmonize their gaming practices and their religion. For example, one gamer plainly dismissed the survey question asking whether he had made "Christian choices" when playing video games: "No! Haha. Like I said, video games are to escape reality. Would I rather be a chaste do gooder or would I rather rob a bank and escape a gunfight? . . . I play games to have fun." For him, the notion that his gaming choices needed to be brought into accord with his religion was literally laughable. And yet, later in the survey, the same Christian who mocked "chaste do gooders" reported that in playing one game with sexual content, he "obviously . . . didn't go to the strip clubs or get with some hooker."[26] His passing comment substantiates my argument that Christian gamers are distinguishable by their effort to apply religious values to their gaming practices. Although this survey participant overtly rejected the notion that his religion influenced his gaming practices, further articulation of his gaming choices indicated that he had made intentional decisions in his gameplay that reflected his religious values.

IMPLICATIONS AND CONCLUSION

By combining a critical reading of select evangelical gaming websites with data generated from an online questionnaire, I aimed in this chapter to distinguish the qualities that characterize a subculture of Christian gamers. First, I identified some ways in which Christian gamers are similar to mainstream hardcore gamers, and second, I identified how Christian gamers distinguish themselves through efforts to make their gaming practices adhere to the communal and ethical standards of their religion. So distinctive are their methods to harmonize their gaming to their religion that I assert the utility of defining a "Christian gamer" as "an evangelical who mediates his or her experience playing video games through the lens of religion."

The study of Christian gamers offers three points of consideration for future gaming studies. The first two address tendencies within video game studies, while the third is aimed at the field of religious studies. First, gaming studies, growing out of media studies, has inherited a propensity to analyze gaming as a solitary pursuit, disconnected from social and cultural influences. The study of religious gamers encourages the field to be mindful of the social and communal aspect of gaming. Christian gaming websites proliferated as evangelicals went online to seek out a like-minded community that shared their values. These websites have both reflected and reinforced particular standards of conduct valued by the community. Anthropological scholarship has modeled approaches that situate video games within their social context. In her book *Ethnographies of the Videogame,* anthropologist Helen Thornham reminds scholars: "Games are not played or experienced in a vacuum, but are contingent upon other relations and other gaming experiences, which frame and produce the practice and meaning of gaming."[27] Studying religious gamers can provide useful insights into gaming as a social practice.

Second, much of media studies continues to, as Stewart Hoover writes, "assume too much about the power and prerogatives of the media and too little about what people do with those media texts and other resources when they encounter them."[28] The study of religious gamers offers insight into how game players employ agency, since Christian gamers do not passively absorb the media before them. Rather, they reinterpret, undermine, filter, and make choices about their experience, employing a range of qualifications and judgments.

Third, this chapter suggests possibilities for approaching games within the frame of religious practice. While religious studies scholars have employed religious categories for studying Graceland, sports, and movies, among other things, there has been little consideration of the relationship between religion, play, and games. Perhaps the self-proclaimed seriousness of religion seems antithetical to the mirthful spirit of play. Yet sixty years ago, Huizinga's *Homo Ludens* noted how the ritual processes required for play reflected undeniable categories of religion. Play, Huizinga argued, requires rituals, performance, symbolic objects, constraints on time and space, and "temporary worlds within the ordinary world, dedicated to the performance of an act apart."[29] *Homo Ludens* considered the boundaries between religion and play to be fluid, and offered a starting point for contemplating their intersections. I would suggest that Christian gaming might be framed within the context of religious practice or lived religion with the intention of encouraging further research to consider the intersection between religion and play.

NOTES

1. www.christian-gaming.com (accessed August 2012).

2. "About," *Hardcore Christian Gamer*, www.christian-gaming.com/about (accessed August 2012).

3. For extended analyses of evangelicalism, see Marsden, *Evangelicalism and Modern America*; and Smith, *American Evangelicalism*.

4. Smith, *Map Is Not Territory*, 290–291.

5. *GameChurch* is accessible at www.gamechurch.com (accessed August 2012), *The Cross and the Controller* can be found at www.thecrossandthecontroller.com (accessed August 2012), and *Christian Gamers Online* is available at www.christiangamers.net (accessed August 2012).

6. www.christandpopculture.com (accessed August 2012).

7. *Follow and Engage* is available at www.followandengage.com (accessed August 2012).

8. I would like to thank Jordan Ekeroth for providing helpful comments and feedback in the early stages of my research. Thanks also to Mikee Bridges for promoting my questionnaire on www.gamechurch.com, and to Brendan Sinclair, senior news editor at GameSpot, for providing video game sales figures. Last, I am most grateful to the Christian gamers whom I met in the forums and to those who took the time to complete my questionnaire.

9. See, for example, Kintz and Lesage, *Media, Culture, and the Religious Right*; Hendershot, *Shaking the World for Jesus*; Schultze and Woods, *Understanding Evangelical Media*.

10. McDannell, *Material Christianity*, 268.

11. Statistics on gender, age, and game genre are based on data from "Console and PC Games."

12. The numbers exceed the total survey participants because I allowed participants to list as many favorite games as they liked, and I derived my scores by counting how many times a game was listed as a favorite.

13. For the 2010 top-selling games, see "Game Software Sales Flat in 2010, Overall Retail Sales Down 6%–NPD," www.gamespot.com/news/game-software-sales-flat-in-2010-overall-retail-sales-down-6-npd-6286347?tag=result%3Btitle%3B4 (accessed August 2012).

14. See, for example, Schiesel, "Choices in Infiltrating a Terrorist Cell"; Horiuchi, "Oh My Tech"; Milland, "'Kill Civilians' Video Game under Attack."

15. "Game Ratings and Descriptor Guide."

16. Richard Clark, "Modern Warfare 2: The Wrong Side of the Gun?," October 29, 2009, www.christandpopculture.com /featured/modern-warfare-2-the-wrong -side-of-the-gun (accessed August 11, 2012).

17. Thirty-six answered "yes," and ten more felt that the differences between Christian and mainstream gamers were slight. The remaining ten indicated that they did not know or they left the question blank.

18. Christian gamer no. 11, online survey, December 6, 2011.

19. Christian gamer no. 43, online survey, December 9, 2011. In their online forum conversations and survey responses, many participants wrote in some version of internet shorthand. In order to maintain clarity and consistency, I took the liberty of punctuating their quotations while being careful to retain the intended meaning.

20. Christian gamer no. 17, online survey, December 6, 2011.

21. I transcribed this conversation from a discussion forum on *Hardcore Christian Gamer*. HCG overhauled its website in mid-2012 and nearly all of the old forum conversations were taken offline.

22. Christian gamer no. 13, online survey, December 6, 2011.

23. Christian gamer no. 74, online survey, January 4, 2012.

24. Christian gamer no. 22, online survey, December 7, 2011.

25. Christian gamer no. 25, online survey, December 7, 2011.

26. Christian gamer no. 27, online survey, December 7, 2011.

27. Thornham, *Ethnographies of the Videogame*, 8.

28. Hoover, *Religion in the Media Age*, 86.

29. Huizinga, *Homo Ludens*, 10.

REREFERENCES

Bainbridge, William Sims, and Bainbridge, Wilma Alice. "Electronic Game Research Methodologies: Studying Religious Implications." *Review of Religious Research* 49, no. 1 (2007):35–53.

"Console and PC Games – U.S." Mintel Reports database. 2010. http:// academic.mintel.com.ezproxy.library .wisc.edu/display/482965 (accessed December 2011).

"Game Ratings and Descriptor Guide." www.esrb.org/ratings/ratings_guide .jsp.

Hendershot, Heather. *Shaking the World for Jesus: Media and Conservative Evan-gelical Culture.* Chicago, Ill.: University of Chicago Press, 2004.

Hoover, Stewart. *Religion in the Media Age.* London: Routledge, 2006.

Horiuchi, Vince. "Oh My Tech: 'Call of Duty' Has Troubling Scene." *Salt Lake Tribune*, November 16, 2009. www.sltrib.com/technology/ci _13799461 (accessed December 2012).

Huizinga, J. *Homo Ludens: A Study of the Play-Element in Culture.* Boston: Beacon, 1955.

Kintz, Linda, and Lesage, Julia, eds. *Media, Culture, and the Religious Right.* Minneapolis: University of Minnesota Press, 1998.

Marsden, George M. *Evangelicalism and Modern America*. Grand Rapids, Mich.: Eerdmans, 1984.

McDannell, Colleen. *Material Christianity: Religion and Popular Culture in America*. New Haven, Conn.: Yale University Press, 1995.

Milland, Gabriel. "'Kill Civilians' Video Game under Attack." *Express*, November 11, 2009. www.express.co.uk /posts/view/139551/-Kill-civilians -video-game-under-attack (accessed December 2012).

Schiesel, Seth. "Choices in Infiltrating a Terrorist Cell." *New York Times*, November 11, 2009. www.nytimes.com /2009/11/12/arts/television/12call .html?ref=activisioninc&_r=0 (accessed January 25, 2013).

Schultze, Quentin J., and Robert H. Woods Jr. *Understanding Evangelical Media: The Changing Face of Christian Communication*. Downers Grove, Ill.: InterVarsity, 2008.

Smith, Christian. *American Evangelicalism: Embattled and Thriving*. Chicago, Ill.: University of Chicago Press, 1998.

Smith, Jonathan Z. *Map Is Not Territory: Studies in the History of Religions*. Chicago, Ill.: University of Chicago Press, 1978.

Thornham, Helen. *Ethnographies of the Videogame: Gender, Narrative and Praxis*. Burlington, Vt.: Ashgate, 2011.

EIGHT

Filtering Cultural Feedback

RELIGION, CENSORSHIP, AND LOCALIZATION IN
ACTRAISER AND OTHER MAINSTREAM VIDEO GAMES

Peter Likarish

USERS DON'T ALWAYS PLAY THE SAME GAME. TWO GAMERS
rush home with copies of a recent entry in their favorite fighting game
series, *Dragon Ball Z: Budokai Tenkaichi* (Atari, 2007). One lives in Japan,
the other in the United States. Both tear open the packaging, choose
their favorite character, and start fighting others from the television series. In numerous bouts with Vegita, Goku, and other popular characters,
the game experience is nearly identical aside from the language displayed
on the screen. Then, a strange thing happens. Both recognize their next
opponent from the *Dragon Ball Z* television series, but the U.S. player
faces off against Hercule, while the Japanese player fights Mr. Satan. Or
the two may be adventuring in the classic role-playing game *Earthbound*
(Nintendo, 1995). Their characters have been gravely wounded and both
head toward a big white building with numerous windows. The Japanese
player sees the nearly universal Red Cross symbol next to the Japanese
kanji for hospital. The American's character approaches the same building in the same location. The word "Hospital" is still emblazoned on the
building, but the cross is gone. In each case, the two purchased the same
game. The vast majority of the content is the same. What accounts for
the differences?

One might assume such differences are only accidents of translation.
In each case, however, a subset of the game's content has been carefully
curated as the game transitioned from Japan to the United States, although nearly everything else remains identical (albeit translated). In
this chapter I examine why religious content, even symbolism that is
only tangentially religious (e.g., the symbol of the Red Cross), is suscep-

tible to alteration. What makes religious terminology and iconography
so sensitive that game producers opt to make these potentially costly
changes? To answer this question I explore the historical role of localization in the game development process and its use to censor objectionable content. By "localization," I mean the process of adjusting the
content and language of a video game for release in a country that did
not produce the game. Using *Actraiser* (Enix, 1991) and *Actraiser 2* (Enix,
1993) as a case study, I argue that localization prevents cultural feedback.
"Cultural feedback" refers to the conceit that, in a global marketplace,
content from one culture is frequently appropriated and reinterpreted
by game developers in a second country, only to be reintroduced into
the original culture in a recognizable but discordant form. I conclude
with a discussion of why religious symbols and iconography differ from
other kinds of censored content (e.g., violent or sexual content). For
instance, many religions encourage their followers to value particular
beliefs. If many followers come to understand such beliefs as dogma,
their incontrovertible nature renders them ill suited to the interactive
narrative of video games in which a player's actions may undermine or
circumvent religious proscriptions.

A GLOBAL PHENOMENON MADE LOCAL

Turning a profit on multiyear projects with seven- to eight-figure bud-
gets requires major studios to release games not only in their country
of origin, but also in countries perceived as receptive markets for the
game's story and aesthetic. This has turned game development into a
global phenomenon. The process of translating a video game for release
in a new market is called "localization."[1] The goal of a localization team
is to make a game as accessible as possible to the target market. This
means that most of the game's content, from art to music to story, is
eligible for revision or excision. The end product is a new version of the
original game that is perceived as better suited to the audience in the
target market.

   The most obvious change that emerges from localization is the translation of the game's text or voice from the original language to the language of the target market. But viewing localization solely as a problem

of translation is reductive: many less obvious changes occur to a game as well. Some of these changes are largely cosmetic and designed to suit local predilections (adjusting the mapping from buttons to character actions is one frequent change). Others go further, potentially altering the experience of playing the game. For example, movement speed in the U.S. version of *The Dirge of Cerberus* (Square Enix, 2006) was faster than that of the Japanese version (reportedly 1.2 times the original rate).[2]

Esselink provides a more general definition of localization as the process of "taking a product and making it linguistically and culturally appropriate to the target locale (country/region and language) where it will be used and sold."[3] This more expansive definition of localization encompasses the cultural (including religious) content in a video game. For the purpose of this chapter, I adopt the definition of "culture" espoused by Friedl and Pfeiffer: it is "a way of life common to a group of people, a collection of beliefs and attitudes, shared understandings and patterns of behavior that allow those people to live together in relative harmony, but set them apart from other people."[4] Video games are cultural artifacts. Even though games are often set in fictional or alternative universes, like any human endeavor games cannot escape their essential nature as a vessel for the ideas and values of the cultures that produce them. Of course, one's religion is a part of one's culture as well. Melford Spiro has suggested that a "religion" is "an institution consisting of culturally patterned interactions with culturally postulated superbeings."[5] Spiro's central conceit – that religion is "culturally patterned" – highlights the interplay of religion and culture and provides a useful starting point for discussing video games as cultural artifacts.

LOCALIZATION AS A CULTURAL FEEDBACK FILTER

As the examples in this chapter will reveal, changes to religious content during localization are often just the superficial renaming of characters and locales and the occasional removal of recognizable religious symbols. If the changes are only cosmetic, however, what purpose does this process serve, and why has it continued for over twenty years? I argue that as the gatekeeper process dictating what content survives the borderland transition between nations, localization serves as a "cultural filter." This filter is designed to prevent cultural feedback, a process in which information from previous events influences current or future outcomes. Most everyone is probably familiar with audio feedback, a high-pitched squealing emitted by a speaker when a nearby microphone picks up on the speaker's signal and retransmits it, forming an audio loop. Borrowing cultural artifacts from abroad and altering them for inclusion in a video game can make a game's story or setting seem believably exotic in the country that produces it. However, when the game is exported, the appropriated cultural material may violate cultural taboos or mores in the target markets. With the term "cultural feedback," I refer to this cycle: the appropriation of religious content, its incorporation into a product, and its eventual reintroduction into the culture of origin. One of the goals of localization is to remove content that seems exotic and exciting in the game's country of origin but negatively impacts the game's appeal abroad.

Here's a concrete example of possible cultural feedback. It's difficult to imagine someone playing *JESUS: Dreadful Bio-Monster* (King Records, 1989) in the United States, especially in 1989 (the year it was released in Japan). The Judeo-Christian concept of the divine, Jesus, is used in an out-of-context manner. But in Japan, a small minority practices Christianity and its iconography is hardly as omnipresent there as it would be in a country in which Christianity is the dominant religion. To a non-Christian in Japan in the 1980s, the word "Jesus" probably felt foreign and strange, yet it was likely to be familiar. Despite the title, the game has few, if any, religious overtones, and Jesus is superfluous to the plot. This is exactly the type of cultural feedback the localization process removes.

Analyzing the localization of religious content as a filtering process is significant because, despite the fact that adjustments made during localization frequently touch on cultural content, little attention has been paid to the potential impact that changes made during localization have on games as cultural artifacts. From the perspective of the game developer, appealing to the broadest possible customer base means excising potentially inflammatory religious content during localization because differences of religion invite controversy and conflict. Of course, religious content isn't the only portion of a game that is vulnerable to censorship during localization. Debates over violent and sexual content receive far more attention from the media and from governmental agencies, in one instance reaching all the way to the U.S. Supreme Court in a 7–2 decision in 2011 that struck down a California law banning the sale of violent video games to children.[6]

For better or worse, a side effect of the scant attention paid to the religious content in video games is a dearth of guidelines outlining the "appropriate" types of religious content in games. The lack of oversight leaves the people in charge of the localization process to serve as de facto (although often amateurish) censors of religious content. This was particularly evident in the United States during the late 1980s and early 1990s when Nintendo of America's content guidelines more or less dictated what content was included in a game and what was removed. If a developer did not obtain the Nintendo Seal of Approval, it would need to circumvent the Nintendo Entertainment Systems' lockout chip in order to run the game on the NES. Unauthorized games, such as *Baby Boomer* (Color Dreams, 1989), were not stocked by major retailers.[7] Aside from religious content, other prohibited content included "sexually suggestive or explicit content . . . random, gratuitous, and/or excessive violence . . . domestic violence or abuse . . . profanity . . . the use of illegal drugs . . . [and] subliminal political messages or overt political statements."[8] These restrictions led game localization expert Ted Woolsey, who was responsible for the effort to localize *Final Fantasy III* (Square, 1994),[9] to lament, "there's a certain level of playfulness . . . that doesn't exist here [in the United States], basically because of Nintendo of America's rules and guidelines."[10]

In general, the censorship of religious references and symbols has a subtle impact on a game; only rarely does it dramatically alter the way one experiences the medium. But the lack of guiding principles, or even a definition of objectionable religious content, has resulted in a series of seemingly arbitrary and capricious decisions as to what passes muster and what is excluded. Red crosses are removed from hospitals. In fact, most crosses are off-limits. In *The Legend of Zelda* (Nintendo, 1986), the Bible is renamed the Book of Magic for international releases. In the United States, references that touch on mainstream religions (e.g., Christianity) are altered while references to deities with a small number of worshipers, or to defunct religions, are left intact. All of these changes have implications for the video game as a transcultural experience: if we're all playing versions of a game tailored to our own aesthetic, are we missing a chance to see our own culture from a different perspective?

LOCALIZATION AND CULTURAL BORDER ZONES

In "Rights of Passage: On the Liminal Identity of Art in the Border Zone," Christopher Steiner contextualizes the transference of an art product from one nation-state to another as a good passing through a "border zone" between the states.[11] As part of this passage, authorities wrestle with the meaning and value of the product after transference. In the case of video games, localization is the major step in this border zone negotiation. In "Imagined Commodities: Video Game Localization and Mythologies of Cultural Difference," Rebecca Carlson and Jonathan Corliss write that games "are translated, and they are adapted for national regulatory boards and regional software requirements. Images, animations, and overall design aesthetics, game mechanics and interface, narrative, and even button mapping might be modified to accommodate the perceived differences between regional markets."[12] But, as they further note, localization involves a negotiation regarding a game's "cultural odor" as well. That is, how "foreign" does the game feel? Sometimes, developers intentionally cultivate a sense of foreignness, but in many cases the localizer's goal seems to be to "deterritorialize" a game entirely, to remove as much of the cultural odor as possible, so that the game can be "reterritorialized" for the new market.[13]

After all, the sensibilities guiding a game's story, design, and aesthetic are rooted in the attitudes, values, and practices of the game's country of origin. During localization, jokes need to be rewritten, references need to be culturally appropriate, and content must be adjusted to suit the mores of a country halfway around the world. The negotiation over the game's meaning between the old market and the new is rife with "gatekeepers" who are responsible for "shaping and channeling (and sometimes preventing entirely) the transnational circulation of these stories and images."[14] It is by shaping, channeling, and preventing the

transference of objectionable content that the gatekeepers of the localization process become censors.

The localization process is full of vaguely defined terms. The phrase
"objectionable content," for example, is an ill-defined notion dependent
on the destination market and the predilections of the game publisher.
In these flashpoint areas, sexually explicit and violent content are the
most frequent candidates for adjustment, since local ratings boards often
have conflicting definitions of the term "objectionable." For instance,
developers are well aware that securing a game's release in Germany
will require them to alter the color of the blood spraying from injured
enemies from red to a less realistic color because Germany's Federal
Examination Department for Media Harmful to Young Persons restricts
the sale of graphic media that glorify war or violence.[15] But how does
one determine what religious content is objectionable? Most games do
not include religions that have living adherents; instead, they're entirely
fabricated.

PRACTICED AND FABRICATED RELIGIONS

There's an important distinction between a religion *practiced* in the real
world, one with millions or billions of believers, and a *fabricated* religion
that exists in-game as part of a story. Video game genres frequently rely
on otherworldly settings, from technologically advanced spacefaring
civilizations to fantasy settings with swords and sorcery. In many cases,
directly transplanting a practiced religion into these fantastical settings
makes very little sense. Instead, characters in such games are more likely
to be adherents of a fabricated religion. Of course, there are instances in
which a game's setting is a simulacrum of our world and the developers
may appropriate and reference a practiced religion in-game.

Even though the religious content in a game may be fabricated – such
as the Yevonites of *Final Fantasy X* (Square Electronic Arts, 2001), the
Andrastrian Chantry of *Dragon Age* (Electronic Arts, 2009), or the Prismatology of *Sam and Max* (Telltale Games, 2006) – these fabricated
religions often have real-world analogues. The Yevonites are a group
of centrally organized (supposed) luddites led by a hierarchical order
of priests (Maesters) who are dedicated to fighting Sin (quite literally, in

this case) and redeeming humanity. The details of Yevonism are a mish-mash of several practiced religions, but an observant player of the game will tease out threads of Calvinism, Catholicism, and, of course, the beliefs of the Luddites. The Chantry has obvious parallels with mono-theistic, evangelical religions: the Chant must be spread to all corners of the earth before the Maker will return. Prismatology is a thinly veiled play on Scientology, and the founder of Prismatology is the author of the fictional tome *Emetics,* a joke version of *Dianetics.*

Fabricating an in-game religion allows the game to operate at a re-move of several steps from any singular practiced religion. Not only does this avoid alienating potential customers who also happen to be devoted followers, but it provides the added benefit of avoiding cognitive dis-sonance between our own experiences with the divine and the super-beings inhabiting our video games – particularly because superbeings worshiped in video games physically manifest with greater frequency than our own experience suggests superbeings tend to do. Fabricated superbeings interact with the game world directly and have a tendency to play the role of literal deus ex machina or to serve as the game's ultimate villain. In what could be termed a form of Orientalism (or Occidental-ism, depending on the game one is discussing), game companies often appropriate religious names and symbols that belong to a foreign culture and include them (or thinly veiled references to them) in their fabricated religions. Such references become prime targets for removal or substitu-tion during localization.

Is it fair to call such changes to a game's content "censorship"? One of the key distinctions between the processes driving religious censor-ship and those driving the censorship of violent or sexual content is that the removal of recognizable religious symbols and references is largely the result of self-censorship. While the Entertainment Software Rating Board (ESRB) and other ratings boards have established requirements concerning violent content, sexual content, drug and alcohol use, and various other types of questionable material, the removal of religious content still occurs at the behest of game companies themselves. Com-panies have gone to great lengths to avoid courting religious controversy while simultaneously pushing the boundaries of allowable violent or sexual content in a game. This emphasizes the differing drivers of religious censorship and of the censorship of other potentially objection-able content. Of course, censorship is in itself a loaded word. It brings to mind banned art and a government that refuses the free exchange of ideas or information. The United States prides itself on a proclaimed aversion to censorship, as do many other Western countries, but game companies are in a unique position to alter their own products at will with little to no awareness from the general public.

CENSORSHIP BY NON-STATE ACTORS

The term "censorship" is most often used to describe a state actor pro-hibiting the distribution of content that the actor believes is harmful to the state. This is a limited definition. More broadly, censorship refers to the act of restricting freedom of expression in order to prevent the release of content deemed objectionable by any controlling body. To see why this expanded definition of censorship is useful, let's consider a few instances in which a non-state entity has acted as a censor. For a non-state actor to be in a position to censor information, the entity must monopolize the flow of that information from source to destination. Consider the historical role of the Catholic Church. For many centu-ries the Catholic Church exercised an outsized role in the distribution of knowledge as one of the only international organizations in existence and through its ability to influence the Catholic countries of Europe. The church's *Index Librorum Prohibitorum* ("List of Prohibited Books") dictated which works could not be printed or read by Catholics. It was published from the sixteenth to the twentieth century and included scientific works and philosophical works as well as lascivious texts.[16] Wielding the threat of excommunication, Catholic officials exercised extreme power over thinkers who promulgated theories contrary to those endorsed by the church. The attempted censorship of Galileo Gal-ilee and the establishment of Copernicanism is an oft-cited example of the church's sway.

In more recent years, Google Inc. has faced similar accusations of censorship due to its outsized ability to act as a "reality filter." That is, if it's not on the front page of Google's search results, it doesn't exist. Google controls well over 50 percent of search traffic and that dominance allows it to wield great power as a censor. A single update to Google's result-ranking algorithm can cause a site's traffic to plummet in a single day. The company's ability to dictate what information is displayed at the top of its search results, and the lack of oversight into just how it makes those decisions, has made it the target of lawsuits from companies that have been harmed by changes to the search-ranking algorithm (e.g., kinderstart.com) and from sovereign nations. For example, the European Union is investigating the possibility that Google manipulates its search results to favor its own services over those of competitors.[17]

Individual game developers do not have the reach of the Catholic Church, nor can they match Google's sway, but as multinational institutions with entrenched monetary interests in the localization process, they are effective censors of information generated within the company because of the pairing of their roles as content creators and distributors. When they transmit content they have produced (such as video games) across national borders, they act as modern-day gatekeepers. Like any digital creation, at the most basic level a video game is just information encoded as an extremely long series of zeroes and ones. There is little public insight into how a company chooses to manipulate the information that it has produced, nor is it at all clear that such insight is desirable.

Our tendency to associate censorship with the state and the lack of public knowledge about the game localization process allows instances of self-censorship by individual corporations to pass unremarked. In the case of the video game industry, relatively few games are outright banned, although some countries, such as Australia and Germany, have a reputation for banning games more frequently than others do. Instead, games are typically submitted to a local ratings board, which assigns a rating based on a review of its potentially objectionable content. Sometimes, as with the ESRB, these boards are not beholden to the state but rather to the game industry itself.

Things did not always operate this way. Before the rise of the ratings board, Nintendo's U.S. branch, Nintendo of America (NOA), long served as the ultimate arbiter of content thanks to its position as the juggernaut of the industry.

NINTENDO OF AMERICA AND
A HISTORY OF CENSORSHIP

Although Nintendo still holds a prominent position in the video game market as one of three companies producing widely distributed video game consoles, the company's current stature scarcely compares with its importance to the industry in the late 1980s and early 1990s. Prior to the release of *Mortal Kombat* (Midway Games, 1993) in September 1993, NOA had almost carte blanche to alter the content of a game prior to its release in the United States. To obtain Nintendo's Seal of Approval, a game had to follow NOA's strict content guidelines, and since no NES developer could release a game without the seal, Nintendo effectively determined what content could be included. Unauthorized games would not even boot on the NES without circumvention of the 10NES lockout system, a hardware chip that synchronized with an authenticated cartridge prior to booting a game.

Nintendo's content guidelines were intended to maintain the company's reputation as family-friendly. Along with the expected guidelines limiting sexual content, coarse language, violence, and graphic depictions of death, there were a number of other stipulations. Most pertinent to this chapter was the prohibition against the release of games that "reflect ethnic, religious, nationalistic, or sexual stereotypes of language; this includes symbols that are related to any type of racial, religious, nationalistic, or ethnic group, such as crosses, pentagrams, God, Gods (Roman mythological gods are acceptable), Satan, hell, Buddha."[18] Several developers from this era have gone on record to denounce the almost Kafkaesque decisions to alter content during this time period, including Douglas Crockford, who was responsible for obtaining NOA's approval for the game *Maniac Mansion* (Lucasfilm Games, 1990). In a now-famous account of the experience posted on his personal website, he ponders – among other absurdities – how to remove nonexistent pubic hair from a statue.[19]

Many games produced in Japan during this time period included iconography appropriated from Western religions, particularly Christianity. When such a game was localized for the U.S. market, these icons and symbols were often removed prior to the game's release to conform to the Nintendo guidelines. The removal of crosses from churches and tombstones occurred frequently in games of this era; see *Duck Tales* (Capcom, 1989) and *Castlevania* (Konami, 1986), although not *Castlevania II: Simon's Quest* (Konami, 1987). Crosses were removed from staves and churches in the U.S. release of *Lufia* (Taito, 1993), except from churches that had been destroyed. They were not removed at all from gravestones in *The Legend of Zelda* (Nintendo, 1986), even though other portions of that game were censored. In general, a survey of such changes reveals that the policy was applied in an ad hoc and confusing manner that frequently ignored the in-game context in which a symbol was used. As mentioned earlier, crosses were removed even when they were not used in a religious context, such as the removal of the Red Cross symbol from a hospital in *Earthbound.*

Religious terminology and references often received the same treatment as religious symbols. *The Legend of Zelda*'s Book of Magic was called "the Bible" in the Japanese release. Places of worship were "temples," "sanctuaries," or "chapels" as opposed to "churches." Even words that referred to general religious concepts rather than to a specific religion were at risk. The "holy" spell in the *Final Fantasy* series was renamed "white" or "pearl," depending on the game. Devils became "imps." Hellhounds were reduced to the much less threatening "heck hounds" in *The Secret of Mana* (Square, 1993). This list is far from complete and, in some cases, it's possible to dismiss these changes as largely cosmetic, having little impact on an individual's gaming experience. The *Actraiser* series, on the other hand, provides an extreme example of the process. Choices made regarding character names neutered the religious connotations of the game even while visual references persisted. The *Actraiser* series borrowed liberally from Judeo-Christianity, albeit with the figure of God transformed into a sword-swinging bodybuilder floating around a palace on top of a cloud.

THE *ACTRAISER* SERIES

Attentive U.S.-based players could hardly fail to note the Judeo-Christian parallels present in *Actraiser* (Enix, 1991). The relationship between the protagonist and antagonist pair, the Master and Tanzra, echoes that of God and Satan. Players are placed in God's shoes, even if they never directly manipulate the Master. Gameplay in *Actraiser* consists of two different types. The first is a top-down simulation in which the player directs the Master's cherubic servant as he attempts to rebuild the civilization wrecked by Tanzra's monsters. Victory is achieved by blocking the monster lairs scattered around the map. The Master's angel-servant not only fights off the flying monsters but also directs the Master to produce miracles. Sandwiching these top-down simulations are two side-scrolling stages in which the player manipulates a sword-wielding statue imbued with life by the Master. With Tanzra's defeat at the end of *Actraiser*, belief in the power of the Master wanes because the successful civilization no longer needs him.

Actraiser 2 (Enix, 1993) takes the Judeo-Christian parallels to greater extremes. This time, the player directly controls the Master/God. During the introduction to the game, we see Tanzra/Satan's fall from paradise, which results in him being cast down into an underworld. Over time, he has recouped his power and his seven lieutenants have taken over various locations in the world. The city simulation portions of the game are gone, leaving the side-scrolling action of the original. The final boss of each stage is one of Tanzra's lieutenants. In the Japanese release of the game, each lieutenant was named for one of the deadly sins. For the English version, many of the names were changed, often to synonyms of the original that thinly disguised the source material: Sloth became Fatigue, Gluttony was unchanged, Wrath became Fury, Lust became Deception, Greed became Doom, Envy became Jealousy, and the final lieutenant remained Pride. Pride resided at the top of the Tower of Souls in the U.S. release, but the description of the level makes it clear it is analogous to the Tower of Babel (the original name in the Japanese release). After defeating the seven deadly sins, the Master crashes his sky palace through the surface of the earth and into hell. When the Master comes face-to-face with Tanzra, he is frozen waist-deep in ice, a visual that clearly references Dante's Satan in *The Divine Comedy*.

The changes imposed on the U.S. releases of *Actraiser* and *Actraiser 2* were typical of Nintendo's enforcement of its content policies. They were applied unevenly and superficially. When possible, the changes were made to in-game text rather than to visuals (which would have required more time-consuming changes). They were applied almost exclusively to Judeo-Christian iconography and references while references to deities from other religions remained unchanged (references to Hindu deities abound in Nintendo games of this era, such as in the *Final Fantasy* series). All of this suggests that between 1985 and 1993 Nintendo of America seemed to view the localization process more as a necessary evil than as an integral part of the game development process. Part of this was undoubtedly due to the immaturity of the industry in general. After all, this was the era that gave us the "all your base" internet meme thanks to a particularly poor translation of *Zero Wing* (Taito, 1989). Nonetheless, the tendency to dismiss the more subtle aspects of localization has persisted far longer than Nintendo's early content guidelines. Chandler's *Game Localization Handbook,* a guide to the localization process from the perspective of a game designer, frames the process almost solely as one of language translation, with less than a page dedicated to the pitfalls of cultural translation. Instead, her primary focus is on making it as simple as possible to make changes to a game during localization by "internationalizing" the game through the organization and design of a game's resources.

MORTAL KOMBAT AND THE RISE OF EXTERNAL RATING BOARDS

Nintendo's role as content gatekeeper ended rather abruptly after the release of *Mortal Kombat.* In 1993, that arcade hit was ported to both the Super Nintendo Entertainment System (SNES) and the Sega Genesis. Despite the fact that the SNES version was graphically superior, the Genesis version outsold the SNES version two to one. The discrepancy was chalked up to the alteration of the blood. In the arcade version, red drops flew from the opponent's character with every hit. In the SNES version, each hit produced a spray of grey, mist-like "sweat." The version of *Mortal Kombat* released for the Genesis was similarly altered but contained one of the more famous cheat codes of the era (ABACABB) to unlock the red blood.

When *Mortal Kombat 2* (Midway Games, 1994) was released the following year, Nintendo's version included red blood. In Sheff's *Game*

Over, a historical account of Nintendo's development into a gaming
powerhouse, Nintendo executive Howard Lincoln is quoted as saying,
"Instead of getting a lot of letters back from parents praising our position, we got a huge amount of criticism – not only by gamers, but even
by parents saying that we had set ourselves up to be censors."[20] The
loss of market share combined with the backlash against NOA's content
guidelines did not immediately stop Nintendo from censoring games,
particularly first-party titles produced by Nintendo, but it did result in
gradual revisions to the content guidelines. The gaming industry knew
that if someone did not censor inappropriate content and provide informative, industry-standardized ratings indicating each game's intended
audience, the government would step in and enact such requirements.

The establishment of the industry-controlled ESRB curtailed the
need for government intervention and brought video game censorship
into the current state of affairs. Although the ESRB is a U.S.-based organization, similar regulatory boards exist throughout the rest of the
world, including the Pan European Game Information rating system
and the Australian Classification Board. The ESRB was established in
1994 as a self-regulatory organization, a legally defined term indicating
that the board has the authority to regulate an industry but the authority
does not necessarily stem from the U.S. government. It was founded by
the Interactive Digital Software Association, which is now known as the
Entertainment Software Association. The Entertainment Software Association counts many of the top game publishers in the world among its
members, including Nintendo, Sega, Microsoft, and Sony. Technically,
submitting a game to the ESRB is voluntary, but unrated games cannot
be licensed on any of the major consoles and are shut out of the major
retail stores. Game submission occurs when a company self-reports instances of potentially objectionable content in its game to the ESRB via
a questionnaire. The ESRB then evaluates the game to ensure that the
content of the game matches the report on the questionnaire. At that
point, the game is assigned a rating, indicating the appropriate audience
age group: Early Childhood (EC), Everyone (E), Everyone 10+ (E10+),
Teen (T), Mature 17+ (M), Adults Only 18+ (AO).

The ESRB supplements game ratings with "content descriptors,"
which are short phrases that summarize the reasons for a game's rating

and provide some insight into the sort of controversial content included in the game. There are currently thirty content descriptors that cover a wide range of content types, such as Language, Blood and Gore, Cartoon Violence, and Sexual Content. Nine of the thirty descriptors describe various kinds of violent content. A further nine descriptors characterize the sexual content of the game. None of the descriptors relate to religious content, once again making it solely the responsibility of the game's producer.

WHAT MAKES RELIGIOUS CONTENT DIFFERENT?

The examples cited in this chapter reveal the (sometimes laughable) lengths to which companies have gone to prevent cultural feedback from religious content. The natural question to ask is whether there is something intrinsic to religious content that makes companies react so strangely. What makes religion different from sex or violence? Rachel Wagner in "The Play Is the Thing: Interactivity from Bible Fights to Passions of the Christ" seeks to answer a related question: Why have depictions of Jesus been largely anathema in mainstream gaming when they are relatively popular in cinema?[21] Wagner argues that part of the answer comes from "how harshly the notion of interactivity clashes with the notion of theological inevitability."[22] Playing as, or alongside, Jesus is unacceptable to people of faith because the interactive nature of a video game challenges the concept that everything is part of God's plan. She relates the idea that a human's actions (your actions) influence the outcome of events to the early Catholic Church's condemnation of the Gnostics and their unorthodox interpretations of the Bible. In contrast to a more or less unwavering "inevitability" of religious doctrine, the acceptability of violent or sexual content ebbs and flows over time as societal mores evolve; as games have become more realistic, so have depictions of violence or sexual situations.

Along with the issues that arise when calling into question religious dogma, Wagner also raises the prospect of player immersion. Playing Jesus via a video game avatar is problematic because "most Christians believe that Jesus is qualitatively different from us in meaningful ways and therefore beyond the possibility of intimate identification through

immersion."[23] Controlling Jesus forces the player into the uncomfortable position of adopting that role, even in a fictional context. This level
of "intimate identification" is uncomfortable at best and certainly blasphemous to many. Many individuals feel repulsed when offered the
choice to kill one of the Little Sisters (children with special powers)
in *Bioshock* (2K Games, 2007); it's even more disconcerting to imagine
making that choice when embodied as an avatar of Jesus.

While Wagner does an admirable job of explaining why games often avoid depicting deities and other important religious characters, her
argument does not account for how strangely overdetermined religion
in video games actually is. Part of this is certainly attributable to a cost-
benefit analysis of leaving objectionable content in versus removing it.
Cultural feedback is difficult to anticipate in advance. Game producers have tended to aggressively censor even remotely religious portions
of video games because leaving this content in is unlikely to increase
their sales. The opposite is true of violent or sexual content. Pushing the
boundaries in these areas has resulted in increased media coverage and
has even directly impacted the sales of a game, as NOA witnessed with
Mortal Kombat. While throttling back the violent or sexual content of a
game can negatively impact a game's popularity, the potential down-
side to producing cultural dissonance by not filtering religious content
strictly enough greatly outweighs the potential gains to be had by leaving
it in. In the twenty-first century, however, it appears that the calculated
avoidance of religious controversy may be coming to an end.

CONCLUSION: PUSHING THE BOUNDARIES
OF RELIGIOUS CONTENT

A rash of games released since 2010 have begun patently eschewing the
trend described in this chapter. Instead of shying away from the inclusion
of sensitive religious content, releases such as *Dante's Inferno* (Electronic
Arts, 2010), *El Shaddai: Ascension of the Metatron* (Ignition Entertainment, 2011), and *The Binding of Isaac* (McMillen and Himsl, 2011) intentionally co-opt Judeo-Christian figures and mythos into the games.
Dante's Inferno is of particular interest because of the manner in which it
skews the original canticle. Dante scholars and feminists have both de-

cried the sexualization of Beatrice (she is transformed into a succubus in the game) and claim that the game misses the entire point of Alighieri's tale: that it is Beatrice who saves Dante, not a scythe- or cross-wielding warrior who rescues *her*. So far, the game companies have seen little out-cry about these games, even when the release of *Diablo III* (Activion-Blizzard, 2012) coincided with Lightside Games' release of its Facebook social game, *Journey of Jesus: The Calling* (Lightside Games, 2012). In fact, Electronic Arts (the U.S.-based producer of *Dante's Inferno*) hired fake protestors from a made-up church to gin up some controversy surround-ing the release.[24] Of course, the use of non-canonical source material (*Dante's Inferno* is based on a work of fiction and *El Shaddai* on the apoc-ryphal book of Enoch) may also have helped them skirt controversy.

A startling transformation occurred in the seventeen years between the release of *Actraiser 2* and *Dante's Inferno*. Game companies transi-tioned from censoring the mere mention of religious figures and symbols to featuring them as a point of provocation. Violent and sexual content may have been pushed so far that they no longer possess the same shock value whereas religious content has been so avoided that it is seen now as a largely untapped source of material. At the same time the United States, at least, has become increasingly agnostic. According to the Pew Forum on Religion and Public Life, a quarter of U.S. citizens aged eigh-teen to twenty-nine are not currently affiliated with any particular re-ligion, and the number of Americans who claim no current affiliation doubled between the 1980s and 2007.[25] Needless to say, this transition paints a picture of a populace that may be less and less likely to outright reject a game with questionable religious content.

This may be especially true given the ease with which video games can adapt fluidly to various markets. The transference of video games across geographic boundaries differs dramatically from that of many other art products. When a painting is reproduced, or a film or book is translated into a new language, most people value faithfulness to the original. We perceive changes to an art product as "selling out" one's artistic vision. This hasn't been an issue with video games since most people only have the opportunity to play the version of the game released in their region and so have no little idea that their experience differs from that of a player halfway around the world.

The frequency with which games change as they cross cultural boundaries provides a unique opportunity for game studies practitioners. Comparing video games localized to different regions allows us to look at our own and other cultures across space and time in a way that media more sensitive to embellishments or alterations do not. Although in this chapter I have looked explicitly at religious content, further examinations of negative or altered spaces in localized video games will provide scholars with other opportunities to examine cultural transference. Of course, one hopes that a mature game industry is better suited than its historical peers to make intelligent decisions regarding the inclusion or exclusion of religious content, decisions that take context into account. Whether religious content in games remains safely sanitized or becomes a flashpoint of controversy is anyone's guess. Regardless, scholars should take the opportunity to examine cultural change through the lens of the games consumed and released and to analyze what is acceptable at a given point in time.

NOTES

1. Chandler, *Game Localization Handbook*, 4.

2. *"Dirge of Cerberus* Features," Square Enix, http://na.square-enix.com /dcff7 (accessed December 22, 2012).

3. Esselink, *Practical Guide to Localization*, 3.

4. Friedl and Pfeiffer, *Anthropology*, 284.

5. Spiro, "Religion," 96.

6. Liptak, "Justices Reject Ban on Violent Games for Children."

7. Woodyard, "Nintendo Keeps Color Dreams Up Worrying."

8. Schwartz and Schwartz, *Parent's Guide to Video Games*, 23.

9. The U.S. version of *Final Fantasy III* corresponds to *Final Fantasy VI* (Square, 1994) in Japan. Not all games in the series were released in the United States during this time period.

10. Quoted in West, "Fantasy Quest," 17.

11. Steiner, "Rights of Passage," 207.

12. Carlson and Corliss, "Imagined Commodities," 64.

13. Ibid., 72–73.

14. Ibid., 64.

15. Bundesprüfstelle für jugendgefährdende Medien, "Portrayals of Violence in Media."

16. Grendler, "Conditions of Enquiry," 45–47.

17. Kantor, "Europe Hints at Impatience in Settling Google Case."

18. Schwartz and Schwartz, *Parent's Guide to Video Games*, 23.

19. Crockford, "Now You're Really Playing with Power."

20. Sheff, *Game Over*, 460.

21. Wagner, "The Play Is the Thing," 47.

22. Ibid.

23. Ibid., 51.
24. Fritz, "E3: *Dante's Inferno* Protest [UPDATED]."

25. Pew Forum on Religion and Public Life, *U.S. Religious Landscape Survey*, 7.

REFERENCES

Bundesprüfstelle für jugendgefährdende Medien. "Portrayals of Violence in Media (Criteria)." http://www.bunde spruefstelle.de/bpjm/redaktion/PDF -Anlagen/portrayals-of-violence-in -media (accessed November 12, 2012).

Carlson, Rebecca, and Corliss, Jonathan. "Imagined Commodities: Video Game Localization and Mythologies of Cultural Difference." *Games and Culture 6* (2011): 61–82.

Chandler, Heather. *The Game Localization Handbook*. Newton Center, Mass.: Charles River Media, 2005.

Crockford, Douglas. "Now You're Really Playing with Power: The Expurgation of *Maniac Mansion* for the Nintendo Entertainment System." http://www .crockford.com/wrrrld/maniac.html (accessed November 12, 2012).

Esselink, Bert. *A Practical Guide to Localization*. Amsterdam: John Benjamins, 2000.

Friedl, John, and Pfeiffer, Jon E. *Anthropology: The Study of People*. New York: Harper's College Press, 1977.

Fritz, Ben. "E3: *Dante's Inferno* Protest [UPDATED]." *LA Times*, June 4, 2009. http://latimesblogs.latimes.com /technology/2009/06/e3-update-on -dantes-inferno-protest.html (accessed November 12, 2012).

Kantor, James. "Europe Hints at Impatience in Settling Google Case." *New York Times*, September 21, 2012. http://www.nytimes.com/2012/09/22 /technology/eu-antitrust-chief-warns

-over-google-talks.html (accessed November 12, 2012).

Grendler, Paul F. "The Conditions of Enquiry: Printing and Censorship." In *The Cambridge History of Renaissance Philosophy*, vol. 1. Edited by Charles B. Schmitt, Quentin Skinner, Eckhard Kessler, and Jill Kraye, 25–54. Cambridge: Cambridge University Press, 1988.

Liptak, Adam. "Justices Reject Ban on Violent Video Games for Children." *New York Times*, June 27, 2011. http:// www.nytimes.com/2011/06/28/us /28scotus.html (accessed December 31, 2012).

Pew Forum on Religion and Public Life. *U.S. Religious Landscape Survey: Religious Affiliations: Diverse and Dynamic*. Washington, D.C.: Pew Research Center, 2010.

Schwartz, Steven A., and Schwartz, Janet. *The Parent's Guide to Video Games*. Rocklin, Calif.: Prima Lifestyles, 1994.

Sheff, David. *Game Over: How Nintendo Zapped an American Industry, Captured Your Dollars and Enslaved Your Children*. New York: Game Press, 1999.

Spiro, Melford E. "Religion: Problems of Definition and Explanation." In *Anthropological Approaches to the Study of Religion*. Edited by M. Banton, 85–126. London: Tavistock, 1971.

Square Enix. "*Dirge of Cerberus* Features." http://na.square-enix.com /dcff7 (accessed December 22, 2012).

Steiner, Christopher B. "Rights of Passage: On the Liminal Identity of Art in the Border Zone." In *The Empire of Things: Regimes of Value and Material Culture.* Edited by Fred R. Myers, 207–231. Santa Fe, N.M.: SAR Press, 2001.

Wagner, Rachel. "The Play Is the Thing: Interactivity from Bible Fights to Passions of the Christ." In *Halos and Avatars: Playing Video Games with God.*

Edited by Craig Detweiler, 47–62. Louisville, Ky.: Westminster John Knox, 2010.

West, Neil. "Fantasy Quest." *Super Play* 23 (1994):14–17.

Woodyard, Chris. "Nintendo Keeps Color Dreams Up Worrying." *LA Times,* October 24, 1990. http:// articles.latimes.com/1990-10-24 /business/fi-2859_1_video-game -market (accessed December 31, 2012).

PART THREE

Gaming as Implicit Religion

LADY BRACKNELL: My nephew, you seem to be displaying signs of triviality.

JACK: On the contrary, Aunt Augusta, I've now realized for the first time in my life the vital Importance of Being Earnest.

OSCAR WILDE, *The Importance of Being Earnest*

NINE

The Importance
of Playing in Earnest

Rachel Wagner

THE ERROR PEOPLE TEND TO MAKE THE MOST IN THINKING
about games and religion is to assume that the primary opposition at
work is the idea that religion is "serious" whereas games are "fun." I propose that a more accurate distinction is between being earnest as opposed to being insincere in one's engagement with the ordered world
views that religions and games can evoke. The importance of constructing systems or worlds of order into which people may willingly enter is a
key feature of both religions and games. The greatest offense in both experiences is to break the rules, that is, to become an apostate, an infidel,
a cheater, or a trifler, to fail to uphold the principal expectations about
how to inhabit that particular experience's world view. To fail in being
earnest in following the rules is to cause a disruption of order, a breach
in the cosmos-crafting activity that both games and religion can provide.
Of course, not all experiences of religious practice and gameplay will fit
this definition, but many of them do. This, I propose, is a fundamental
similarity between religion and games, generally speaking: both are, at
root, order-making activities that offer a mode of escape from the vi-
cissitudes of contemporary life, and both demand, at least temporarily,
that practitioners give themselves over to a predetermined set of rules
that shape a world view and offer a system of order and structure that is
comforting for its very predictability. While it is true that games offer
such ordered worlds on a temporary basis and religion attempts to make
universal claims to such rule-based systems, the root impulse of entering
into ordered space reveals a deep kinship between religion and games
that is startling and evocative.

PLAYING BY THE RULES

In *Homo Ludens: A Study of the Play-Element in Culture,* Johan Huizinga admits that "we are accustomed to think of play and seriousness as an absolute antithesis," but he argues that such a separation "does not go to the heart of the matter."[1] Play infuses both religious ritual *and* games, according to Huizinga. Since play itself depends upon rules to happen, play is part of the very process that instantiates an ordered cosmos, a play arena, a system for being in the world. Accordingly, definitions of games are often closely related to definitions of play, since play can be seen as a clarification for how interaction with the rules of a game actually works. Eric Zimmerman, for example, in an essay in *First Person* defines play as "the free space of movement within a more rigid structure."[2] The "more rigid structure" in most cases is, put simply, the rules of the game, and play is how you interact with those rules. His observations can also apply to the "rules" of religious activity and the "play" with which a practitioner engages when enacting a ritual, such as vocalizing a liturgy or moving in regulated embodied ways.[3] Play happens, Zimmerman says, in the "interstitial spaces" that exist "between and among [the system's] components." Play works against and in response to the structures of the system, but it is also "an expression of a system, and intrinsically a part of it."[4] Such play with the system is characteristic of religious activity and of games, and in both cases it depends upon the "more rigid structure" of rules and often also upon any stories or texts that inform the shape of how the rules are to be enacted. As Alexander Galloway explains it in *Gaming: Essays on Algorithmic Culture,* "The imposition of constraints also creates expression."[5]

Such a rigid structure offers a reliable sense of order, even if the rules are agitated against, even if the point is seeing how you might bend or break them within the allowable parameters. There are always rules where there are games and, I suggest, also where there is religious activity. It's the rules that allow the construction of a ritual or game-defined other space; it's the rules that deposit the practitioner into this what-if world; and it's the rules that define the system of user or worshiper engagement, creating a world that we experience temporarily or, in the case of religion, perhaps for a lifetime. Rules tell believers how to live.

They articulate who can make authoritative decisions in the day-to-day world, and why. Rules dictate how sacred texts are read. Rules give us guidelines for behavior, often anchoring them in past sets of rules or the authority of previous rule makers. Rules tell us how to treat special objects and sometimes even tell us what to say. Rules are at the root of many of the most common features of games, and rules are a key basic feature of religious practice, especially ritual.[6]

Religious ritual and gameplay, Huizinga writes, are deeply connected. Indeed, "the Platonic identification of play and holiness does not defile the latter by calling it play, rather it exalts the concept of play to the highest regions of the spirit."[7] Religion and play have a long history of demarcating other worlds, other spaces in which rules adhere. Indeed, as Egenfeldt-Nielsen, Smith, and Tosca observe in *Understanding Video Games,* the desire to make and to play games may well be "a fundamental human tendency," as old as religious activity itself.[8]

RELIGIOUS GAMING: BETWEEN RULES,
STRUCTURE, AND BELIEF

It appears that many ancient games may have been used for religious purposes. In ancient Egypt, one can find "draught boards" drawn on certain tombs, with squares "decorated with benefic hieroglyphics." The player inscriptions around the game board "refer to decrees of judgment of the dead" as "the deceased gambles his fate in the hereafter and either wins or loses blissful eternity."[9] In Vedic India, there is evidence that worshipers performing sacrifices would sometimes balance on a ritual swing, the motion of which was believed to "link the heavens with the earth" such that "the cosmic swing sweeps the universe away in an eternal coming and going in which beings and worlds are carried along."[10] Mary Flanagan explains in *Critical Play* that the Chinese game *WeiQi* (called Go in Japan) is "believed to have developed from divination practices by emperors and astrologers in Zhou culture."[11] Go was also closely connected to staple ritual practices, was given as a gift at weddings, and was a "documented pastime of Zen monks, shoguns, and tea ceremony masters."[12] In all of these examples, the order-making principles of games and religion are evident in the intersection between rules, structure, and belief.

One of the most obvious places where religion and games converge
is in divination practices, which frequently incorporate game-like components. Games and divination practices do similar cultural work: both
present structures that propose an ordered cosmos in a temporary space,
creating a safe arena in which to play by known rules. Game theorist
Roger Caillois identifies the ancient religious divinatory practices of *alea*
games as the basis for one of his major divisions of contemporary types
of games. Derived from the Latin alea, meaning "dice," in these games
"winning is the result of fate rather than triumphing over an adversary"
and "destiny is the sole artisan of victory."[13] For Caillois, alea games are
shaped by the "capriciousness of chance." In their religiously motivated
form, of course, it is the gods who affect the role of the dice (or bones),
who cause cracks in a tortoise shell, or who arrange sticks after they are
thrown onto the ground. Alea games function as "a negation of the will,
a surrender to destiny."[14] Such a view assumes no greater order apart
from generalized fate. Yet even the secular play of games of chance is a
performance of a desire for order: "For nothing in life is clear, since everything is confused from the very beginning, luck and merit too. Play,
whether *agon* [competitive] or alea [chance], is thus an attempt to substi-
tute perfect situations for the normal confusion of contemporary life....
In one way or another, one escapes the real world and creates another."[15]
For religious folk, games of divination are just as much a resistance to
chaos as secular games of chance; they merely ground the performance
in a belief in a divine power that shapes all of life, experiencing a game
of chance as a game of revelation.

Clearly, games and religion have an intimate and long-lasting relationship, characterized deeply by a shared concern for crafting rules,
shaping worlds, and creating spaces in which predictable ordered systems shape our experiences. However, despite these similarities in purpose and function, most people today tend to see religion and games as
occupying separate realms of cultural experience, largely because of the
profound difference in mood that seems to manifest when one is playing
a game versus when one is performing religious activities. I argue that
mood is not the determining difference here. Religion can be serious or
fun, just as games can be. Rather, the opposite of serious or earnest play
is insincere play. Indeed, both games *and* religion are at their best when

players are earnest, when they take the experience seriously, that is, when they are fully committed to the rules of the experience or world view into which they have entered. The root similarity of religion and games, then, what I call order-making, is affiliated with the most ideal form of player engagement in both games and religions, namely, earnest play.

I must admit, of course, that even though hardcore gamers and deeply pious believers can both be earnest in their commitment to the rules of play, they enact their commitment in different ways. To overgeneralize, religious believers are typically earnest in an *ultimate* way, meaning that to "win" is to define one's purpose in life and to claim success in achieving it. They play a game that is believed to encompass all of life. Some believers (though by no means all) argue that everyone must play by the same rules, a proposal that can lead to conflict when two separate systems of rules clash with one another.[16] Most secular games, including most video games, by contrast, are experienced as temporary, ephemeral systems. Some games have definite win states, as is the case with *Portal* (Valve, 2008) and *Halo* (Bungie, 2001), for example. Some virtual worlds, like *World of Warcraft* (Blizzard Entertainment, 2004) and *Rift* (Trion Worlds, 2011), exhibit many game-like qualities, involving discrete quests and point-accumulation mechanisms and offering players prestige with increasing levels of skill. But for almost all video games, even if one is earnest in terms of devotion to play, the game involves entry into a *temporary* world of gameplay. The experience typically has little measurable effect on real life. As systems of rules, however, religion and games can both offer a form of relief for the practitioner from the temporary chaos of ordinary life, a means of imposing upon one's life a sense of order, predictability, purpose, and discoverable meaning. Today's video games increasingly offer richly crafted worlds in which there are predictable rules, in which winning is a possibility attainable by anyone with enough devotion.

Is it any surprise, then, that so many people are being drawn to the screened, ordered, rule-based spaces in which video games take place? Galloway defines a video game as "an algorithmic machine and like all machines [it] functions through specific, codified rules of operation."[17] In *Rules of Play*, Katie Salen and Eric Zimmerman say that playing a game means "interacting with and within a representational universe, a space of possibility with narrative dimensions."[18] Playing a game is, in short, a form of cosmic play. And it may be that we are increasingly enchanted with computers because they do what our religion has always done for us, but in some ways they do it better. Our machine-based, digital culture is shaped precisely by ordered, coded, rule-based systems, by visionary experiences of rule-based environments in which we can be sure that life is dictated by a programmer who has shaped our experience in a manageable way. Computers never forget what to say or when to say it, and the code is almost unfailingly predictable. Both religion and games, then, promise us some kind of respite from the chaotic interaction of competing views so prevalent in twenty-first-century life. What Galloway calls our "algorithmic culture" is infused with massive – and growing – numbers of game worlds that entice us with effective rituals, discernible missions, and promises of quantifiable rewards in the here and now.

So far I've been writing as if we all know what "religion" and "games" are. But these are two of the slipperiest concepts out there. As Salen and Zimmerman note, "If you wanted to study everything that might relate in some direct or indirect way to games and play, you could easily spend many lifetimes reading."[19] We could say the same of religion. Scholarly discussions of religion must address complex modes of engagement with the world that can be assessed via texts, traditions, and views of authority that go back thousands of years. Some religions include belief in a supernatural deity, and others do not. Some religions point to texts as authorities; others do not. Some point to an otherworldly reality as the ideal, and others say that what we do on earth is all that matters. Do we define religion functionally? Phenomenologically? Anthropologically? Socially? Do we look at observable human practices, beliefs, rituals, texts, stories, or histories? How do we decide what is a "religion" and what is simply a cultural practice? Religion scholar Georg Simmel lamented over a hundred years ago that "no light will ever be cast in the sybillic twilight that, for us, surrounds the origin and nature of religion as long as we insist on approaching it as a single problem requiring only a single word for its solution. Thus far no one has been able to offer a definition of religion that is both precise and sufficiently comprehensive. No one has been able to grasp its ultimate essence."[20]

The situation hasn't improved much today, over a hundred years and thousands of scholarly tomes later, but we do have a few key definitions of religion that scholars find useful for particular purposes. For example, we have social definitions like Emile Durkheim's, which posits religion as a "sacred" activity binding a community together in commitment to a common focus of worship that itself represents social cohesion. For Durkheim, religion is "a unified set of beliefs and practices relative to sacred things, that is to say, things set apart and forbidden – beliefs and practices which unite [into] one single moral community, all those who adhere to them."[21] Others are more drawn to phenomenological definitions like Mircea Eliade's, which depends upon Platonic notions of the "sacred" as the most "real." Some more contemporary definitions of religion, like Thomas Tweed's, relinquish the notion of belief altogether for the proposal that "religions are confluences of organic-cultural flows that intensify joy and confront suffering by drawing on human and superhuman forces to make homes and cross boundaries."[22] If boundaries include screens, then Tweed's definition points powerfully toward the ability of virtual spaces to evoke religious responses.

Jonathan Z. Smith has famously criticized Eliade's definition of religion, particularly his "dramatic wager" that the "mundane world, the human world, takes on reality only to the degree that it participates in that which is 'beyond,' in that which is transmundane and transhuman."[23] For anthropologists, social scientists, and humanists of all stripes, such assumptions are dangerous, since they depend upon unverifiable belief. However, we can use the sacred-profane dichotomy simply as a tool for understanding the beliefs of those human beings who *do* tend to see the world this way and, with Smith, "reverse the polarities of the maxim 'as above, so below,' yielding the formula 'as below, so above,' thereby suggesting some theory of projection in the service of legitimating human institutions and practices."[24] Eliade's notion of sacred and profane is actually more about rules anyway than it is about space. Eliade has argued that one of religion's principal activities is creating means for making sense of what he calls "inhabited" and "uninhabited territory."[25] What he really seems interested in, though, is how order is imposed on spaces via rules and structure. Everything that exists "outside" of the inhabited, ordered world, Eliade says, is a "chaotic space, peopled by ghosts, demons, [and] 'foreigners,'" those entities that we believe we cannot possibly understand. The gods, however, have the ability to "consecrate" chaotic space and therefore render "chaos" into "cosmos."[26] Eliade uses the analogy of occupation as the principal means of creating cosmos in such an area through the imposition of a ritual of cosmogony.[27]

The dismal implications for interreligious encounter are obvious. If occupation and colonization are the only means of dealing with the "foreign," then such human impulses can only create trouble. But Eliade is also up to something more fundamental. The urge to ritually create cosmos out of chaos is at its root an order-making activity. It is the desire for a systematic, knowable world with rules that we can recognize. For Eliade, this act is a "repetition of . . . the divine act of creation," an observation which, in our context, could be read as the mythic time when God is said to have imposed order onto meaninglessness, cosmos onto chaos, the rules of the game onto an unmanaged play space. God created the game board, so to speak, and put people on it. If myth reflects desire, the mythic construct of chaos-to-cosmos is, in its most basic form, a wish that the world could *have* knowable rules so that it might be played like a (very serious) game.

In *Between Sacred and Profane*, Gordon Lynch proposes a "rehabilitation" of Eliade that, like Smith's, requires a rejection of Eliade's reliance on the "binary opposition" between sacred and profane. Eliade's division, says Lynch, establishes a "false distinction between mundane everyday life, and the realm of the transcendent mediated through specific spaces, rituals, and personnel."[28] For Lynch, Eliade's sacred and profane hinge upon a division of the world into the sacred ("up there") and the profane ("down here") and is thus also problematic for its resulting implicit reliance on "Western" notions of a divine godhead in a transcendent spatial realm. However, if we look afresh at Eliade's categories and consider the ways they are instantiated through actual ritual practice, we find that the functional purpose of the division into sacred and profane is that the sacred is characterized by rules and order and the profane exhibits no obvious rules or order. We need not take Eliade's belief in the supernatural seriously in order to see the applicability of his categories for how humans behave. That which is governed by rules and structure is cosmos. That which is without known rules is chaos. The movement from chaos to cosmos, from profane to sacred, is accomplished by laying a system of rules over the world – that is to say, by determining, or perhaps even manufacturing, the rules of the game.

Whereas Eliade depended on the notion of an ordered "up there" that earthly rituals reflect, I need only propose that the ritual performers *themselves* assume that there is an order up there that is instantiated down here, and that rituals work as a sort of rule-based system. Put in terms of games, I argue that the problems inherent in contemporary humanistic applications of Eliade's distinction between sacred and profane are resolved when we see the sacred as demonstrative of a rule-based, ordered cosmos, as a "game" that makes sense, and when we see the profane as those lived spaces that are not game-like. Eliade is in fact drawing a distinction between those spaces that are played like a game, and those that are not.

My own rehabilitation of Eliade involves the recognition, with Lynch, that we need not assume the reality of a transcendent realm upon which all earthly order is modeled, but we should instead utilize Eliade's distinction between sacred and profane functionally, recognizing that the *desire* for rules, for order, for cosmos is nothing more nor less than the desire to play a meaningful game, to live in a world governed by knowable and predictable rules. This desire might be visible in existing religious practices, but may also be visible in the cultural practices of ordinary gameplay, and it is certainly present in many manifestations of religious ritual. It even allows us to see deeply immersive secular gameplay as a kind of sacred practice. In such an argument, the sacred need not have a spatial existence beyond the human realm, but need only be recognized as the assumption that life can be played like a (very serious) game, and that to do so is exceedingly comforting.

GAMES AS ORDER-MAKING RULES

Games are no easier to manage in terms of definition and analysis, but they too reflect a deep concern with producing order. Apart from this

foundational concern, however, approaches and definitions abound.
Do we define games according to systems of logic and probability? Do
we employ systems theory? What about aesthetics? Do we look at educational games, outdoor games, card games, board games, ball games,
children's games? How do toys and other props relate to the definition
of a game? And when we think about video games, how do we integrate
things like programming, hardware interface, and game design theory?
Many scholars have offered their own distinctive definitions of religion
and of games, and there is a lot of disagreement. But it does seem that
most, if not all, definitions of religion and of games gesture toward the
notion of order-making, especially as expressed in what I am here des-
ignating as "rules," the instructions that determine what kind of play is
allowed.

As part of his analysis of language, philosopher Ludwig Wittgenstein advises that there is no reliable set of defining features of games,
and offers a caution that could as easily apply to attempts to define religion. Inviting his reader to consider the wide breadth of activities that
we call "games," he asks what is common to all of them: "For if you look
at them you will not see something that is common to all, but similarities, relationships. . . . Look for example at board games. . . . And we can
go through the many, many other groups of games . . . [and] see how
many similarities crop up and disappear. And the result . . . is: we see
a complicated network of similarities, overlapping and criss-crossing:
sometimes overall similarities, sometimes similarities in detail."[29] Egenfeldt-Nielsen, Smith, and Tosca make a similar argument about video
games, admitting that genres of games are somewhat "arbitrary," mere
"analytical constructs imposed on a group of objects in order to discuss
the complexity of their individual differences in a meaningful way."[30]

Zimmerman admits of games what we might also say of religions,
namely that "there are no right or wrong approaches." In the study of
both, the approach one takes "depends on the field in which a particular
inquiry is operating and exactly what the inquiry itself is trying to ac-
complish."[31] Nonetheless, some of the most commonly cited definitions
of games evoke rules as the foundation. Salen and Zimmerman, for example, define a game as "a system in which players engage in an artificial
conflict, defined by rules, that results in a quantifiable outcome."[32] Jesper

Juul says something similar, defining a game as "a rule-based formal system with a variable and quantifiable outcome, where different outcomes are assigned different values, the player exerts effort in order to influence the outcome, the player feels attached to the outcome, and the consequences of the activity are optional and negotiable."[33] Definitions by other key voices in gamer theory,[34] including Roger Caillois, Bernard Suits, and Elliott Avedon and Brian Sutton-Smith,[35] also include rules as a primary, possibly essential, feature of games.

It is not that surprising that rules and order-making are linked, with one producing the experience of the other. Where there are rules, it matters if the players adhere to them, as this affects the ability of the system to provide a predictable, reliable experience. Thus it is important that players take the game or religious experience seriously, that is, whatever mood they may be invited to express in a game or religious experience, they also must be earnest in their engagement with the rule-based experience and willingly invest themselves in it. The opposite of play, then, is not seriousness. Play can be both serious *and* fun; the real opposition is between those who play earnestly and those who play insincerely, thereby disrupting the rule-based, ordered, cosmos-producing system of a game.

NOT PLAYING IN EARNEST: RELIGIOUS TRIFLERS, CHEATERS, SPOILSPORTS, AND NIHILISTS

Borrowing principles from scholar of play Bernard Suits, video game theorists Salen and Zimmerman also express a deep interest in the concept of play, defining the playful or "lusory" attitude as "the state of mind whereby game players consciously take on the challenges and obstacles of a game in order to experience the play of the game itself" through "accepting the artificial authority of the magic circle, submitting behavior to the constraints of rules in order to experience the free movement of play."[36] Suits notes that we submit to rules in the lusory attitude "just so the activity made possible by such acceptance can occur."[37] The player wants to enter into an ordered system; entry requires an earnest investment in the rules of that system. Drawing on Sutton-Smith, Jon Dovey and Helen Kennedy argue in *Game Cultures* that play requires an attitude, a "particular frame of mind" or "sense of 'what if?'"[38] Suspension of disbelief, then, at times may work just as well as belief since both involve temporary acquiescence to the rules of the larger system.

To be earnest in play is to buy into the system willingly and fully, to say yes to the world created by the rules. Sometimes this entry involves the pressing of a button on a gaming console or the donning of a costume. In religious contexts, the response to an altar call is a commitment to new rules for life. A rite of passage moves one into a new state of commitment, via the articulation of new formulations of expectations. But we all know that not everyone enters a game or religious experience with the same commitment, the same earnest attitude. Some make up new rules that apply only to themselves, or scoff at the expectations placed on them. In a religious context, some perform the ritual, but don't really mean it. Insincerity can ruin the most compelling game or religious ritual. By considering the types of insincere engagement that someone might enact in regard to a system's rules, we can recognize some of the key similarities between games and religion, even as we also expose the most compelling differences between ordinary games and religion. Here I draw upon gaming scholars to develop a taxonomy of four modes of non-serious, non-earnest players – triflers, cheaters, spoilsports, and nihilists – and I consider the implications for these categories on religion when it too is viewed as a game.

As Suits explains, a "trifler" is a "quasi-player of the game who conforms to the rules of the game but whose moves, though all legal, are not directed to achieving a checkmate."[39] Triflers may make up their own rules even while playing a game with rules that they are expected to follow, but refuse to follow fully. Triflers don't always take the game seriously; they may go through the motions, but do not care about the outcome. They lack zeal and commitment. They can spoil the fun for everyone in the game by becoming a weak element, by refusing to play with any real devotion. In the game of religion, then, a trifler would be one who *seems* to be following the rules of faith, but in fact does not believe at all: "although he is not really playing the game, he has not abandoned the game's institution. On the contrary, his continuing to operate in the terms of the institution is a necessary condition for his exploitation of the game and of his opponent."[40] Perhaps, in religious terms, the trifler doesn't attend services or scoffs in the back of the worship area. Triflers, says Suits, "recognize rules but not goals."[41] Triflers thus threaten to undermine the assumption that the rules matter, that the game means something, and that winning is worth working for. It's not difficult to see what form trifling might take in religious worship, nor how dangerous it may seem to those who are fully earnest in their own religious activity.

Another form of non-serious or insincere player is the "cheater." As Salen and Zimmerman explain, the cheater "transgresses the operational rules, the actual rules of play." The cheater "surreptitiously takes actions that are not proscribed [sic] by the rules, in order to gain an advantage."[42] Cheaters seem to be scoffing at the game much as a trifler might; but cheaters, by contrast, remain invested in one aspect of the game: the hope of winning, since "being the victor still has meaning to the cheater."[43] The cheater's investment in winning the game is usually tied up with some larger social prize: "to reap the rewards of glory external to the game."[44] To win, though, even by cheating, the cheater must in some way remain committed to *most* of the rules of the game.

If one goal of gameplay is to create a system of rules that are knowable, constructing what we might call a cosmos in religious terms, then we can easily understand why cheaters are resented. In an essay called "Fun and Games," Erving Goffman discusses the social qualities of games, pointing out that "by locating the power of determining the outcome of the play in the arrangements made by one player, cheating, like mismatching, destroys the reality-generating power of the game."[45] In other words, the world created by the game is no longer corporately constructed, no longer evolving in tension with the prescribed rules. Consequently, the element of ordered play is disrupted for everyone. Instead of maintaining a shared world view and set of rules, one cheating player despotically creates a world for everyone else, denying the assumption of shared rules and fragmenting the illusion of order. In so doing, cheating "punctures and deflates a world that has already developed."[46]

The practice of "bending" rules is technically in the same category as cheating, but usually without the same damaging consequences. Game theorist Bernard DeKoven explains that the most important quality of a game is that everyone agrees, upfront, on how it will be played and that everyone follows known rules. This means that if rules are changed, everyone must know about it and agree upon it. Bent rules, then, are acceptable in solitaire, since you are the only one affected. Bending rules is also acceptable, with proper negotiation and open acceptance by all players, in group games. The overall social cohesion, in this case, is not disrupted despite the violation of the original rules. Using the example of dodgeball, DeKoven says: "We didn't really change a rule, we bent it. We made an exception, and it was clear to all of us that it was all right."[47] Social cohesion is maintained when there is an agreed-upon system of rules and there is a shared understanding that everyone must acquiesce to any changes made to the system. Furthermore, rules must remain consistent while play is in motion. In religious terms, one could see, for example, changes made to liturgical formations to account for unusual or changing circumstances as an agreed-upon form of bending rules.

So who is the "cheater" in religious practice? There is, of course, the worshiper who takes communion even though he or she isn't the right denomination, but that might be mere trifling. There is the religious leader who doesn't actually possess the credentials he or she claims to have, and thus breaks the rules about ritual performance. But these forms of cheating are complicated by the apparent lack of an obvious "win" state that emerges as a result of the cheating. Is it really cheating if there is no win state? For a more extreme case of religious cheating, consider, for example, the Christian controversy about lapsed believers in the third century, a disagreement that hinged on whether bishops who had compromised their faith under the persecution by Emperor Decius still had the authority to baptize believers and engage in other official actions sanctified by the emerging church authority. In other words, the question was whether the "lapsed" Christians were cheaters who had failed to accept death and were willing to break the rules of earnest belief to save themselves.

This application reveals one of the most intriguing comparisons between cheating in ordinary secular games and cheating in a religious game. Winning by cheating in an ordinary game might bring one an undeserved trophy or monetary reward, but always on a physical plane.

Winning by cheating in a religious game might mean defeating death or avoiding martyrdom by refusing to follow the rules of faith. However, perhaps paradoxically, for those who remain in the faith despite the threat of martyrdom, "winning" might indeed mean dying – and thus "winning" a place in heaven. For the former, the "game" is an earthly one, and a win involves staying alive. For the latter, the "game" is ultimate, and a win involves dying. Identifying cheating, then, depends very much on the frame of reference for the game, that is, on the rules themselves.

The "spoilsport" is, in some ways, the most dangerous insincere player because, as Huizinga explains, the spoilsport "shatters the play-world itself."[48] The spoilsport's power comes through exposing the rules as a human-made construct crafting a temporary world, revealing the known but temporarily unacknowledged fact that real life doesn't adhere to such fixed rules. Accordingly, says Huizinga, we could say that the spoilsport "shatters civilization itself."[49] The spoilsport is constantly reminding us that games are "just" games, that order is constructed and malleable. Huizinga explains that "by withdrawing from the game [the spoilsport] reveals the relativity and fragility of the play-world in which he had temporarily shut himself with others." In so doing, he "robs play of its illusion – a pregnant word which means literally 'in-play.'"[50] As a result of disturbing the game, the spoilsport "must be cast out, for he threatens the existence of the play community."[51]

It is easy to see how such an idea applies to religious worlds too. The list of religious spoilsports includes "apostates, heretics, innovators, prophets, conscientious objectors," and so on: "The outlaw, the revolutionary, the cabbalist or member of a secret society, indeed heretics of all kinds are of . . . a sociable disposition, and a certain element of play is prominent in all their doings."[52] The spoilsport may object to the rules of one game, only to start a new game with transformed rules. Spoilsports, then, might include religious reformers, splinter groups, controversial contemporary interpreters of sacred writ, or even the proliferation of individual interpreters of all kinds as new readers approach ancient traditions and reassess what the rules of the game are and make new arguments for what the rules *should* be.

The urge to have a complete cosmos is tantalizing. Stephen Sniderman points out that even though no set of rules can possibly cover every eventuality, people "almost always play [a game] as if the rules were not only complete but knowable and statable."[53] This is a powerful reflection of our desire for order. The spoilsport is dangerous because "a player who argues about rules risks disapproval, sanctions, and even ostracism." Other players will be threatened by the spoilsport because "without necessarily being aware of their reasons, [they may] perceive [his activity] as a threat to pleasure, continuity, and stability."[54] And where the game is perceived as ultimate, as with religion, the spoilsport's ability to puncture it is all the more powerful. The work of spoilsports, however, may at times be necessary and useful – especially in those circumstances where religion is played as a game with absolute and ultimate rules. There are some extreme forms of religious practice, terrorist groups for example, that desperately need more spoilsports. The spoilsport typically argues about rules in order to change them, but still wants to play. The next type of game player would willingly abandon the game altogether.

Caillois explains that a game can be ruined by the "nihilist," who refuses to buy into the rules at all. A nihilist "denounces the rules as absurd and conventional" and refuses to follow them, asserting instead that "the game is meaningless." As opposed to the trifler or the cheater, the nihilist doesn't pretend to follow the rules. As opposed to the spoilsport, the nihilist doesn't try to create new rules, seeing all games as senseless. Because he or she has, by design, just refused to buy into the rules at all, the nihilist's "arguments are irrefutable." Furthermore, by asserting his or her refusal to accept the rules, the nihilist reveals that the game "has no other but an intrinsic meaning."[55] That is to say, the nihilist reveals the game *as* a game, as constructed, as a sort of deliberate sham, and what's more, he or she takes delight in exposing it. When applied to religion, the nihilist is the public atheist who exposes religion's absurdities. Some of today's most vocal nihilists regarding the game of religion are Bill Maher, James Randi, Christopher Hitchens, and Sam Harris. As Caillois explains, the nihilist's claims reveal that one should only play a game (or religion) if one *chooses* to; the nihilist disruptively exposes the voluntary nature of belief in a game's rules.[56] The fallout of such a claim, for the nihilist, is the affiliated argument that the game itself is a waste of time.

CONCLUSION

In games as we normally think of them, the rules are "not ultimately binding." As Suits points out, commitment to a game's rules is "never ultimate," because "there is always the possibility of there being a non-game rule to which the game may be subordinated."[57] Values larger than those expressed in the game will, or should, always trump the game's own limited rules. Put another way, our world is larger than the world of any game, and our ongoing human relationships should matter more than those relationships circumscribed by the limited temporary world of the game. So if the game begins to do real harm, we should stop playing. Suits explains that rules are "lines that we draw," but we should always draw them "short of a final end or a paramount command."[58]

In religious games, however, the rules are often believed to govern the cosmos itself and to define the ultimate conditions of how an ordered universe works. Thus for some overly zealous players, the game of religion itself is threatened with exposure as a constructed system of rules, unless players demand that everyone adhere to exactly the same rules and claim everlasting consequences for not taking the game seriously, for not playing earnestly. It is in situations like these that terrorism erupts, that lives are taken, that martyrs die, and that tyrants punish.

But perhaps religious game players have something useful to learn from non-ultimate game players. The recognition of triflers, cheaters, spoilsports, and nihilists reveals that not everyone *wants* to play the same game in the same way. Furthermore, our world reveals that there is more than one set of rules for every game. And religion, like any human construct, is bound by rules that can never be complete, can never cover every situation or every person's needs. As Sniderman writes, "No two people can possibly follow the same set of rules in exactly the same way."[59] We can thus ask with Sniderman: "What follows from the acknowledgment that no human system has a completable set of 'rules'?"[60] One of the things we may realize, he says, is that "no set of rules is inherently superior to any other."[61] Put in theological terms, all play systems, all games, all modes of cosmos crafting (religions included) consist of human-made rules that we voluntarily accept. If we recognize that much, then perhaps we can also acknowledge that others may choose to play by different rules or perhaps even play different games.

The imposition of rules is a performance of the *desire* for order, not the recognition of preexisting order in the cosmos. Religion, as a game, is an expression of how we *wish* things could be, what we want, what we dream. The comparison of religion with gaming reveals its constructed qualities, and requires that we question preconceived notions of what it means to commit to a set of religious beliefs.[62] Despite the initial strangeness of my argument, religion can be viewed as a game too, and in some of its manifestations the game of religion can devolve into assumptions of certainty where certainty does not exist. A recognition of religion as play exposes its constructed nature. Caillois makes a similar point when he proposes that play exposes artifice and is fundamentally "to the detriment of the secret and mysterious, which play exposes, publishes, and somehow expends."[63] If we know that we are being *invited* to play a game, religious or otherwise, we can look with open eyes at the rules and make careful decisions about whether to even play those games that have deep implications for our values. We can recognize that in accepting a religious world view, we are building a cosmos and perpetuating it through our earnest investment in it. Accordingly, we should ensure that any religious game we play contributes to human thriving, encouraging potential and nourishing hope.

Thinking critically about play can give us the freedom to take responsibility for the games we choose to play. Caillois remarks that "thanks to the nature of play, man is able to counteract monotony, determinism, nature's blindness and brutality. Play teaches one to build an order, to conceive an economy, to establish fair dealing."[64] The lusory attitude is, and always has been, a choice. All play, all rules, all order-making is at its root a human constructive activity, a human attempt at meaning-making. The comparison of games and religion urges us to play in more mature ways, to bear the burden of the rules to which we commit, and, if necessary, to change them. With religion and with games, to be earnest is to be aware, to be responsible, and to engage with a modified sense of what it means to "win." To be earnest is to only play those games we have decided to play, but to play them with full sincerity.

NOTES

1. Huizinga, *Homo Ludens*, 18.

2. Zimmerman, "Narrative, Interactivity, Play, and Games," 159.

3. Ibid.

4. Ibid.

5. Galloway, *Gaming*, 7.

6. For more on how rules interact with rituals, games, and beliefs, see Wagner, *Godwired*.

7. Huizinga, *Homo Ludens*, 19.

8. Egenfeldt-Nielsen, Smith, and Tosca, *Understanding Video Games*, 45.

9. Caillois, "Unity of Play," 95.

10. Ibid.

11. Flanagan, *Critical Play*, 69.

12. Ibid., 105.

13. Caillois, "The Classification of Games," 133.

14. Ibid., 134.

15. Ibid., 135.

16. For more on this perspective and its implications, see Wagner, "First-Person Shooter Religion."

17. Galloway, *Gaming*, 5.

18. Salen and Zimmerman, *Rules of Play*, 378.

19. Ibid., xix.

20. Simmel, "A Contribution to the Sociology of Religion," 101.

21. Durkheim, *Elementary Forms of Religious Life*, 46.

22. Tweed, *Crossings and Dwellings*, 54.

23. Smith, "Introduction," xiv.

24. Ibid., xv.

25. Eliade, *The Sacred and the Profane*, 29.

26. Ibid., 30.

27. Ibid., 31.

28. Lynch, "What Is This 'Religion,'" 136.

29. Wittgenstein, *Philosophical Investigations*, 66–67.

30. Egenfeldt-Nielsen, Smith, and Tosca, *Understanding Video Games*, 41.

31. Zimmerman, "Narrative, Interactivity, Play, and Games," 155.

32. Salen and Zimmerman, *Rules of Play*, 96.

33. Juul, "The Game, the Player, the World," 35.

34. Following McKenzie Wark, I use the term "gamer theory" here intentionally to distinguish between theory relating to video games and "game theory," which relates to the advanced study of mathematics and probability. See Wark, *Gamer Theory*.

35. Caillois, *Man, Play, Games*; Suits, *Grasshopper*; Avedon and Sutton-Smith, *The Study of Games*.

36. Salen and Zimmerman, *Rules of Play*, 574.

37. Suits, *Grasshopper*, 54.

38. Dovey and Kennedy, *Game Cultures*, 29.

39. Suits, *Grasshopper*, 58.

40. Ibid., 59.

41. Ibid., 60.

42. Salen and Zimmerman, *Rules of Play*, 274.

43. Ibid., 275.

44. Ibid.

45. Goffman, "Fun and Games," 130.

46. Ibid.

47. DeKoven, "Changing the Game," 522.

48. Huizinga, *Homo Ludens*, 11.

49. Ibid., 211.

50. Ibid., 11.

51. Ibid.

52. Ibid., 12.

53. Sniderman, "Unwritten Rules," 498.
54. Ibid., 499.
55. Caillois, "The Classification of Games," 126.
56. Ibid.
57. Suits, *Grasshopper*, 42.
58. Ibid.

59. Sniderman, "Unwritten Rules," 501.
60. Ibid., 499.
61. Ibid., 500.
62. Ibid., 501.
63. Caillois, "The Definition of Play," 124.
64. Caillois, "Unity of Play," 94.

REFERENCES

Avedon, Elliott M., and Sutton-Smith, Brian. *The Study of Games*. New York: Wiley, 1971.

Caillois, Roger. "The Classification of Games." In *The Game Design Reader: A Rules of Play Anthology*. Edited by Katie Salen and Eric Zimmerman, 129–147. Cambridge, Mass.: MIT Press, 2006.

———. "The Definition of Play." In *The Game Design Reader: A Rules of Play Anthology*. Edited by Katie Salen and Eric Zimmerman, 123–128. Cambridge, Mass.: MIT Press, 2006.

———. *Man, Play, Games*. 1958. Urbana: University of Illinois Press, 2001.

———. "Unity of Play: Diversity of Games." Translated by Elaine P. Halperin. *Diogenes* 19 (1957):92–121. http://www.gamesmuseum.uwaterloo.ca/Archives/Caillois/index.html.

DeKoven, Bernard. "Changing the Game." In *The Game Design Reader*. Edited by Katie Salen and Eric Zimmerman, 518–538. Cambridge, Mass.: MIT Press, 2006.

Dovey, Jon, and Kennedy, Helen. *Game Cultures: Computer Games as New Media*. New York: Open University Press, 2006.

Durkheim, Emile. *Elementary Forms of Religious Life*. 1915. New York: Oxford University Press, 2001.

Egenfeldt-Nielsen, Simon, Smith, Jonas Heide, and Tosca, Susana Pajares. *Understanding Video Games: The Essential Introduction*. New York: Routledge, 2008.

Eliade, Mircea. *The Sacred and the Profane: The Nature of Religion*. Translated by Willard R. Trask. New York: Harper and Row, 1957.

Flanagan, Mary. *Critical Play: Radical Game Design*. Cambridge, Mass.: MIT Press, 2009.

Galloway, Alexander. *Gaming: Essays on Algorithmic Culture*. Minneapolis: University of Minnesota Press, 2006.

Goffman, Erving. "Fun and Games." In his *The Goffman Reader*. 1961. Edited by Charles Lemert and Ann Branaman, 129–146. Malden, Mass.: Blackwell, 1997.

Huizinga, Johan. *Homo Ludens: A Study of the Play-Element in Culture*. Boston: Beacon, 1955.

Juul, Jesper. "The Game, the Player, the World: Looking for a Heart of Gameness." In *Level Up: Digital Games Research Conference Proceedings*. Edited by Marinka Copier and Joost Raessens, 30–45. Utrecht, Netherlands: Utrecht University Press, 2003.

Lynch, Gordon. "What Is This 'Religion' in the Study of Religion and Popular

Culture?" In *Between Sacred and Pro-fane: Researching Religion and Popular Culture*. Edited by Gordon Lynch, 125–142. New York: Tauris, 2007.

Salen, Katie, and Zimmerman, Eric. *Rules of Play: Game Design Fundamentals*. Cambridge, Mass.: MIT Press, 2004.

Simmel, Georg. "A Contribution to the Sociology of Religion." In his *Essays on Religion*. 1898. Translated by Horst Jürgen Helle, 101–120. New Haven, Conn.: Yale University Press, 1997.

Smith, Jonathan Z. "Introduction." In *The Myth of the Eternal Return; or, Cosmos and History* by Mircea Eliade. Translated by Willard R. Trask. Princeton, N.J.: Princeton University Press, 2005.

Sniderman, Stephen. "Unwritten Rules." In *The Game Design Reader: A Rules of Play Anthology*. Edited by Katie Salen and Eric Zimmerman, 476–503. Cambridge, Mass.: MIT Press, 2006.

Suits, Bernard. *Grasshopper: Games, Life, and Utopia*. 1978. Orchard Park, N.Y.: Broadview, 2005.

Tweed, Thomas, *Crossings and Dwellings: A Theory of Religion*. Cambridge, Mass.: Harvard University Press, 2006.

Wagner, Rachel. "First-Person Shooter Religion: Algorithmic Culture and Inter-Religious Encounter." *Cross Currents* 62, no. 2 (June 2012):181–203.

———. *Godwired: Religion, Ritual and Virtual Reality*. London: Routledge, 2012.

Wark, McKenzie. *Gamer Theory*. Cambridge, Mass.: Harvard University Press, 2007.

Wittgenstein, Ludwig. *Philosophical Investigations*. Translated by G. E. M. Anscombe. Oxford: Blackwell, 1953.

Zimmerman, Eric. "Narrative, Interactivity, Play, and Games." In *First Person: New Media as Story, Performance, and Game*. Edited by Noah Wardrip-Fruin and Pat Harrigan, 154–163. Cambridge, Mass.: MIT Press, 2004.

TEN

"God Modes" and "God Moods"

WHAT DOES A DIGITAL GAME NEED TO
BE SPIRITUALLY EFFECTIVE?

Oliver Steffen

"I'M NOT SURE HOW MUCH RELIGION YOU'LL FIND IN *THE PATH*," writes Michaël Samyn, director of the Belgian independent studio Tale of Tales, in response to an inquiry.[1] After all, *The Path* "is a short horror game inspired by older versions of Little Red Riding Hood, set in modern day."[2] Six sisters, aged nine to nineteen, are sent on an errand to their sick and bedridden grandmother. Mother tells them to stay on the path that leads through a thick and dangerous forest. The woods, however, promise adventures that can hardly be resisted by the girls. In the forest, they find strange areas and objects related to their characters and life situation. Most important, they find their personal wolf – a traumatic encounter, after which grandmother's house becomes a place of surreal nightmares that end with the death of each girl.

The Path, which won awards for innovative game design, shows little overt religious symbolism, apart from some Christian crosses at the graveyard and the girls' reflections about death. However, a glance at the developer's forum reveals that players relatively often tie their play experiences to religious themes.[3] Therefore, the game might be an example, on one hand, of the suggestion of William Sims Bainbridge and Wilma Alice Bainbridge that it is "possible that certain categories of games satisfy some of the same psychological needs satisfied by religion,"[4] and on the other hand, of game researcher and designer Ian Bogost's approach that games may have a spiritually relevant persuasive effect through their procedural representations and interactions rather than through their contents.[5] In this chapter, I suggest a ludologically influenced religious studies approach to digital games.[6] I am interested

214

10.1. Rose off the path. *The Path* (2009).

in the basic structural elements of games that generate religiously or spiritually relevant experiences in players. As a start, I examine a number of scientific and journalistic publications that, in their discussion of digital games' effects, not only refer to religious terms, metaphors, and themes, but also provide details about the characteristics of the corresponding ludological structure. I offer a list of criteria to compare the spiritual efficacy of digital games – an essential aspect of the implicit religious potential of games. I then show that this efficacy may be understood and compared in terms of flow, meditation, empowerment, disempowerment, and morality. This catalog becomes the basis for my analysis of *The Path*, which is followed by a discussion from a religious studies perspective.

So even if Michaël Samyn is not sure how much religion is in *The Path*, I'll gladly follow his friendly invitation: "But have a look. . . . And do please let us know what you find!"

THEORIES AND CONCEPTS

The following key theories and concepts will be used to unpack the "religious" experiences reported by game players.

Implicit Religion and Spiritual Efficacy

In this chapter, "religion" is defined according to the sociological theory of "implicit religion," which covers cultural phenomena that are not attributed to traditional religions, but have the same or similar structures and functions for individuals. Here, I focus on a single theme of implicit religion, spiritual efficacy, as expressed by the German sociologist of religion Günter Thomas. First, through rituals and other strategies, the religious communication process induces and interprets experiences of altered states of consciousness. These experiences show two typical poles: an operation of consciousness that is to the greatest possible extent hetero-referential, that is, the individual consciousness is absorbed by external stimuli, as in practices of ecstasy; and an operation of consciousness that is to the greatest possible extent self-referential, for example, phenomena of silence, meditation, and mystical experience. Second, religious communication provides cognitive, affective, and evaluative orientation. Third, it suggests specific ways of behaving and acting. Thus, the individual consciousness of the participants, or their self-perception and social perception, is meant to be shaped permanently.[7] As I will show, parallels can be found for these three interdependent factors in digital game literature.

"God Mode" and "God Mood"

To examine spiritual efficacy in digital games in more detail, let me introduce the twin concepts of "god mode" and "god mood." In digital gaming, "god mode" is a common term for the practice of permanently maximizing the avatar's attributes, that is, achieving a state of immortality, by altering the game rules. This process has several aspects that are relevant to this chapter. It emphasizes the ludological structure of digital games by dealing with the rule system. It conveys a particular religious notion, namely that of an omnipotent and immortal deity. Finally, it induces an altered game experience in the players, including feelings of absolute power and of "playing God."[8] Based on these aspects, I use the term "god mode" to identify ludological structures that are spiritually effective, according to the literature I reviewed. This means that these structures do not merely convey religiously or spiritually relevant notions, but also bring about "god moods," which is defined as the corresponding changes in the players' consciousness.

To determine the ludological structures, I focus on three of Aki Järvinen's "compound elements": the procedurally actualized "rule set"; the game's "mechanics," the diegetic possibilities of player action; and the "theme," the integration of the game elements into a system transcending the contexts of meaning.[9] These compound elements can be expressed and accessed only by means of other compound and systemic elements: "components," the game elements that can be manipulated and owned; the "environment," which is the spatial organization of the game; "information" about events, roles, and states of the system; and the human-computer "interface." To take these perceptually accessible elements into account, I summarize them into another category: "aesthetics."

APPROACHES TO SPIRITUAL EFFICACY IN DIGITAL GAMES

I now examine the concrete phenomena of the above-mentioned religious experience, orientation, and disposition of actions in terms of their psychic effects (god mood) and ludological structure (god mode). First, I discuss religious experience in terms of flow and meditation. This is followed by a discussion of cognitive, affective, and evaluative orientation in terms of empowerment and disempowerment.

Religious Experience: Flow

Flow and the problem of its measurement in digital games is a known topic in game studies. Though flow cannot be directly identified with ecstasy, it fits the description of an operation of consciousness that is to the greatest possible extent hetero-referential: in flow state, the player's consciousness and reaction are fed and operated on by external stimuli. Flow is a psychological concept, but it may have religious significance in both religious and nonreligious contexts.[10]

Such significance is given to flow in a series of transpersonal psychology studies by Jayne Gackenbach and colleagues. The authors investigate if and how digital games can be described as cultural amplifiers for the process of consciousness development. The results of their extensive surveys show that flow and lucid dreaming are the most frequently experienced altered states of consciousness in digital gaming that can be associated with "higher state of consciousness."[11] Unfortunately, Gackenbach pays little attention to the genre or elements of digital games. Therefore, I turn to game designer Xinghan (Jenova) Chen, co-founder of the game development studio Thatgamecompany. In his M.F.A. thesis, "Flow in Games," he investigates game design requirements in order to create games appealing to a broad audience.[12] He takes the concept of flow as a source of inspiration and starting point. Based on the flow elements most important to game design – rewarding the player, balancing between the game's challenges and the player's abilities, and the player's control over the game activity – he suggests a flow system including the following criteria: "1) a wide spectrum of gameplay covering different difficulties for all types of players; 2) a player-oriented active Dynamic Difficulty Adjustment (DDA) system to give the players control over their gameplay, allowing them to play at their own paces; 3) embedment of DDA choices into the core mechanics of gameplay to adjust flow experiences directly through diegetic behavior."[13]

Thatgamecompany implemented these principles in its widely recognized and successful game flOw (Thatgamecompany, 2006). Programmer Eddy Boxerman from Hemisphere Games, who worked on Osmos (Hemisphere Games, 2009), a game similar to flOw, has adopted Chen's approach and mentions further elements of flow games: intuitive gameplay and controls; appealing visuals, sounds, and music; and the absence of time pressure.[14] For its flow-based games, Thatgamecompany introduced the genre "Zen."[15] Sony Computer Entertainment, which has published Thatgamecompany's more recent games for the PlayStation 3, adopted the term to promote the release of flower (2008).[16] Boxerman suggests that "flow" would have been more appropriate, but "'Zen Gaming' sounds better, and perhaps it paints a broader picture for the genre."[17]

Religious Experience: Meditation

The digital game genre Zen also points to the other type of religious experience: the operation of consciousness that is to the greatest possible extent self-referential. According to Thomas, an example of that experience would be meditation. This comes close to what Bogost calls "zen-gaming." Here, Zen is not equated with flow, but is thought to imply notions of meditative practices: Zen games, Bogost insists, must be "lean back" or relaxing games; they are not about control, engagement, and time pressure, but embrace simplicity, austerity, and calmness in visuals, themes, and controls.[18] Thus, good examples of Zen games are casual puzzle games: they provide abstract aesthetics and demand repetitive gestures, and achieving the goal becomes secondary. Other types of Zen games, according to Bogost, are gardening games and wandering games: the first include tilling, planting, and weeding as core mechanics and are said to induce the meditative effect of *karesansui* (Japanese dry gardens). The latter provide the spatial exploration of open virtual worlds and may be connected to historical and mythological accounts of meditative wandering.

Sus Lundgren and colleagues in 2009 approached the issue without referring to the history of religion. They used the term "meditation" to describe one of several aesthetic ideals of gameplay design; more specifically, meditation is the result of a specific set of variable gameplay properties. It seems promising to amend the authors' approach by clarifying the relationship of these properties to historical accounts of meditation. For the most part, Lundgren and colleagues support Bogost's idea of Zen, in which meditation games should be simple ("simplicity") and avoid non-goal-related work, therefore minimizing the possibility for reflection ("minimal excise"); their rules should be consistent and cohesive; and they should eschew complex themes, accurate simulations, varying strategies, different meaningful choices, and emergent gameplay, that is, complex situations that arise from simple rules and mechanics. All of these requirements point to small and simple games, for example, puzzle or skill games like *Tetris*. In contrast, by attributing a great deal of micro-management – small tasks requiring immediate attention – and, contradicting Bogost, limiting play time to the meditation aesthetic ideal, play moves and rounds are clearly repetitive. This resembles the meditative repetition of prayers (*ruminatio*)[19] rather than silent nondiscursive observation. And some use of chance, as well as a tempting challenge based on pattern recognition and analytical skills, suggests an understanding of meditation that emphasizes the investigation

of contingent phenomena or the revealing of hidden truths – similar
to how the term was used in European medieval academic theology.[20]

Cognitive Orientation: Empowerment

In participants, the religious communication process seeks to bring
about cognitive, affective, and evaluative orientation. Digital games, too,
aim to channel players' thinking, feeling, and evaluating through challenges, selective multimedia communication, rules, and reward systems.
In the reviewed literature, authors sometimes identify game structures
that refer to the subject of empowerment. More precisely, they refer to
the "empowerment of the mind, will, and imagination,"[21] that is, the re-
alization of special powers that may result from cognitively, affectively,
and evaluatively adopting a particular religion's rules and ideals. Aaron
Oldenburg's art game *After* provides an example of the extra-psychic
or supernatural acquisition of information.[22] An alternative temporary
perspective presented in a separate window conveys counterintuitive information that is relevant for progress in the game. The source of that information seems to be a deceased person close to the player's character.
Depending on the interpretation of how this information is transmitted
to the player's character, this perspective may be considered to be a simulation of channeling, clairvoyance, or out-of-body experience. Based
on this example, I suggest the consideration of the transmission and
representation of relevant information in first- and third-person games.
Besides alternative perspectives in separate windows, directional arrows, marks, and other hints also may be interpreted – depending on the
thematic context – as psychic or intuitive attention-directing processes,
as extraordinary knowledge, or as the "omniscience" of the avatar.

Structures of empowerment can also be identified when studying
god games, which include construction and management simulations
as well as strategy games, in which the player takes on the role of a deity,
as in *Black & White* (Electronic Arts/Feral Interactive, 2001), or an all-
powerful mundane decision maker, as in *Sim City* (Maxis, 1989–). In the
reviewed literature,[23] several god game properties are mentioned that
may induce feelings of superhuman powers in players: extensive control
over individuals, cities, or civilizations, which manifest in game mechan-

10.2. Integrating the deceased's perspective. *After* (2010).

ics of terraforming, building, exploring, expanding, and conquering and even in nondiegetic level design; a narrated time often exceeding a human lifespan; and a top-down or isometric perspective ("god view"). Making use of a typical feature of digital games – the ability to achieve a huge effect with a small effort[24] – god games may be interpreted as the simulation of an aspect of spiritual empowerment, namely that "willing and thinking become transfigured in such a way that whatever one thinks or wills immediately comes to pass."[25]

While in god games great power is often given from the start, action and role-playing games emphasize the path to power. In the course of the game narrative, the action or role-playing hero has to level up in order to become a match for superhuman challenges. There is reason to consider this empowerment process as implicitly religious. Dan Pinchbeck and Brett Stevens refer to Victor Turner's ritual theory to understand digital game narratives as highly structured liminal phases: avatars undergo a conflict-laden transformation of world and self, in the process of which the conflict is resolved and a stable end-state is brought about.[26] Ludologically, the liminality becomes evident in the player's progress through increasingly challenging levels (FPS, action games) or in the mechanics of leveling up (RPGs).

Cognitive Orientation: Disempowerment

I generally use the term "disempowerment" to describe all sorts of processes that relativize and confine human possibilities of being and acting.
At least two forms of disempowerment may be religiously relevant: first,
the fundamental contingency of life, that is, a human being's helplessness
vis-à-vis bodily and psychic dependencies; and second, overwhelming
experiences of any sort that induce feelings and psychophysical reactions
like wonder, shivering, or awe and may likely be perceived as superhuman or sacred. Both forms may contribute to an awareness of the individual's limitations; in both cases, religions provide a frame of interpretation; and both situations may bring about the individual's submission
and devotion to the assumed source of life or power experienced. I suggest that religiously relevant disempowerment is actualized in games that
consciously limit the player's control and thus make a counterpoint to the
usual control in digital games. Such processes are easily associated with
religiously relevant themes like metaphysical uncertainty, fear of death,
and self-abandonment, as the following examples illustrate.

    The adventure game *Cosmology of Kyoto* (Softedge, 1995) is an ex-
ample of limiting cognitive control. Each of the protagonist's acts in medieval Kyoto influences his karma and determines his rebirth. However,
since this important process remains nontransparent, we find reports
containing phrases like "I don't know if this [giving money to the beg-
gars] affects your karma,"[27] or "I developed a sort of faith that performing these rituals [praying in a Buddhist monastery] would affect my
karma points."[28] Based on this example, I suggest that generally every
act in a game whose effects are not, or not immediately, evident to the
player opens up the possibility for the questioning of meaning and faith.
To players who are accustomed to "meaningful play"[29] – a developer's
design ideal implying that every interaction must be relevant to local
and global goals – this questioning is urgent.

    Limiting the control of affective tendencies is another type of con-
trol confinement. This is vividly experienced in action game situations
of persistent and imminent threat which cannot be properly dealt with
due to the player character's low skills, inadequate equipment, poor
health, or lack of ammunition. The capture or demotion of the pro-

tagonist, implying the loss of skills or equipment, may be narrative manifestations of the player's confined agency. This is carried to the extreme by survival horror games like *Amnesia: The Dark Descent* (Frictional Games, 2010). The protagonist, hunted by obscure but powerful creatures, lacks the means to defend himself: running away and hiding are the only options. The protagonist's fear and terror are simulated as blurred views and the player's loss of direct control over the character. Situations like these may induce feelings of powerlessness, helplessness, and fear in players. Referring to "predation games," Elena Bertozzi describes states like these as "simulated near-death experience[s]."[30] She cites the Hegelian motif of the struggle to the death for recognition, among others, to also consider the empowering effects of these experiences. Thus, shooters and horror games simulate the trial to reach higher states of freedom and consciousness through self-sacrifice and overcoming the fear of death.[31]

Finally, some games urge players to abandon agency in order to progress. Meditation games like *Guru Meditation* (Ian Bogost, 2007), *Wii Fit Zazen* (Nintendo, 2007), and *Journey to Wild Divine* (Wild Divine, 2001) not only refer thematically to the abandonment of agency but, using input devices like balance boards and biofeedback finger sensors, even realize it on a vestibular and psychophysiological level. Furthermore, the abandonment of agency has a somewhat different quality if it unexpectedly defies genre conventions. For example, in *Star Wars Jedi Knight: Mysteries of the Sith* (LucasArts, 1998), the player has to realize that in order to win the final battle, his character needs to stop fighting. Such simulations of the abandonment of self or control are most likely found at the intersection of art and digital games. In *The Night Journey,* an experimental video game by Bill Viola and others, the "mechanic of enlightenment"[32] requires the player to give up control of moving and looking in order to gain new perspectives and to progress in the game. According to Oldenburg, these strategies are religiously relevant. On one hand, the limiting of control and agency parallels the requirement of many religions to give up control over worldly affairs and to surrender one's life to the assumed transcendent reality. The defiance of genre conventions, on the other hand, often induces disorientation, which may culminate in a "transcendent religious experience."[33]

Disposition to Act: Morality

From this discussion we can see that the religious communication process seeks to bring about dispositions to act in the participants, here
considered as moral behavior. Generally, religions function as a breed-
ing ground and a basis of legitimacy for cultural "codes of conduct,
procedures for reasoning morally, and standards of virtue. To support
commitment to the moral life, they help configure the world as a moral
order. Finally, they are prepared to qualify or refine this order so as to
permit anyone to attain the highest level of moral excellence."[34] Like
fairy tales and myths, some digital game narratives establish a moral
order to which the protagonists are subjected. However, only a small
number of games make their moral system an object of interactive decisions. This is rare even – or perhaps especially – in faith-based games.[35]
Technically, the simulation of morality is based on simple arithmetic
systems that distribute different points for the player character's different actions, giving the player corresponding feedback sooner or later. A
closer look at the concrete implementation of such systems highlights
the different dimensions of historical religious morality. The avatar's
moral attributes in some games function as a strategic resource. In the
Christian real-time strategy game *Left Behind: Eternal Forces* (Inspired
Media Entertainment, 2006), for example, the believers' "spirit" level
increases through praying and decreases when in bad company. Increasing spirit is essential for the player to keep control of the believers and to
convert enemies into believers.

Another example is the role-playing game series *Ultima* (Origin,
1981–2009), which provides open virtual worlds with far-reaching possibilities to act. Misconduct in *Ultima IX* (1999) is clearly defined and
reduces the "karma" value of the avatar. Low karma is punished by the
system by weakening other attributes of the avatar. In contrast, *Black
& White* and *Star Wars: Knights of the Old Republic* (BioWare, 2003) do
not overtly punish or reward the player's deeds, but clearly qualify them
as "good" or "evil" through textual and aesthetic feedback. The central
ludological element in all of these games is some kind of moral meter, a
closer examination of which will reveal some historical and philosophical characteristics. Moral meter games have an ethical effect because

they objectify presuppositions that are implicit to morality, like "right" and "wrong," as well as the idea of retribution. At the same time, they allow players to consider their own acts from a position of objectivity and impartiality – a requirement for ethical reasoning. Moral meter games usually exclude eschatology: retribution has its effect in the game's here and now, no later than the final sequence. Regarding the source of morality, the systematic rational character of moral meter games suggests less a personal deity than an impersonal body of rules, similar to the Hindu or Buddhist notion of karma. Finally, moral meter systems do not usually provide redemption or the qualification of moral rules. Unless such is foreseen in the game's narrative, digital game protagonists are not saved by remorse or by some god's grace; they do not overcome the "samsaric" good-evil scheme.

In contrast, the consequences of moral decisions in the action and FPS games *Deus Ex* (Ion Storm, 2000) and *Bioshock* (2K Games, 2007) are not expressed by moral meters or any other form of numeric or aesthetic evaluation of the player's acts; the consequences are expressed by the narrative itself – a process closely corresponding to a moral interpretation of life events and situations. Usually, these games provide a set of different options to act in each ethically delicate situation; players choose their protagonist's next move by their ludic preferences and ethical sense alone, because the game provides little or no information about the effects. Later in the game, players are confronted with how the game world or the protagonist has been affected by their earlier choices. Promoting the players' imaginative empathy and the notion that one's own conduct influences others' welfare, *Deus Ex* and *Bioshock* contribute to the expansion of ethical reasoning.

Except for a few cases (e.g., *Left Behind*), the moral systems of digital games are not embedded in the explicit theological, metaphysical, or ritual dimensions of historical religions. They are based on fictional religious or religion-like systems (e.g., *Star Wars* or *Ultima*) or on the developer's ideas. In any case, digital game morality may be understood as a set of highly simplified and individualized behavioral principles to meet current needs for action. These principles follow the Golden Rule known from many cultures, including prohibitions to kill, injure, and lie, and the support of the socially disadvantaged and people in need.

Violent games usually qualify the prohibition against killing according
to a morality close to that of Abrahamic religions: killing human beings
to protect oneself and one's own people is justified; killing animals and
other nonhuman creatures does not have any moral implications.

A QUESTION SET TO DETERMINE THE
SPIRITUAL EFFICACY OF *THE PATH*

I have developed a question set to consider the spiritual efficacy of digital
games, focusing on flow, meditation, empowerment, disempowerment,
and morality. I use these five terms to describe particular psychic states
(god moods) that are induced by particular sets of ludological elements
(god modes). In other words, flow and the other categories are at the
same time god moods and god modes, depending on the corresponding
view. In figure 10.3, I have assigned the game elements or god modes to
the main categories of rule set, game mechanics, theme, and aesthetics.

In this chapter, I apply this question set to *The Path*. Each affirmatively answered question increases the score of a particular god mode
by 1, indicated as "(+1)" in the analysis below. Negatively answered questions add no points, indicated by "(+0)." Since the number of questions
about each god mode varies, the final scores are scaled to a ten-point
system[36] in order to compare the god modes. My analysis of *The Path*
reveals the picture shown in figure 10.4.

The Path has some potential for flow. The game does not provide
different degrees of difficulty, goals, or scenarios. For example, the narrative, as well as some areas and objects, are adapted according to the per-
sonality traits of the girl chosen at the beginning (act 1), but the gameplay
remains the same (+0). In the second act, however, the player has some
control over the pace and progress of the game. He may choose to stay
on the path and directly head to the grandmother's house, confront the
wolf in the forest, or go back to act 1 and start over with another girl (+1).
Most of these options are realized through the core mechanics of walking and, therefore, are more or less consciously chosen by the player (+1).
As the developers write on their website, "*The Path* is a slow game."[37]
Indeed, there is no time limit for exploring, discovering, and experimenting (+1). Though the game's mechanics – walking, running, and interact-

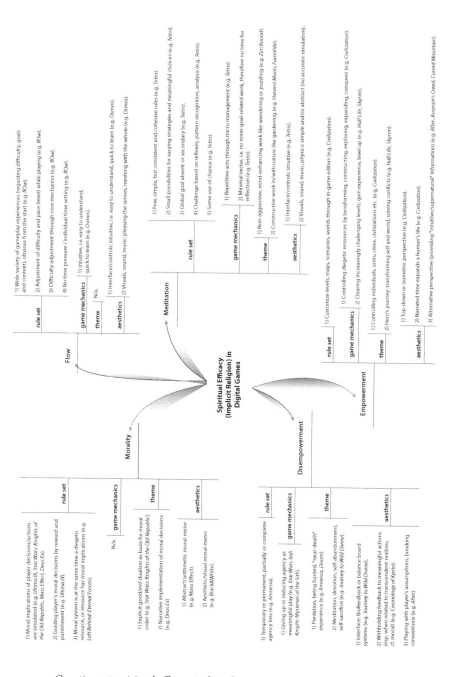

10.3. Question set: spiritual efficacy in digital games.

Spiritual Efficacy (Implicit Religion) of *The Path*

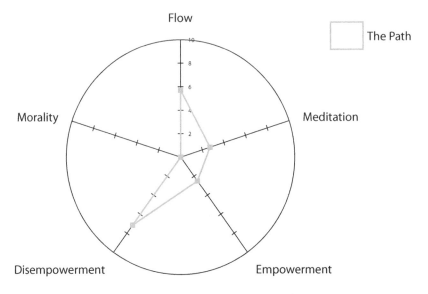

10.4. *The Path*'s god modes' potential to induce the corresponding god moods.

ing – are simple and easy to perform, the meaning of the interactions with objects and protagonists is not easy to understand and therefore is subject to interpretation (+0). The controls are a combination of conventional inputs – for example, moving by pressing the left mouse button or the keyboard keys W, A, S, and D – and unconventional elements like interaction through letting go of the controls. Also, the confusing hint system, which takes the form of scribbles and overlays on the screen, does not contribute to an intuitive understanding of how the game works (+0). Aesthetically, *The Path* is a beautiful game with lovely animations, colors, and sounds, sensibly embedded into the virtual world's narrative (+1).

The Path does little to bring about meditative states. Regarding rules, the art game's cunning instruction to stay on the path causes confusion, especially for players who are used to trusting a game's information. The generally consistent, but not cohesive, rules become evident to the player only gradually (+0). The possibilities for interacting with objects are rather low, but the game definitely provides opportunities for differ-

ent strategies and meaningful choices, for example, the free exploration
of the forest as opposed to the aim of unlocking all of the hint system
by collecting flowers (+o). *The Path* has no predetermined goal (+1). To
face the challenge, emotional skills and the urge to discover are more
promising than sensorimotor and analytical skills (+o). There is also
some element of chance. Every time one plays, the layout of the forest
is different, and the objects and attractions are distributed randomly
(+1). The game mechanics are not repetitive in terms of Lundgren and
his colleagues' micro-management (+o); some interactions, like looking
into a well or playing with the Girl in White, seem to be ludologically
redundant, but they invite the player to pause and reflect (+o). Though
a "horror game," *The Path*'s main theme is wandering and exploring the
forest; it is neither aggressive (+o) nor constructive (+o). As already mentioned in the discussion of flow, the controls have original elements, but
are not as intuitive as meditation (and flow) games would require (+o).
The visuals and sounds are, in the main part of the game, sensual and
realistic rather than abstract or simple – although they are continually
superimposed by abstract and associative images, and in act 3, surrealism
completely breaks through (+o).

Like meditation, empowerment is not much of *The Path*'s business.
There is no built-in or external editor to adapt the game world (+o). Even
though there are aspects of the hero's journey – like exploring, discovering, and transformation – embedded into the core mechanics (+1), there
is no classic improvement of the avatar's abilities (leveling up) (+o) nor
is there control and increase of the game world's resources (+o). *The
Path* is not a control simulation (+o). There is no top-down or isometric
perspective (+o) and no narrated time exceeding a human lifespan (+o).
There is, however, an alternative perspective: depending on the direction
and movement of the player's character, the screen is overlaid with flash-
ing, sketch-like figures such as faces, wolf paws, lips, or eyes, as well as
abstract forms like color stains and scribbles, arguably representing the
girl's intuitive or even supernatural anticipations and perceptions (+1).

The Path disempowers players in a variety of ways. The need to start
interactions with objects by letting go of the controls limits the player's
power over the protagonist; in act 3, which runs like a film with minimal
interaction, even the girl's moving direction is preset (+1). In addition

to walking, running is an option to move through space, but the "slow game" palpably restricts it: in some special areas, the girl just won't run. And the player is generally best advised to refrain from running since running makes the collectible flowers disappear and zooms out the camera from an over-the-shoulder perspective to a bird's-eye view, literally forcing the player to lose sight of his virtual aims (+1). *The Path*, as a horror game, deals with death and near-death: the girls, who occasionally hang out in the cemetery and philosophize about death, die in their grandmother's house after they encounter their personal wolf. But there's no apparent threat or necessity to experience these traumatic encounters – the girls, or the player, freely choose it (+0). This is why the sacrifice of the girls' innocent and childish selves and their surrender to the adolescent or adult world seem to be the main themes of the game (+1). On the aesthetic level, the game defies conventions as well (+1): though feedback is given for the player's actions, it often appears cryptic because of missing information (+1) or surrealistic aesthetics. The meaning of the girls' thoughts, the hint system, and the events in their grandmother's house become only gradually clear to the player. Until then, feelings of disorientation and confusion are likely to arise. The input devices of mouse and keyboard are conventional (+0).

The Path does not convey morality in the sense I outlined above. There is no moral system (+0) or resource associated with morality (+0) as a foundation for player actions; accordingly, there are neither numerical (+0) nor aesthetic (+0) moral feedbacks. Player decisions are not guided; the final score screen, like a school report card that evaluates one's accomplishments ("Success," "Failure," rank of A to D), informs the player about possible goals, but appears to be too ironic to seriously guide the player's actions (+0). Also, there is no indication of any dualism of good and evil (+0).

CONCLUSION: SOME REMARKS FROM A RELIGIOUS STUDIES PERSPECTIVE

To answer Michaël Samyn's invitation, *The Path* is neither a faith-based or religious digital game, nor does it contain a striking quantity of symbols that are known from historical religious traditions. According to my analysis, *The Path* has some potential to keep players in the flow by providing interesting characters and a fair amount of control regarding the gameplay. On the other hand, it disempowers players with unconventional information and controls. My analysis suggests that the feelings associated with flow and disempowerment might be religiously relevant to some users. But to what extent can this finding be generalized? And are flow and the other concepts discussed here necessarily related to religion? I will conclude by considering these questions focusing on three contingencies of the method outlined and applied above.

1. God Mode: The Compilation of Ludological Elements and
   Their Identification in Games
   I have used the term "god mode" to describe religious ideas that
   are actualized in digital games in the form of ludological elements
   arranged according to specific themes. Since the god modes were
   compiled based on only a small number of articles, I understand
   this question set as an instrument that suggests a method to investigate implicit religion in digital games, open for amelioration
   and change. Moreover, it is evident that assigning these ludological elements to structures existing in a particular game is also a
   question of interpretation and taste. To minimize this effect, the
   question set could be operationalized into an (online) survey
   which would be completed by the fans of a particular game.

2. God Mood: Feelings Induced
   The reviewed literature implies that god modes induce religiously relevant feelings: god moods. However, the relationship
   between god modes and god moods is contingent. Just like
   religious communication may draw individuals' attention, but
   cannot enforce perceptions and states of consciousness,[38] god
   modes may induce in players the corresponding god moods, but
   not necessarily. *The Path*, for example, provides the structural
   preconditions to induce a state of flow, but whether players really
   experience flow depends on them. This is true also for the question of whether the experience of flow and so on is relevant to
   players beyond the gaming context – apparently a precondition
   for any cultural phenomenon to be qualified as religious. To Old-

enburg, for example, "Mechanics alone are not generally enough to turn a feeling of faith in a game system into a belief in the supernatural, but must rely on the meta-aspects of play: how the player cognitively intersects the game with his or her life outside the game's imaginary structure."[39] God moods, therefore, are potential and contingent rather than determined.

3. God Mode, God Mood?: Determining the Reference to Religion
To limit the scope of this chapter, the ludological structures and the feelings they supposedly induce have been required to refer to religion, that is, they have been required to be "god" modes and "god" moods. This reference is a construction to which several authors have contributed, including me, a white male, raised in a Christian environment, trained in secular religious studies, and interested in altered states of consciousness. A critical review of the main points of how god modes and god moods are related to religion will reveal the constructed nature of this approach.

Flow and meditation refer to religion through their association with altered states of consciousness. While altering consciousness is central to some religions' ritual practices, it is not exclusively religious. This is suggested by the psychological concept of flow. Meditation, on the other hand, has stronger ties to religious or spiritual traditions, but even more than flow, it is used inaccurately in the reviewed literature. There, neither flow nor meditation refer to a particular religion, even if they are associated with Zen, because the authors' usage of "Zen" does not consider traditional Japanese Zen Buddhist schools and practices. It is rather a product of Western adoption starting with nineteenth- and early twentieth-century Orientalist discourse.[40] Today, Zen often means "a sense of liberation, spontaneity, and oneness with the world that can be sought not only in highly technical forms of meditative practice but also in archery, gardening, tea ceremonies, and even the most mundane matters, such as motorcycle maintenance"[41] – or gaming, according to some authors.

All of this suggests that the reference of flow and meditation to religion is based on concepts that are characteristic of a popular notion of spirituality, which is focused, among other variables, on "mystical experiences."⁴² These concepts are used by some individuals with in-terests in research, development, or marketing to give special impor-tance to different genres, to alternative gaming, and to the phenomenon of players' distance from everyday life while playing – often described by game scholars as the "magic circle," a concept borrowed from Johan Huizinga.⁴³ Of course, this does not touch on the question of authentic-ity. Whether a player is having a religiously or spiritually genuine ex-perience – regardless of its contents and characteristics – or whether he simply enjoys himself by being "in the zone" can only be answered by the experiencing individual or by a particular religious community.

Likewise, empowerment and disempowerment are used as meta-concepts, not referring to a particular religious tradition. I have intro-duced these terms to subsume ludological elements to the theme of granted or restricted player control, as well as to describe the subjective feelings associated with that control. Reference to religions is established by the notion of a particular contrast between human powerlessness and superhuman or godly power. Rather than essentializing "power" as a religious object, I observe that powers tending toward omnipotence and omniscience are part of many religious reflections and myths; still, they are also communicated outside of particular religious traditions – es-pecially in popular media. Similarly, disempowering contingency may, but does not have to, be experienced or dealt with in a religious context.

Finally, even though morality is a classic theme of many religions, most authors writing about digital games' morality or ethics are inter-ested in aspects other than religion. This is not surprising since digital games' moral systems rarely explicitly refer to a religious tradition. Thus, god mode morality stands for the ludological evaluation of players' de-cisions in terms of dualistic judgmental concepts like "good and evil," "light and dark," "spiritual and mundane," and so on. In this chapter, sim-ilarities to general or particular religious morality have been established in a somewhat superficial way. Further investigation should include the developers' perspective.

It must not be forgotten that these contingencies fit the logic of im-plicit religion: the god modes and god moods outlined here are part of a broader polythetic definition of religion. They answer the question of how the religious communication process affects the consciousness of participants. In order to call a phenomenon like digital gaming "religious," other factors have to be considered, like the symbol system, the question of imagined personal beings, rituals, and the development of communal structures. All of these factors, efficacy included, are not specific or exclusive to the religious communication process. But when it comes to religion, they often show typical characteristics. To identify the characteristics of the factors collectively called "efficacy," I applied the same polythetic model: the efficacy of digital games – spiritual or not – consists of a number of ludological elements, which themselves are not obviously religious or spiritual. In this sense, the question set developed here supports a modern and critical understanding of religion, acknowledging the contingent interplay between material base, human interaction, and subjective interpretation. In the case of implicit religion, this contingency usually is assumed by those interacting with the phenomenon in question. For many, it is an incredibly long way from, say, graphical simplicity and abstraction, to consciousness change, to meditation, and to the explicit religiously or spiritually relevant effect. For others, however – and the results presented in this chapter indicate that, too – this long way is overcome with the ease of a *Super Mario* jump.

NOTES

Figures 10.1 and 10.2 are screenshots taken from games. They are used according to the copyright law doctrine of "fair dealing/fair use." Figures 10.3 and 10.4 are by the author.

1. This inquiry and this chapter are related to "Between 'God Mode' and 'God Mood': Religion in Computer Games and the Meaning of Religion for Gamers," a research project of the Institute of Science of Religion, University of Berne, Switzerland, funded by the Swiss National Science Foundation, http://www.god-mode.ch.

2. http://tale-of-tales.com/ThePath.

3. Tale of Tales, "The Path – Discussion."

4. Bainbridge and Bainbridge, "Electronic Game Research Methodologies," 35–36.

5. Bogost, *Persuasive Games*; cf. Oldenburg, "Simulating Religious Faith."

6. I use the term "religious studies" in the sense of the "science of religion," that is, the study of religion conducted according to the approaches and methods of secular disciplines like sociology, anthropology, and so on, rather than theology or phenomenology. Scholars of secular religious studies have largely ignored digital and nondigital games as a research topic until now. A rare and recent publication is Burger and Bornet, *Religions in Play*.

7. Thomas, *Implizite Religion,* 441–446.

8. Consalvo, *Cheating,* 93, 97.

9. Järvinen, *Games without Frontiers,* 63–98.

10. Steffen, "High-Speed Meditation?," 93–96.

11. Gackenbach, "Video Game Play and Consciousness Development."

12. Jenova Chen, "Flow in Games" (M.F.A. thesis, University of Southern California, 2006), http://jenovachen .com/flowingames/thesis.htm (accessed December 18, 2012).

13. Ibid.

14. Boxerman, "Zen Gaming, Part 2."

15. Chaplin, "Video Game Grad Programs."

16. Totilo, "Sony Introduces New Genre to Video Games."

17. Boxerman, "Zen Gaming, Part 2."

18. Bogost, "Persuasive Games: Video Game Zen."

19. Baier, *Meditation und Moderne,* 32–37.

20. Ibid., 37–42.

21. Hollenback, *Mysticism,* 150.

22. Ibid., 156–167.

23. Neitzel, "Die Frage Nach Gott oder Warum Spielen wir Eigentlich so Gerne Computerspiele"; Wiemker, "To Win, You've Got to Think Like a God"; Atkins, *More Than a Game,* 115.

24. Klimmt, *Computerspielen als Handlung,* 80.

25. Hollenback, *Mysticism,* 150.

26. Pinchbeck and Stevens, "Ritual Co-Location."

27. "Cosmology of Kyoto Event List V1.1."

28. Oldenburg, "Simulating Religious Faith," 55.

29. Salen and Zimmerman, *Rules of Play,* 30–37.

30. Bertozzi, "The Feeling of Being Hunted."

31. Ibid., 13–15.

32. Fullerton, "Reflections on *The Night Journey.*"

33. Oldenburg, "Simulating Religious Faith," 56–57.

34. Green, "Morality and Religion," 6189.

35. Cf. Bogost, *Persuasive Games,* 292.

36. For example, god mode "flow" consists of a total of seven questions (number of questions [nq] = 7). In the analysis, four of these seven questions are answered affirmatively (final score [fs] = 4). This score is scaled from a seven-point system to a ten-point system by the formula $fs*10/nq$, resulting in the value of 5.71 for "flow," which is shown in figure 10.4.

37. http://tale-of-tales.com/The Path.

38. Thomas, *Implizite Religion,* 445.

39. Oldenburg, "Simulating Religious Faith," 56.

40. Cf. King, *Orientalism and Religion.*

41. Ahn, "Zen, Popular Conceptions of," 923.

42. Zinnbauer et al., "Religion and Spirituality."

43. Huizinga, *Homo Ludens,* 25.

REFERENCES

Ahn, Juhn. "Zen, Popular Conceptions of." In *Encyclopedia of Buddhism*. Edited by Robert E. Buswell Jr. New York: Macmillan, 2004.

Atkins, Barry. *More than a Game. The Computer Game as Fictional Form*. Manchester, England: Manchester University Press, 2003.

Baier, Karl. *Meditation und Moderne*. Würzburg: Königshausen and Neumann, 2009.

Bainbridge, William Sims, and Bainbridge, Wilma Alice. "Electronic Game Research Methodologies: Studying Religious Implications." *Review of Religious Research* 49, no. 1 (2007):35–53.

Bertozzi, Elena. "The Feeling of Being Hunted: Pleasures and Perils of Predation in Play." *Myweb @ C.W. Post*. http://myweb.cwpost.liu.edu/ebertozz /game/readings/Bertozzi Predation-Draft.pdf (accessed January 15, 2012).

Bogost, Ian. *Persuasive Games: The Expressive Power of Videogames*. Cambridge, Mass.: MIT Press, 2007.

———. "Persuasive Games: Video Game Zen." *GamaSutra*, November 29, 2007. http://www.gamasutra.com /view/feature/2585/persuasive_games _video_game_zen.php (accessed October 25, 2011).

Boxerman, Eddy. "Zen Gaming, Part 2." *Hemisphere Games*, December 14, 2008. http://www.hemispheregames .com/2008/12/14/zen-gaming-part-2 (accessed October 25, 2011).

Burger, Maya, and Bornet, Philippe. *Religions in Play: Games, Rituals, and Virtual Worlds*. Zurich: Theologischer Verlag, 2012.

Chaplin, Heather. "Video Game Grad Programs Open Up the Industry." *NPR*, March 23, 2009. http://www .npr.org/templates/story/story.php ?storyId=102246406 (accessed October 25, 2011).

Consalvo, Mia. *Cheating: Gaining Advantage in Video Games*. Cambridge, Mass.: MIT Press, 2007.

"Cosmology of Kyoto Event List V1.1." *Mennekecheats*. http://www.menneke cheats.nl/walkthroughEng/c/Cos mologyofKyoto.htm (accessed January 15, 2012).

Fullerton, Tracy. "Reflections on *The Night Journey*: An Experimental Video Game." 2009. http://www.tracy fullerton.com/assets/Reflectionson TheNightJourney_tfullerton.pdf (accessed December 30, 2011).

Gackenbach, Jayne. "Video Game Play and Consciousness Development: A Transpersonal Perspective." *Journal of Transpersonal Psychology* 40, no. 1 (2008):60–87.

Green, Ronald M. "Morality and Religion." In *Encyclopedia of Religion*. 1987. Edited by Lindsay Jones. New York: Macmillan, 2005.

Hollenback, Jess Byron. *Mysticism: Experience, Response, and Empowerment*. 1996. University Park: Pennsylvania State University Press, 2000.

Huizinga, Johan. *Homo Ludens: A Study of the Play-Element in Culture*. Boston: Beacon, 1955.

Järvinen, Aki. *Games without Frontiers: Theories and Methods for Game Studies and Design*. Tampere, Finland: Tampere University Press, 2008. http:// acta.uta.fi/english/teos.php?id=11046.

King, Richard. *Orientalism and Religion: Post-Colonial Theory, India and "The Mystic East."* London: Routledge, 1999.

Klimmt, Christoph. *Computerspielen als Handlung. Dimensionen und Determinanten des Erlebens Interaktiver Unterhaltungsangebote.* Cologne, Germany: von Halem, 2006.

Lundgren, Sus, Bergström, Karl J., and Björk, Staffan. "Exploring Aesthetic Ideals of Gameplay." In *Breaking New Ground: Innovation in Games, Play, Practice and Theory: Proceedings of DiGRA 2009.* http://www.digra.org/dl/display_html?chid=http://www.digra.org/dl/db/09287.58159.pdf (accessed January 15, 2012).

Neitzel, Britta. "Die Frage Nach Gott oder Warum Spielen wir Eigentlich so Gerne Computerspiele." *Ästhetik und Kommunikation* 32, no. 115 (2001):61–67.

Oldenburg, Aaron. "Simulating Religious Faith." *Journal of Gaming and Virtual Worlds* 3, no. 1 (2011):51–66.

Pinchbeck, Dan, and Stevens, Brett. "Ritual Co-Location: Play, Consciousness and Reality in Artificial Environments." *Proceedings of Connectivity: The Tenth Biennial Symposium on Arts and Technology.* 2006. http://www.thechineseroom.co.uk/PinchbeckStevens.pdf (accessed January 15, 2012).

Salen, Katie, and Zimmerman, Eric. *Rules of Play: Game Design Fundamentals.* Cambridge, Mass.: MIT Press, 2004.

Steffen, Oliver. "'High-Speed Meditation'?: Eine Religionsästhetische und Ritualtheoretische Betrachtung des Computerspiels." M.A. thesis, University of Berne, 2008. http://www.god-mode.ch/assets/downloads/oliver-steffen_high-speed_meditation – lizentiatsarbeit%20_mai-2008.pdf.

Tale of Tales. "*The Path* – Discussion." *Tale of Tales Forum.* http://tale-of-tales.com/forum/viewforum.php?f=39 (accessed December 27, 2011).

Thomas, Günter. *Implizite Religion: Theoriegeschichtliche und Theoretische Untersuchungen zum Problem Ihrer Identifikation.* Würzburg: ERGON, 2001.

Totilo, Stephen. "Sony Introduces New Genre to Video Games." *MTV Multiplayer,* December 12, 2008. http://multiplayerblog.mtv.com/2008/12/10/sony-introduces-new-genre-to-video-games (accessed October 25, 2011).

Wiemker, Markus. "To Win, You've Got to Think Like a God: An Introduction to Religiousness and God in Games." Paper presented at the Seventh International Crossroads in Culture Studies conference, Kingston, Jamaica, 2008.

Zinnbauer, Brian J., et al. "Religion and Spirituality: Unfuzzying the Fuzzy." *Journal for the Scientific Study of Religion* 36, no. 4 (1997):549–564.

ELEVEN

Bridging Multiple Realities

RELIGION, PLAY, AND ALFRED SCHUTZ'S

THEORY OF THE LIFE-WORLD

Michael Waltemathe

IN *RESISTANCE: FALL OF MAN*, A FIRST-PERSON SHOOTER SET IN
an alternative history, aliens have attacked earth and enslaved most of
humankind and transformed them into supersoldiers. Some of the fighting in the game takes place in what is left of Manchester Cathedral in
England, which in the alternative history is now infested by alien forces.
As a result of this depiction, in the real world the Church of England
took legal action against the publisher of the game, the Sony Corporation. The legal argument was that Sony had not asked permission to use
graphic depictions of the cathedral in its product.[1] The official reason for
the legal action can be seen in the following quote from Church of England officials: "We are shocked to see a place of learning, prayer and
heritage being presented to the youth market as a location where guns
can be fired. . . . For many young people these games offer a different
sort of reality and seeing guns in Manchester Cathedral is not the sort
of connection we want to make."[2]

What is clear is that for the Church of England the virtual representation of the cathedral still retains its religious character, which is seen
as being damaged by the virtual weapon fire. Even more interesting is
another development that followed the publication of the game – independent of the lawsuit. Surprisingly, in the months after the game was
published tourist attendance at Manchester Cathedral soared. Especially
interested were young people, who wanted to come and see a building
they had fought in against alien invaders. Some even explained that they
wanted to see if the building was real.[3]

This example raises a number of questions. What is the relationship between play, religion, and virtual worlds? Are there certain aspects of computer worlds that enable them to communicate religious thought and ideas more "effectively"? Are they a playground in which to explore religion? Is it possible to describe religious symbols – which are often used in computer games – as samples of "real" religiosity?

Often, religious spaces in video games are dismissed as inconsequential. Using Alfred Schutz's theory of the enclave, however, I argue that humor and play are the bridge between the worlds of video games and the actual world, because both the religious experience and the comic relieve us of the tense and fundamental anxiety of what Schutz calls the "paramount reality," the pragmatic world of working in daily life.[4] In other words, what makes a video game "religious" is not only the occasional mention of a deity or other overtly religious aspects, but the relation between the mode of playfully experiencing symbolic universes and transforming those experiences to other parts of the life-world. Describing computer games within the framework of social phenomenology and the sociology of knowledge highlights that they are not "unreal," but are human worlds revealed to be symbolic universes accessible through a machine. Using a sociophenomenological approach, I show the nature and place of computer worlds in the life-world of the individual. I discuss the basic nature of the different areas of the life-world and the place computer worlds take in it. The result is a concept of the structure of the human-computer interaction in accordance with social phenomenology. Using examples from different games, I argue that computer worlds connect different areas of the life-world.

A sociophenomenological approach is crucial for understanding religion and games because it takes the individual player's perspective into account and describes the structure of human-machine interactions from this perspective. People who play computer games immerse themselves in these universes and play by or with the rules of these universes. The way people interact with these symbolic universes is defined by the human-computer interface. A phenomenological analysis of this situation can help us gain insight into the primary mode in which the computer-manifested universes can be experienced: playfulness. This playfulness while interacting with the computer and the worlds embodied in or represented by the machine can be described as one of the fundamental characteristics of what is commonly called "virtuality." When looked at from this perspective, computer games enable us to understand the relation between the individual player and the symbolic references within the game world that show themselves as religious universes.

SCHUTZ'S PHENOMENOLOGICAL
THEORY OF THE LIFE-WORLD

Alfred Schutz in *On Multiple Realities* describes the life-world as resting on the paramount reality of the "world of working in daily life." This paramount reality is "the inter-subjective world which existed long before our birth, experienced and interpreted by others, our predecessors, as an organized world."[5] The world of working in daily life is only one of several worlds constituting the life-world of human beings. The others, according to Schutz, are "the world of dreams, of imageries and phantasms, especially the world of art, the world of religious experience, the world of scientific contemplation, the play world of the child and the world of the insane."[6] Schutz gives a detailed account of the possibilities to act, interact, and communicate in these provinces of meaning, but grounds his theory in the "reality of the world of daily life and its pragmatic motive."[7] It is the setting for our actions and interactions.

THE STRUCTURE OF THE LIFE-WORLD

The life-world (*Lebenswelt*) is constituted from various multiple realities.[8] Using the world of everyday life as an example, Schutz develops six characteristics of finite provinces of meaning that apply to all of them, but he also offers a specific characteristic for each of the different provinces. Contra the American philosopher and psychologist William James, he accepts the world of everyday life as real not because it enables sensual perception, but because it has a pragmative motive.[9] This makes the world of everyday life the paramount reality in Schutz's concept of the life-world, especially because it is the province of meaning, which enables us to communicate. As long as our experiences par-

take of the cognitive style of the world of everyday life, we will consider
this province of meaning as real. This is easy in the paramount reality,
because our working in it proves its unity and congruity and itself as
valid. All the experiences in a single province of meaning share the same
cognitive style, because they are compatible and consistent within that
particular province of meaning.[10] Schutz calls these "finite provinces
of meaning."[11]

This idea enables us to understand computer worlds within the
framework of the various finite provinces of meaning. Their structure
within the framework is not clear, however. If human-computer interaction is to be understood as similar to human-human interaction, the
computer worlds will have some aspects of the finite province that enables communication, the world of everyday life. But computer worlds
have other characteristics as well. To better understand the place of computer worlds in the life-world, we need to take a closer look at the boundaries of the different finite provinces of meaning and the ways humans
organize their lives within these provinces.

Schutz argues that we cannot shift the accent of reality from one
province of meaning to another without having a shock experience.[12]
Schutz uses the term "shock experience" in a specific way: shock experiences are as numerous as there are different provinces of meaning,
and they befall us frequently during our daily lives. Schutz gives some
examples, including falling asleep, waking from a vivid dream, going to
the theater and seeing the world transformed as the curtain rises, and
especially humor, as we accept the foolish ways of the joke as reality
and thus experience the comic, or the imaginary world when suddenly
a simple cardboard box becomes a child's time machine or a spaceship.
A prime example for Schutz is religion – for instance, Kierkegaard's experience of the "instant" as the leap into the religious sphere. Another
example of such shock is the decision of the scientist to replace all pas-
sionate participation in the affairs of "this world [with] a disinterested
contemplative attitude."[13]

The shock experience, however, is not something that befalls us
when we enter certain domains of our life-world, which have a special
place or time attached to them, but something ordinary, which befalls
us frequently during the course of our daily lives. Sometimes the shock

experience does not even take us from one province of the life-world to another but rather mixes provinces of meaning. Schutz states that some provinces of the life-world can be bridged by our actions, implying that there are areas of the life-world, "enclaves," that belong "to one province of meaning enclosed by another."[14]

COMPUTER WORLDS IN THE LIFE-WORLD

There is one fundamental fact concerning the status of computer worlds in the life-world that arises from Schutz's thoughts on the structure of the life-world: the world of working in daily life remains the paramount reality. It is not possible to live in computer worlds alone. Sherry Turkle in *Life on the Screen* quotes a user who describes real life as just one more window among others, and not usually his best one.[15] This of course does not fit with Schutz's theory of the life-world. Real life, according to Schutz, is the world of working in daily life. If, for the sake of the argument, we uphold Turkle's windows metaphor, according to Schutz real life would be the desktop and all the other worlds just windows on it. I can shift my attention to computer worlds, the worlds of dreams and phantasms, and in a sense *be* in them, but my body will always stay in the world of working in daily life. But even if the body is not necessarily engaged in conquering the worlds of dreams, daydreams, fantasies, media, and scientific theorizing, it does get involved in the world of play and the computer worlds. The worlds of play and the computer worlds are interactive worlds. They react to our working and performing in them. The computer worlds combine quite a few aspects of the world of working in daily life with the worlds of phantasms and playing. They seem to be not a finite province of meaning of their own, but rather an enclave of the world of working in the world of phantasms and playing.

COMPUTER GAMES AS VIRTUAL SPACES WITH BODIES

The enclave-like character of computer worlds becomes even clearer when we look at the part our body plays while interacting with them. The interesting point concerning virtual space is the idea that it seems to have no regard for the body. The virtual space seems bodiless. This idea, popular as it may be, can be challenged from a sociophenomenological perspective. Indeed, it can be shown that the virtual world relies far more on bodily interactions than do other media, such as film or print.

One could thus argue that using the computer is hardly virtual at all. The virtual space itself is only understandable from a bodily perspective since communication in it underlies the general thesis of the alter ego. The "general thesis of the alter ego" is Schutz's assumption that the other, another individual, has to be equal to the self for communication and sociality to be possible. This means that humans are principally able to understand each other by trying to take the other's perspective, while differences in world views stem from different individual perspectives. Communication therefore can be the means to try and annihilate the differences between two people. Schutz's general thesis of the alter ego even states that under ideal circumstances points of view can be made interchangeable and systems of relevance can be made overlapping so that the different perspectives of two individuals can be theoretically one. Schutz calls this the "thesis of the reciprocity of perspectives." Both theses state that I understand others as "like me." This means that my perception of a social interaction is grounded in my understanding of myself as the center of my universe. I can only grasp the Other as another representation of myself and understand his or her intentions from projections of my own intentions and perspectives on the world. This idea has consequences for trying to understand the nature of computer worlds. If all communications are predetermined by my understanding of the communication partner, human-computer interactions will be shaped by the same process. In the theory of Alfred Schutz, the human-computer interaction is firmly in the world of working in daily life.

The experience of bodies enables virtual worlds to be understood as other human beings, as the Other whom I can understand through a reciprocity of perspectives. Since communication in Schutz's theory relies on the world of working in daily life and within it on bodily modifications of that same world, communication with a machine can be understood as relying on bodily interactions more so than do other media. In this sense, reading a book is a lot further away from the paramount reality than surfing the internet. This places at least part of the experi-

ence of computer worlds firmly within the realm of the paramount reality and is a strong argument for their enclave-like character.

ALMOST MYSTICALLY SCREENING THE WORLD OF WORK

Both gaming and religion have an almost mystical quality. Their time
experience is distinct from the experience of social time. Even virtually modified social interaction is drawn into *durée*, the time perspective of the inner self. This almost mystical quality occurs because when
entering computer worlds, the user usually sits in front of a computer
screen or a video game. Even if he uses his mobile phone, he will still be
fixated on a tiny screen. The screen is the mediator between the worlds
"inside" the computer and the world of everyday life. The screen as a
mediator also has the function of a filter between worlds. Not everything
that happens in one world is transferred into the other world. Keystrokes
and other haptic work have direct impacts on the world "behind" the
screen. Optical feedback gives the world behind the screen "reality" in
daily life. My working on the keyboard changes the world behind the
screen and with it the output on the screen – reverberating back into
the world of daily life. I do not see, however, the bits changing in the
memory chips of my computer. My only feedback is a visual representation through the screen, filtered from many of the other channels of perception I would normally employ in daily life. Death in a virtual world,
for example, does not smell. A virtual encounter with a loved one has no
physical contact. The screen and other devices filter several possibilities
of perception from the computer user. Still, the interaction with the virtual world via the computer interface is in general terms bodily. There
are some fundamental differences from the world of working in daily
life, however.

   The *epoché*, in which we suspend judgment about the actuality of
daily life, is no longer valid once we are in front of the computer screen.
Everything is possible in computer worlds; this assumption is not in itself illogical, and it might even be acceptable in the appropriate setting.
The epoché of the computer worlds is like that of the world of phantasms.[16] The situation in front of the screen is the specific shock experience that lets the user leap into the computer world, and the shock expe-

rience manifests when the border between closed provinces of meaning is breached. Some of the characteristics of the world change when looked at from a different province of meaning. The world might seem less real; we might feel untethered, insecure. For computer worlds, this shock, the leap between worlds, happens in front of the screen of my machine. Everything I perceive now is to be treated differently than in the world of working in daily life. There are similarities in perception, but also huge differences.

Unlike other shock experiences Schutz mentions, the specific situation when approaching computer worlds still places some responsibility on the body. Computer worlds are interactive worlds. The prevalent form of spontaneity in computer worlds is still somewhat similar to working in the world of daily life. It is not pure "working," because in contrast to Schutz's idea that working in the outer world is irrevocable and as such distinguished from performing, for computer worlds, the "working" – the bodily movements – is merely a vehicle for a specific form of performance, which happens on the screen. When my fingers work on the keyboard, they bring about this text, which has not changed the world of working in everyday life but rather the computer world, the enclave of theorizing in the world of working. This working *is* revocable; it does not even need sophisticated countermoves to undo it. (In my word processor, pressing CTRL-Z will do.) We still seem to need a body, however, since the body is a vehicle for the real action (not in the Schutzean sense), which happens in the computer world. While I only move part of my body to manipulate the computer controls, different actions take place in the computer world as a result. This is even more profound in the various gaming environments in computer worlds.[17]

But still, there will be differences between the epoché of the various worlds of phantasms. A play world that heavily relies on bodily objects from the world of working in daily life will not entirely question the validity of these objects, even if they have slightly different meanings in a specific play world. The computer and its screen are such objects, since they are produced in the world of working in daily life. When compared to the worlds of play, one could argue that, similar to a toy, the computer itself provides a connection from computer worlds to the world of working in daily life. Thus the *epoché* of computer worlds will still rely on the world of working in daily life, even when it brackets several aspects of everyday life. The importance of working as the means by which computer worlds can be discovered is what makes them interactive. Although the working of the computer controls gains a performance aspect in the computer worlds, the conquering and changing of the world remain. As in the reality of working in daily life, I change the world through my actions. I interact with computer worlds. The difference from mere fantasy is that the user of computer worlds wants to see his actions fulfilled. Therefore computer worlds have a much more pressing intention of realizing the actions one wishes to perform in them, and in this aspect, they resemble the world of scientific theorizing much more closely than they do the world of phantasms.

The "specific tension of consciousness" in the world of daily life, according to Schutz, is "wide-awakeness," originating in one's full attention to life. Although life gets a certain secondhand quality when it is happening beyond the boundaries of our body and is only experienced by our sense of sight and restricted to manipulating the computer controls, the specific tension of consciousness of computer worlds is still wide-awakeness, only in this case originating in full attention to a combination of actions in the computer worlds (my virtual life) and my working on the computer controls (my real life). This action-oriented characteristic of my being in computer worlds is the cause of the full attention to life in them that defines my tension of consciousness.

A PLAYFUL WORLD: HUMOR, HUMILITY, AND RELIGION

The playful world of humor is closely aligned with religion and games. The sociologist of religion Peter Berger, basing his thoughts on Schutz's theory of the life-world, has given a compelling account of the connection between playfulness, religion, and humor that can help us understand the connection between computer worlds and religion even better. The experiential similarities between humor and faith can help us understand the relationship between computer worlds, real life, and religion. Humor threatens the social order of our reality and at the same time (or by the same means) enables us to transcend the pragmatic motives of working in everyday life and leap into other realms. The world of working in daily life loses its paramount character for the period of time that a joke is funny. Humor forces us to concentrate on the essence of an issue and to make sure we analyze every possible meaning of what is said (maybe even in advance). Humor as communication imposes outside perspectives on problems and provides ways to gain new insights and show the relativity of the problems at hand.

Both the religious experience and the comic relieve us from the tension and the fundamental anxiety of the paramount reality. They enable us to look at our problems and ourselves from a perspective well outside this world. Relying on Schutz's analysis of Don Quixote, Berger points out that the act of faith brings about a shift in the accent of reality.[18] As we leap between different the provinces of meaning of the life-world every day, the paramount reality stays the same. Berger argues that what he calls the "epistemological reversal" is such a strong shift in the accent of reality that consequently the act of faith, which brings this reversal about, replaces the paramount reality of the life-world permanently.

In Schutzean terms, every leap temporarily shifts our accent of reality from the paramount reality to the province of meaning we are currently in. Berger's idea is that the act of faith is strong enough to make this shift permanent. An example of this is the person who has just had a religious revelation. Everything she has based her life on is now changed forever. She takes a completely different stance on life, because she has just experienced a different reality than before. That means that a religious person grounds his or her life-world not in the paramount reality of the world of working in daily life, with its pragmatic motives, but in the province of religion, with its different characteristics than the world of working in daily life. As Berger notes: "The paramount reality of everyday life is relativized; conversely, the specific finite province of meaning to which faith pertains is absolutized. Needless to say, it is finite only in the perspective of the paramount reality. As the epistemological reversal occurs, it is, on the contrary, the threshold of infinity; conversely, the empirical world, far from being paramount, is disclosed as being very finite indeed."[19]

The epistemological reversal means nothing less than turning one's world view upside down. What was before the safe ground upon which one's life rested is now just another province of meaning, although not the paramount reality of the world of working in daily life. This makes the religious person's world view vastly different from that of the nonreligious.

But computer worlds usually do not allow this kind of revelation. Their nature is similar but still different from an epistemological reversal. Just as in humor, the leap into computer worlds is not as consequential as the epistemological reversal. While laughing about a good joke enables us to leap between provinces of meaning temporarily, religion makes this leap permanent. A person who changes his or her life permanently for religious reasons is different from a person who suddenly understands a joke and sees the humorous side of a cartoon for just the duration of the laugh. While the religious leap is by Berger's definition life changing, the leap of comedy is short-lived.

Like religion, the comic can provide us with a sense of epistemological humility. Berger argues that humor can give a brief insight into what religion or the religious attitude describes as the other world, the transcendent world. While humor is fleeting, temporary in nature, religion in the full, proper sense of the word gives the impression of a world changed permanently. One could argue that humor is a weak example of the epistemological reversal that defines religious faith in Berger's theory. Berger talks about the redeeming quality of laughter, which he sees as the weak equivalent of experiencing transcendence in its religious meaning. There is no direct route from humor to religious experience; they are only connected by their structure: "There is a secular and a religious mode of comic experience, and the passage from one to the other requires an act of faith."[20]

The relation between gaming and religion is similar to the secular mode of comic experience. Through gaming, one can taste the nature of the religious experience; it is even reality shifting for a moment, but it is not as consequential as the act of faith. Computer worlds thus allow the player to experience this shift in reality without the consequences that a leap of faith has for the true believer. The act of faith is what distinguishes the religious sphere from the secular. In virtual worlds, one can encounter various models of religion and various systems of faith. Computer games, such as those from the *Star Wars* universe, can confront the player with certain moral or even religious choices. The player can act within the game in accordance with the religious or moral code or against it. The consequences, however, are restricted to the gaming experience. Only if the game experience is strong enough to bring about a leap of faith will the religious code of the game become life changing. But playing in computer worlds usually gives the player just a hint of what the leap of faith would be like, without actually taking it. Thus humor and the use of computer worlds as tools for gaining knowledge can provide us with a certain epistemological humility, that is the ability to look at different systems of faith and play with them, recognize their ultimate value for their followers, and, depending on the way we deal with computer worlds, simulate what it would be like to take this system for granted.

Such epistemological humility is what makes religion in computer games more than just a joke. As computer worlds bring phantasms and daily life closer together, they demand a specific way of dealing with them in a scholarly and educational context. Play and games have always been the bridge between phantasms and reality. I therefore suggest using a phenomenologically inspired idea of playfulness as the bridge between different provinces of meaning and the paramount reality of the life-world. Michael Kolb has shown that play, in a phenomenological sense and in phenomenologically oriented play theories, is the construction of identity-defining spheres in our life-world.[21] Play is a flexible, subjectively constructible relationship between human beings and the world, between inner fantasies and outer reality.[22] Computer worlds are such a relationship. They help us to realize ourselves as a totality in our working acts while at the same time we perform through them in computer worlds.[23]

The analysis of computer worlds as enclaves, according to Schutz's theory, implies that there always is an aspect of self-construction and individual learning to these worlds. When working and performing are combined as means of conquering a world, the reflective attitude comes naturally. The mode in which we interact with computer worlds can be seen as a stop-and-go motion between performing in the computer worlds and working on the computer controls. This bipolar mode of access already incorporates the reflective attitude, which is vital for learning and gaining knowledge.

A computer game like *Star Wars: Knights of the Old Republic* (Lucas-Arts, 2003), for instance, lets the player deal with the religious codes and symbols of the Jedi order. Certain rules apply to Jedi behavior, which define their nature as "good" or "bad." The game offers challenging situations that force the player to choose between different courses of action. Killing innocent bystanders forces the player toward the Dark Side, while protecting the innocent and sometimes even the bad guys themselves turns the player's path toward the light. The game gives the player the possibility to choose over and over again and thus experience the consequences of his actions without really permanently changing the course of his life. A different example is the game *Fallout 3* (Bethesda Softworks, 2008), where a side quest confronts the player with the choice of disarming or detonating a nuclear bomb in an inhabited area. The choice the player makes changes the gaming experience, but has no direct consequences for the player's life-world. Still, it represents the moral choices that play a huge role in one's behavior in the world of working in daily life.

The specific advantage of computer worlds is this unique bond between daily life and playful fantasizing. If computer worlds are to be understood as a medium with religious connections, their interactive side is probably the most important. Computer worlds are a type of proving ground for religious ideas, an interactive playground in which to explore religion, morals, and ethics. If we take the interactive nature of computer worlds seriously and accept their playful nature, religion is even more at stake in computer worlds than in other provinces of the life-world. There is one aspect to the relation between religion and computer worlds, however, that takes away a bit of the pressure of the transformative aspects of computer worlds. On one hand, while they threaten religious tradition due to their experimental nature, on the other hand their structure enables us to understand their playfulness as only temporary and thus largely non-life-threatening to religious tradition. Even if the player chooses to act against religious dogma within the game, the distinction between the paramount reality and the computer world saves religious tradition from the consequences of the player's actions. This can be seen in the original example of Manchester Cathedral.

CONCLUSION: COMPUTER RELIGIOUS WORLDS
AS PLAYFUL ENCLAVES IN THE LIFE-WORLD

A phenomenological description of computer worlds following Schutz's phenomenological theory shows their enclave-like character: connecting the world of working in daily life with the world of play and other worlds of phantasms, including religion. Computer worlds are not a single province of meaning. They combine different characteristics of different provinces of meaning in a single enclave. One could even argue that from the player's perspective computer worlds are superior to reality in some respects. The example of Manchester Cathedral in the game *Resistance: Fall of Man* makes this clear. For players, the cathedral was more "real" in its virtual representation than in the actual building in Manchester, because the game allowed the players to work in it in the Schutzean sense and thus make it part of their life-world. The building in Manchester had no reality for most of the players. The virtual representation, however, was part of their life-world.

The question we now need to ask is: Does the cathedral retain its religious character despite the discrepancy between the working in the virtual building and the working in the real building? Can the theoretical thoughts from this chapter give a deeper insight into the relation between real and virtual worlds in the example of Manchester Cathedral? Like humor, this playing with the seemingly impossible – firing a gun in church at an alien invader – enables users to approach all their preconceptions about the religious from a different angle. Also, like a religious joke, playing with religion may offend. The lawsuit by the Church of England has helped save the religious character of the cathedral by emphasizing the difference between reality and virtuality. Firing guns in a cathedral in reality is against all the Church of England stands for. This makes up the religious character of the actual building in large part and thus gives the virtual representation character as well. The discrepancy between the game use and the real-life use of the cathedral emphasizes the distinction. The debate about the game combined with the rising number of visitors to the cathedral, however, shows that the players gained new insight into the possibly religious character of a building they had never seen in reality before.

As this chapter has shown, computer worlds differ from other forms of fantasy because they let one work in the Schutzean sense in them. That is the main difference between phantasms and the world of working in daily life. Computer worlds make those differences crumble. Although computer worlds tend to have the same time perspective as the worlds of phantasms, because of their prevalent form of play they connect the time perspectives of different provinces of meaning. They therefore represent a bridge between different provinces of meaning and as such gain specific potential to be of use in an individual's construction of their spheres of meaning. It is commonly feared that the use of computer technology will rob humans of their sense of the real world, pull up the roots they have in reality, and transport them to virtuality. The thoughts in this chapter on the analogy to humor and the analysis of the interface situation might help prevent that from happening and might even extinguish the fear it could happen. Being able to look at myself, my situation, and the different worlds of the life-world around me from the perspective of humor, I will be able to group these experiences, reflect on them, and sort them. Humor is a facilitator for these actions because it has the power to take us outside the current focus of our life-world.

Combining their modes of grasping knowledge and reflecting it, religion in games becomes a powerful tool chest for gaining insight about the world. No matter which finite province of meaning we are concentrating on at the moment, humor can take us away from that focal point, if only for a short time. This gives us a certain sense of epistemological humility that puts all our experiences in perspective, especially with regard to other provinces of meaning. Thus the experience of our life-world gets clearer and more organized. Virtuality then can be understood not as a total and ultimately demanding reality, as is widely feared, but rather as a mode of leaping between worlds, as an analogue to humor.

In computer games, you can play god and reflect on your morals as a deity; you can fight evil with evil or with good, thus challenging your understanding of religiously motivated ethics; or you can interact with other human players and incorporate and transform religious rituals into a virtually acceptable new form. Computer worlds are a playground for playing with content from different provinces of the life-world, even though religion is not just like other content because of its relation with the life-world. There is a fundamental difference between the leap of faith and the reflective attitude of the enclave of computer worlds.

NOTES

1. BBC News, "Cathedral Row over Video War Game."

2. PS3News, "Church of England Sues Sony over *Resistance: Fall of Man*"; see also BBC News, "Cathedral Row over Video War Game."

3. Richardson, "*Resistance* Fracas a Blessing for Church."

4. Schutz, *On Multiple Realities.*

5. Ibid., 208.

6. Ibid., 232.

7. Ibid.

8. With William James, Schutz argues that there are different sub-universes that make up the life-world. However, Schutz decides to speak of "finite provinces of meaning" to free the concept from its ontological character. Schutz understands the life-world as a social construction based on our experiences, not on any inherent characteristics. Schutz, *On Multiple Realities*, 230.

9. "Sie ist der Bereich, in dem wir handeln und handelnd die Wirklichkeit verändern" (It is the province in which we act and while acting change reality). Knoblauch, "Transzendenzerfahrung und Symbolische Kommunikation," 158.

10. Ibid., 159; Schutz, *On Multiple Realities*, 234.

11. Schutz, *On Multiple Realities*, 231.

12. Knoblauch, "Transzendenzerfahrung und Symbolische

Kommunikation," 159; Schutz, *On Multiple Realities*, 231.

13. Schutz, *On Multiple Realities*, 231.

14. Ibid.

15. Turkle, *Life on the Screen*, 13.

16. Even if one is interacting with, say, an ATM, there is still a certain amount of fantasy involved. Although ATMs are much closer to the world of daily life than is a science fiction computer game, what they are doing still happens in a virtual space. ATMs transform the fruit of one's working in the world of daily life, which has been transferred into the computer world, back into the bodily world. The successful outcome of one's interaction with an ATM lies in the bodily world. The interaction itself happens through bodily working, through the interface situation, in the virtual reality of the computer world. And this we can only grasp in the enclave of the theoretical attitude, which in a way is close to the world of phantasms.

17. Fritz, *Warum Computerspiele faszinieren*; Fritz and Fehr, *Handbuch Medien*, 207–215.

18. Berger, *Redeeming Laughter*, 205.

19. Ibid.

20. Ibid.

21. Kolb, *Spiel als Phänomen*.

22. Ibid., 377.

23. Schutz, *On Multiple Realities*, 212.

REFERENCES

BBC News. "Cathedral Row over Video
    War Game." http://news.bbc.co.uk/2
    /hi/uk_news/england/manchester
    /6736809.stm (accessed September 4,
    2012).
Berger, Peter L. *Redeeming Laughter:
    The Comic Dimension of Human Expe-
    rience.* New York: de Gruyter, 1997.
Fritz, Jürgen. *Warum Computerspiele
    faszinieren.* Weinheim, Germany:
    Juventa, 1995.
Fritz, Jürgen, and Fehr, Wolfgang, eds.
    *Handbuch Medien: Computerspiele,
    Theorie, Forschung, Praxis.* Bonn, Ger-
    many: Bundeszentrale für Politische
    Bildung, 1997.
Knoblauch, Hubert. "Transzendenzer-
    fahrung und Symbolische Kommu-
    nikation." In *Die Phänomenologisch
    Orientierte Soziologie und die Kom-
    munikative Konstruktion der Religion.*
    Edited by Hartmann Tyrell et al.,
    147–186. Würzburg: Ergon, 1998.

Kolb, Michael. *Spiel als Phänomen – Das
    Phänomen Spiel: Studien zu Phänome-
    nologisch-anthropologischen Spiel-
    theorien.* Sankt Augustin, Germany:
    Academia, 1990.
PS3News. "Church of England Sues
    Sony over *Resistance: Fall of Man.*"
    http://www.computerandvideo
    games.com/165667/church-of
    -england-sues-sony-over-resistance
    -fall-of-man (accessed September 4,
    2012).
Richardson, Ben. "*Resistance* Fracas a
    Blessing for Church." http://www
    .gamesradar.com/resistance-fracas
    -a-blessing-for-church (accessed Sep-
    tember 4, 2012).
Schutz, Alfred. *On Multiple Realities.*
    Edited by Maurice Natanson. The
    Hague: Martinus Nijhoff, 1962.
Turkle, Sherry. *Life on the Screen: Identity
    in the Age of the Internet.* New York:
    Simon and Schuster, 1995.

TWELVE

They Kill Mystery

THE MECHANISTIC BIAS OF VIDEO GAME
REPRESENTATIONS OF RELIGION AND SPIRITUALITY

Kevin Schut

THE VIDEO GAME MEDIUM IS IDEALLY SUITED TO REPRESENT one aspect of religion: the experience of being a god. Game after game gifts players with supernatural powers. *From Dust* (Ubisoft, 2011) has players take the role of a Polynesian deity that protects The People mostly via reshaping entire islands. The title character of *Bayonetta* (Platinum Games, 2009) is a witch who can take on and destroy the forces of heaven. *The Sims* (Maxis, 2000) series of games goes small-scale and gives players the power of a local deity to micro-manage practically all aspects of an individual's life. But such power fantasies, in the end, represent a rather limited engagement with religion. Imagining what it is like to be a god is an interesting thought experiment, but it does not really get to the heart of the meaning and practice of religion – at least from the perspective of religious adherents. Finding games that really deal with the internal experience of faith and its sociocultural impact is somewhat more difficult, but such games *do* exist. Historical simulations examine the role of religion in the building of empires, and narrative games engage religion on a wide range of levels. Books like Detweiler's *Halos and Avatars* and Wagner's *Godwired: Religion, Ritual and Virtual Reality* indicate that scholars are also starting to note the religious implications of both mainstream, big-budget video games and the smaller set of clearly religious games.

Despite this scholarship and the growing diversity of video games dealing with religion, however, certain patterns are common. This may be due to the relative adolescence of the medium: film took quite a few decades to mature as a tool for art and expression. This chapter, however, argues that the construction of the medium itself has an impact on the manner in which games handle religion, although that impact is not insurmountable. Specifically, the argument here is that the systematic nature of game rules and computer programming bias the video game medium toward a mechanical, demystified representation of religion. At the same time, other factors, such as the ability of video games to weave narratives, to invoke non-game texts and themes, and to give a space for emergent play, complicate the video game bias toward mechanized religion.

MACHINE GOD: THE SYSTEMATIC BIAS OF VIDEO GAMES

Harold Innis – along with many subsequent theorists of media ecology – argued that all media have a bias.[1] That is, all media are predisposed toward certain patterns of communication. So what might be the bias of video games? Jesper Juul[2] and many other game scholars note that video games always have a system of rules that govern what can happen when someone starts playing a game. This suggests that video game religions might tend toward a systematic or mechanistic representation of faith, something amply demonstrated by a popular and complex strategy game, *Civilization*.

Case Study: Civilization: Religion as a Strategic Tool

The later versions of Sid Meier's *Civilization* series of games, such as *Civilization IV* (Firaxis, 2005), take a bold and serious look at the role of religion in history. *Civilization* is a turn-based strategy game that allows the player to guide a culture from prehistory through the colonization of space. From a disembodied global perspective, the game simulates a wide range of social phenomena, such as agriculture, art, commerce, and warfare. Players create cities that produce structures and units, research for technology, money for maintenance, and culture for the expansion of territory. Players strategically manage all these factors in order to either gain global dominance or be the first to colonize a planet revolving around Alpha Centauri (later versions also allow for cultural or diplomatic victories).

The earliest iterations of the simulation series only provide a few religious structures like temples to improve the happiness of a culture, or world wonders (super-powered structures, essentially) like the Oracle of Delphi. The first three versions of the game include several historical religious developments as researchable technologies, such as monotheism. That, however, is the extent of explicit religion in the game. But the fourth version of the game makes religion a significant part of gameplay, allowing players to research and found one of seven major historical faiths: Hinduism, Buddhism, Confucianism, Taoism, Judaism, Islam, and Christianity. The producers of *Civilization V* (Firaxis, 2010) removed these major world religions, but reintroduced them in the *Gods and Kings* (Firaxis, 2012) expansion, and added Shintoism, Sikhism, Tengriism, and Zoroastrianism.

The experience of religion in the 2012 version of the *Civilization* series is quite complex. Players can construct religious buildings in their cities that generate "faith points," which the civilization accumulates. The player can spend these points several different ways. Early in the game, the primitive civilization has no formal religion, but with enough points, it can select a "pantheon belief," which the game documentation describes as "an early approach to Religion" that is "the first step towards founding a full Religion." In *Civilization IV*, all the religions have exactly the same characteristics in the gameplay, but in the *Gods and Kings* expansion, players have a long list of pantheon beliefs to choose from, each providing benefits to the civilization. For example, the "desert folklore" belief provides one extra faith point for every desert tile a city uses; the "goddess of love" gives an extra happiness point to the civilization for every city with a population of six or more. Players can also spend faith points on generating the "great prophets" necessary for founding a full religion that, when unlocked, provides access to another menu of religious benefits, regardless of which historical faith players choose. For example, the "founder belief" called "interfaith dialogue" gives the players technology research points every time a missionary converts another city to the specified religion. The player can also use faith points to purchase these proselytizing missionary units and inquisitor units that eliminate foreign religions. Finally, the player can also use faith points to purchase religious buildings, such as pagodas or cathedrals, each of which has unique civilization benefits. To sum it up, these games present religion as a strategic tool.

Theory: Video Game Systems

As simulations of religion go, this is pretty complex. The preceding description doesn't actually do the game justice; religion is only *part* of the overall game and interacts with all the other factors. To choose one small example: faith points come from buildings that are constructed with resources generated by workers in cities that require economic support from trade and adequate food supplies grown on farms, whose productivity is determined partly by the natural fertility of the land and partly by agricultural upgrades. I mentioned none of this above. Yet for all the game's complexity and the boldness of its social modeling, it should be apparent that this is an incomplete representation of religion.

Outside of a simulation, it is truly impossible to quantify spiritual fervor or religious devotion, even on a macro scale. Disentangling faith motivations from economic, political, relational, or aesthetic factors is also nearly impossible to do. Likewise, even if we *could* count such a thing as faith points, they certainly could not be channeled into predictable achievements or products. And even if we grant the fantasy of the player being able to shape a culture à la carte, the variable social effects of religions are not historically stable things, because religions change in different contexts. In terms of their cultural implications, Pauline Mediterranean Christianity was not the same as the high medieval scholastic Christianity of Northern Europe nor the modern Korean Presbyterian Christianity.

Anyone who works in game design is aware that all simulations are simplifications of the real thing, as Frasca notes: "all simulations are constrained, limited approaches to (real or fictional) systems."[3] If a game truly approached the complexity of real life, it would no longer be a game! But what is important to note here is the *kind* of simplification the gamer experience. Novels also simplify the experience of reality – even the most complex literature leaves out a lot of life – but not in the same way as video games do.

The key thing I want to highlight here is the systematic nature of both the game form and the computer medium that houses the video game. To start, games are, at the very least, systems of rules and defined elements.[4] The pieces of a game, whether they are little counters that move around the Monopoly board or the racing vehicles of *Mario Kart Wii* (Nintendo, 2008), cannot be ambiguous objects for a game to function. Players must know what things are and what is possible with those things. And what a player can do with a game element is governed by the game's rules. The little pewter top hat must move in a clockwise fashion around the board the number of spaces determined by the roll of the dice, and Princess Peach slows down when the player presses the B button. In short, a game functions like a machine: various parts are arranged like cogs and gears that impact one another based on input from the user. This is not to say that all game elements have a clear function: the artwork on a board often does not directly impact the gameplay, but clearly it is part of the game, and often an important part, creating a particular mood or providing motivation for play (more on this below). But the point is that such elements are, in a sense, purely decorative and not necessary for a game to be a game.

The systematic nature of the game form is further reinforced in video games by the computer itself. It is possible with a board game to modify rules on the fly: halfway through a game, players might discover something in the rulebook that they were not aware of, and they can improvise a method to deal with this discrepancy. In contrast, it is possible for a program to have mistakes in its crafting, but when the computer uses those lines of code, the program will most likely crash. Whether a computer program is a game or not, its code must be fully systematic, completely defined by rules, and its object cannot be ambiguous at all. Computers do not truly improvise.

Rules are, of course, hardly limited to games. As Rachel Wagner points out in *Godwired*, religious rituals are themselves constituted by rules, which might suggest that the rule-bound nature of games and programming is hardly antithetical to religion. This is an important point, but there are still significant differences between a rule-bound ritual and a rule-bound video game. For one thing, if an adherent breaks a rule of a ritual, it complicates the experience (often, but not always, in negative ways), but if a player breaks a rule, the game ceases to function properly. More important, all the different rules of a video game must work together in a complete system; the relationships between all the rules must be airtight, perfect. Most video games have bugs or design flaws that players can exploit, but even with those imperfections game systems are far simpler and more coherent than any religion. In *Civilization*, the connection between a battle of two units and a civilization's faith points may be a bit convoluted, but it can, in the end, be precisely mapped. The connection between the rosary and the mass, on the other hand, is far less neat: it's not that there's no connection, but rather that there is a potentially limitless number of connections, and they don't interact in a simple cause-and-effect manner. The rules of religion are more organic and less mechanical than the rules of a video game. In other words, religious guidelines and instructions are fully social: they allow for reinterpretation, they can be negotiated, and they allow for mystery and the unknowable.

Regardless of the subject addressed, a video game is likely to systematize it in some way, to use a kind of mechanized representation. Both the game form and the nature of computer programs push in that direction. The effects of this bias on game representations of religion are pronounced and show up in a number of different ways.

MANIFESTATIONS OF SYSTEMS

A great many video games that feature or represent religion in some way tend to have a kind of mechanical theology that sees gods as technologies to be manipulated for power. Complex as they are, the *Civilization* games reduce religion to a matter of predictable social and cultural effects. A shrine produces one faith point per turn, and a temple produces two. Great prophets found religions and convert cities. Fertility cults lead to better agriculture. The effects and uses of religion are tightly restricted, as they would be in a machine. Games that map the inner workings of the divine also tend to show formulaic deities. The most common manifestation of this is that the power of a deity is directly related to the number of worshipers that he or she or it has. The *Dungeons and Dragons* world of Forgotten Realms has a pantheon based on this premise, as do the classic Peter Molyneux titles in the *Populous* (Bullfrog, 1989) series.

Perhaps the most mechanical theological concept of games is the quantification of faith or religious action. In the evangelical real-time strategy game *Left Behind: Eternal Forces* (Inspired Media Entertain-

ment, 2006), for example, each person in the game has a spirit value
between zero and one hundred that indicates his or her spiritual health:
high values are Christian, low values are anti-Christian, and the rest are
neutral. *Civilization*'s faith points are another manifestation of the same
thing. As Dante battles the minions of hell in *Dante's Inferno* (Electronic
Arts, 2010), he earns redemption points, which fill a meter that give combat boosts when it is full.

The common thread that runs through all of this is an inorganic,
rigid theology. Even the most systematic of theologies typically has
room for grace, for mystery, for divine unpredictability. Very few theologians really claim to have figured everything out about their god. There
is no denying, of course, that religion has social, political, and economic
effects. There is also no shortage of theologies that draw clear and simple
lines between human action and divine action: plenty of prophets attach
divine favor or punishment to certain actions by adherents. However,
many – perhaps most – religions do not have such neat formulations.
Even prophetic calls for repentance may not guarantee divine mercy.
"Who knows?," says the Jewish prophet Joel after calling his people to
repentance, "[God] *may* turn and relent and leave behind a blessing."[5]
There are plenty of theological insights that are far more complex; Augustine's *City of God,* to take one classic example, argues that the city
of God and the city of the world are tremendously hard to disentangle
in this life.

Video game religions frequently not only imply mechanistic theologies, but they function as or provide supernatural technologies. Flip
the right switches, and religion becomes a power tool. In some games,
religion can function as a form of mind control, as in *Age of Empires* (Ensemble, 1997), where priests can convert enemy units. In other games,
such as the Caribbean dictatorship simulation *Tropico* (PopTop, 2001)
and its sequels, religion functions as Marx's "opiate of the masses," keep-
ing a population from becoming dangerously unhappy.

Far more commonly, religions – or, more precisely, deities – are supernatural power generators. In some games, this can be a creative, constructive force: in *From Dust,* the animistic Breath can shape the earth
of a Polynesian island in order to protect and grow nascent tribes of set-
tlers. This kind of positive god-like power is not unusual, but far more

common is destructive, weaponized divine force. Gods or their servants can unleash fireballs, create or destroy the undead, freeze their foes, and manipulate the forces of nature, to name just a few of the many war-like powers employed in a myriad of games, such as *Age of Mythology* (Ensemble, 2002) or any dungeons-and-dragons game.

Magic, a quasi-divine or religious element in countless games, is typically as well defined as the technical specs of any machine that runs games. Fantasy genre games typically have long lists of spells with a wide range of effects. But it is normal for the description of spells to be filled not with arcane concepts or language, but rather with lists of numbers giving precise parameters for the effect of the magic, such as its duration, the area of its effects, the possible range of points of damage or healing, the casting time, and so on.

Technology is a tool that, if properly handled, can augment human capabilities.[6] Throughout the centuries, many people have tried to turn their religions into just such a thing: devotees try to use sacrifices or divination or deals with the gods to get a desired effect. But few religious systems teach that the divine is a force to be easily and predictably manipulated with the appropriate actions. Yet this is precisely how the supernatural functions in many video games. Magic or the gods or spirits, all those mysterious forces, have been reduced to a fancy type of gun or an extra-strong bandage.

Finally, video games tend to turn religions into simple markers of faction. Melodramas need heroes and villains, and so do most video games. The stark contrast between protagonist and antagonist makes for strong conflict, which facilitates engaging play. Religion provides excellent justification for just such white hat versus black hat clashes. The plot of Electronic Arts' highly unfaithful adaptation of *Dante's Inferno* is typical: the player controls the crusader warrior Dante as he seeks salvation by battling the hordes of demons while descending the circles of hell. The forces of Satan feature in countless other games too, battling either the righteous forces of good or flawed-but-ultimately-good characters.

The cosmetic differences in games between angels and demons, or Christians and Muslims, or followers of the fictional Tyr and Tiamat, however, mask a remarkable similarity. In order to keep gameplay balanced, video game factions must be roughly equal. They also usually will have similar win conditions. In other words, both heaven and hell must have similar strength, and both must seek to kill and conquer the other in most video games. Similar strength can manifest as exactly the same unit with different decorations – minions of light and darkness both have the same attack value, defense value, and so on. But it also might mean that the overall force of one side balances the other side. In the *Heroes of Might and Magic* series (e.g., *Might and Magic: Heroes VI* [Black Hole Entertainment, 2011]), angels and demons do not have exactly the same statistics, but their overall factions have different strengths and weaknesses that tend to compensate for each other, meaning that they're about equally powerful if handled the right way. In other words, while the angels look holy and the devils infernal, they do about the same thing. Religion, in these games, functions as a badge, a sports jersey, an army uniform.

Again, there is something legitimate about such models. Religion is often a motivator of struggle and conflict; it can separate people into antagonistic functions. But most devout practitioners of a faith would argue that their devotion springs from much more than that their god gives them a fan club to join; meaningful religious practice takes right and wrong or the sacred and the profane more seriously than just as a decorative marker of which team someone belongs to. Different religions are not always antagonistic either, as the long and complex history of the relationship between Judaism, Christianity, and Islam illustrates. And it is ridiculously reductionist to argue that all religions are, at base, essentially the same thing.

THE DEATH OF FREE RELIGION

The upshot of all this is that video games have a bias toward creating and modeling mechanically restricted religions. The overly systematic religions noted above do two major things. First, they kill mystery. That is, a video game cannot tolerate that which is unknowable because it is greater than human comprehension. The story of the prophet Elijah and the fire from heaven[7] is very dramatic and leaves a great deal unexplained: the reader knows Yahweh is responsible for a miracle, but does not really understand how that miracle came to pass. A video game version of that event would likely either use it as a non-interactive cutscene (a mini-movie, in essence) or would precisely quantify the damage done by the flames from heaven and offer a clear trigger (perhaps the right number of prayer points?). A great deal of religious narrative and theology emphasizes the uncontrollable, unpredictable, and incomprehensible nature of the divine. This is directly at odds with the video game's need to clearly define and govern all its working elements – and whatever cannot work that way becomes decoration.

Second, mechanistic video game religions focus almost entirely on the *functions* of religions: the effects they have and the machinery that leads to those effects. Again, it is impossible to deny that religions have effects. They are fully cultural phenomena and impact the way people handle politics, economics, agriculture, art, and much more. But many religious adherents believe that their faith means much more than just its sociological impact. The internal and collective experience of religion can be deeply moving, powerful, emotional, and irrational, going beyond self-interest and the survival instinct. In other words, people who are committed to following a god or some divine principle do not necessarily do so just to serve themselves or to produce some kind of desirable social outcome. The exact nature of belief varies from person to person and from community to community, but it is safe to say that many, if not most, believers do not adopt their religious commitments cynically. And it is possible to argue that any simulation or discussion of religion that assumes that faith is nothing more than a sociological tool for power or survival relies on a kind of religious viewpoint – the idea that there is nothing more than material reality. Perhaps this is too strong, but the vision of religion that video games often adopt is fairly reductionist in nature.

IMAGINATION CAPTURED BY THE MACHINE:
THE POWER OF WORLDS AND NARRATIVES
TO DE-MECHANIZE RELIGION

Given the heavily systematic representation of religion so often on display, it may come as a bit of a surprise to discover that most scholarly analyses of spirituality in video games are bullish on the medium's potential. This scholarship focuses on the aspects of games that are not so machine-like, such as the elaborate stories and complex signs deployed. A close look at one popular role-playing game will illustrate these other dimensions of games.

Case Study: Dragon Age

The role-playing game *Dragon Age: Origins* (BioWare, 2009) has a very different approach to religion than the *Civilization* series; this is not entirely surprising, given the differences of genre. However, the richer narrative of *Dragon Age* suggests how video game representations of religion can be somewhat less mechanistic than the games described above.

Dragon Age is set in the land of Ferelden on the continent of Thedas, with a rather typical fantasy genre assortment of warriors, clerics, cutpurses, rangers, witches, and mages, as well as elves, werewolves, animated dead, demons, and dwarves. The scope and detail of this world is impressive, even compared to the most popular fantasy role-playing games (RPGs). The history of this world, doled out in scattered conversations and books, is intimately tied in with religion, and religion makes prominent and repeated appearances. While the story of the game changes significantly based on the player's choice of character and the decisions made while playing, *Dragon Age* has a relatively consistent narrative arc. Regardless of the backstory, the player becomes a Grey Warden, an ancient order of warriors, spellcasters, and others dedicated to protecting Thedas from a race of corrupted, near-mindless corpses called the Darkspawn.

The peoples of the game have many different faiths. Dwarves, for instance, practice a kind of ancestor worship, while elves have a kind of polytheistic pantheon, and the Witches of the Wilds have an animistic perspective. But the two main religions – the most relevant to the main plot arc – are those of the Old Gods and the Chantry. According to the lore of the game, the world was created by the Maker. The great mages (spellcasters) that governed the powerful Tevinter Imperium, however, worshiped a pantheon of seven dragons called the Old Gods. Hungry for power, the mages attempted to enter the Maker's Golden City, which resided in the dream reality called the Fade. This reach for power corrupted paradise, turning the Golden City into the Black City, and sent the mages back to earth as the first Darkspawn. These evil creatures constantly seek out the Old Gods, who have been imprisoned deep beneath the earth by the Maker. Whenever the Darkspawn find an Old God, they corrupt it, and the insane dragon then leads a Darkspawn army on a rampage of death and destruction; the Grey Wardens were founded to stop this blight.

The final religious twist in this complicated plot was the arrival of the prophet Andraste, a woman who was the Maker's greatest servant. She led a crusade against the Tevinter Imperium, only to be betrayed by her mortal husband and burned at the stake. Her death, however, instigated the religion of the Chantry, which preaches the "Chant of Light," a missionary creed designed to reconcile the world with the Maker. The Chantry is clearly modeled on medieval European Christianity, complete with robed priestesses and militant Templar warriors, who maintain a careful eye on both orthodoxy and managing the mages, who are continually in danger of demonic possession (which is another angle of the religious and magical reality of this world). The Chantry also police mages on the illegal use of blood magic, a dangerous and arguably foul creation of the Tevinter mages.

Convoluted as this brief summary must sound to someone who has not played the game, it is integral to getting full value from *Dragon Age*. It is possible to complete the game without paying much attention to the narrative, but the story provides crucial motivation and direction to players. Many times, the player must make decisions that become critical plot points; if these are not to be completely random, knowledge of the narrative – both the immediate plot *and* the backstory – is necessary. For instance, if players choose to be a mage, they must decide whether to turn in a friend who is accused of practicing blood magic. Such a choice means nothing without the supporting mythology about the gods and magic.

The religions of *Dragon Age* are complex, multifaceted things that are deeply integral to its fictional world. The fictitious religious practitioners whom the player encounters span all kinds of character types, from inflexible fanatics to sincere and balanced adherents to struggling agnostics to jaded cynics to nominal but self-interested believers. The game, interestingly, does not attempt to resolve the apparent incompatibilities of the different religions, adopting a postmodern neutrality and letting every party speak for itself. The faiths in the game are clearly modeled on real-world systems, but there is enough ambiguity that a player can make those connections or ignore them. In short, these religions do not belong to an airtight system of spiritual cogs and gears.

Theory: Narrativists Strike Back

This is a notably different approach to religion than what is on offer in the *Civilization* series and is more in tune with many current evaluations of spirituality in video games. Detweiler's *Halos and Avatars,* a book of essays, features analyses of *Bioshock* (2K Games, 2007),[8] *Ultima IV* (Origin, 1985),[9] and Islamic games,[10] and the authors argue that the games have important theological implications. Likewise, Wagner's *Godwired* does an excellent job of connecting game studies scholarship with the religious significance of video games. Commentators on the internet have posted blog entries and articles on religion in video games,[11] and there are plenty of other examples.

These serious evaluations of religion and games are possible because the video game medium is more than just a system of rules. There are two main elements that work against the mechanization of the player experience: the fiction of a game and emergent play. To start, most video games use elements that might function as decoration, but are very much part of the gaming experience, although the exact role they play is a matter of some debate. In the first few years of the nascent discipline of game studies, academics coming from a literary studies background waged a war of theories over the role of narrative in video games. The so-called ludologists, responding to the incorrect extension of literary theory to video games, insisted that games were not stories and any apparent connection between them were either corruptions of the game form or the result of academic misinterpretation.[12] Others, often labeled "narrativists" or "narratologists," argued that stories clearly *were* important parts of video games. While this issue is perhaps not quite as central to game studies now as it was a decade ago, the tension between the game system and the game fiction still remains. Nevertheless, it seems clear that although video games are clearly different as a form or medium from the novels and movies upon which the discipline of narratology was founded, plots, characters, and the fictional worlds of games can all be engaged by players and be meaningful. The best game theory notes that video games are both "rule-based formal system(s)"[13] *and* "spaces ripe with narrative possibilities."[14] As Juul argues in *Half-Real,* a complete analysis of a video game representation cannot ignore either aspect.

Games have always been able to create fictional worlds, but the capacity to do so expanded immensely when the form jumped to a computerized medium. Computers, in the broadest sense of the word, including game consoles and smartphones, remediate other media.[15] A video game can be the pages of a book, a radio broadcast, a movie, a photo, a pen and paper, and much more. While few of these imitations are exactly the same as the original medium, this means that most of the communicative capacities of older media are at the disposal of video games. If a movie can show a story, so can a video game. If a book can give a backstory (as do the many tomes lying around Ferelden in *Dragon Age*), so can a video game. While the tools of communication are not identical, and always exist within a framework of a playable system of rules, the remediation capabilities of the medium allow for culturally familiar representations of religion.

Game studies scholars identify one other aspect of video games that de-mechanizes the experience of a game: emergent play. Salen and Zimmerman define "emergence" as "systems generating complex and unpredictable patterns of behavior from simple rules."[16] Emergent play occurs when players do unexpected things with video games. YouTube is full of examples of gamers exploiting bugs or design features in ways the game makers almost certainly did not anticipate – videos demonstrate loopholes that allow players to rack up unlimited money or experience points, become impossible to kill, and so on. The entire field of machinima – recording and editing videos of gameplay to make movies and tell stories – is a kind of emergent play, as it turns games into a kind of video production tool.

Humans often exercise a great deal of creativity when they are given restrictions. Many artistic forms rely on this very thing: poems like limericks or haiku use set structures, spurring creative choices of words. The hit game *Minecraft* (Mojang, 2010) is an excellent illustration of this. A graphically primitive game that gives players the ability to build just about anything they want – it's a kind of giant Lego box – it has spawned an international community of enthusiasts who revel in creating surprising, obscure, and amusing virtual sculptures, like a highly accurate recreation of the Death Star in *Star Wars*.[17] Religion operates in much the same way, as Wagner notes: a great deal of religious thought, experience, and practice involves play within forms, rules, and structures.[18] Even highly systematic representations of religion in video games, then, may allow for a greater variety of play and meaning-making than might be immediately apparent.

PRACTICE: HOW COUNTER-MECHANICAL FLEXIBILITY SHOWS UP

So what do nonmechanical representations of religion look like in actual games? The description of *Dragon Age* above should make clear that games are capable of delivering multifaceted religious stories and characters, and creating fictional worlds in which religion is an integral part. But games do not have to be as sprawling and detailed as that massive RPG in order to tell provocative religious tales. The popular indie game *The Binding of Isaac* (McMillen and Himsl, 2011) has simple art and equally simple gameplay in addition to a fairly small number of short cutscenes, yet it crams some challenging religious questions and ideas into its lean frame. It opens with the story of a woman who watches too much televangelism and starts to hear the voice of God asking her to abuse and eventually kill her only son, Isaac, who barely escapes into the basement. The gameplay consists of simple combat in a disturbing and dysfunctional world that features flies, dung, blood, and grotesque monsters, all drawn in a simple, yet powerful style. In its short narrative sections and via its unnerving fictional world, the game questions the nature of religious obedience.

The decorative aspects of games also allow them to employ religious symbolism, both overt and subtle. Even mechanistic strategy games invoke historical visuals to represent different faith traditions. For example, *Europa Universalis* (Paradox Entertainment, 2000) and its sequels use a series of icons to indicate the dominant faith of a particular territory. *The Binding of Isaac* has an obvious connection with the Jewish story of Abraham and Isaac[19] and frames the story as a tale of contemporary American Christian fundamentalism with the iconic use of the TV (for televangelism) and the Christian Bible. The many appearances of angels and demons in video games draw on the imagery of many different religions.

But the religious symbolism of games is often more subtle. Clothing is an important but often unnoted element of video games, and it frequently suggests certain associations with real-life faiths. For instance, the robes of the Chantry in *Dragon Age* suggest medieval European monasticism and the priesthood, but are different enough that the clergy only indirectly evoke contemporary religious leaders. The architecture of virtual worlds likewise suggests cathedrals or mosques or pagodas without being identical to physical religious buildings.

One of the more powerful tools at the disposal of game makers is the ability to piggyback on well-established narratives, ideas, or imagery – to make intertextual connections. A video game, for example, does not have to do a lot of work to explain the idea of a crusade, since the concept and its history has wide currency. Players of *Civilization V* or *Gods and Kings,* when choosing the religions they found, are able to tap into whatever narrative they already attach to Taoism, Zoroastrianism, or Islam. *Dante's Inferno* relies to some degree on gamers' already established ideas about hell.

This points to the final, and probably most powerful, way that non-mechanical religion appears in video games: players interpret, imagine, and play. It is a truism in communication studies that texts do not interpret themselves,[20] and this is just as true of cybertexts – Espen Aarseth's term for texts that are part of information feedback loops and thus require user input[21] – like video games. The models of religion presented in some games may indeed be mechanistic, but that does not mean players will necessarily understand religion that way. Emergent play means divergent interpretations and real creativity. Games also often provide opportunities to play in a way that does not maximize the efficiency of the system. For example, while chopping down a forest in a *Civilization* game may be advantageous for building, an environmentalist player may, due to beliefs and interests formed outside the game, decide to never do such a thing. Likewise, the *Dragon Age* player may ignore advantageous actions in order to role-play a character intent on religious purity or some other goal not strictly necessary to completion of the game.

And when it comes to filling the gaps of a fictional world – explaining all the bits not seen or never written into a game – players can vividly construct any range of understandings. As noted above, *Dragon Age* does not assert which religion in its world is correct, so it is up to players (if they care) to figure out how that all works. This means that the religious elements of a game may become organic and nonmechanistic in terms of the player's actual understanding; the fictional world is, in a sense, only limited by the player's imagination. This can explain why interviews with gamers show that some, at least, clearly see religious significance in their play.[22]

FINAL ANALYSIS: THE POWER OF MEDIA BIAS

Is There a Bias?

Given these two very different patterns, is it fair to say there is a religious bias built into video games? Might it be better to say that there are at least two major trends: that some games are likely to mechanize religion, while others are likely to produce fuller and more organic representations? It is certainly possible and reasonable to make that case.

But my account of nonmechanistic representations of religion is a bit misleading, because it isolates those textual features that counter the systematic bias of video games. In reality, players encounter both the fiction and the system, as Juul argues.[23] *Europa Universalis* might employ Muslim and Eastern Orthodox symbols, but it is a strategy game just as mechanical as *Civilization*. *The Binding of Isaac* has a fascinating and difficult religious narrative, but it is a "rogue-like" game: a genre that uses algorithms to generate maps that are all rather repetitive variations on a theme. *Dragon Age* has detailed religions and cosmologies, but it also has the mechanistic spell systems, to say nothing of the combat system that is at the heart of the gameplay.

The main point here is that while video games can do without much in the way of fiction – see abstract games like *Tetris* (Spectrum Holobyte, 1987), *Geometry Wars: Retro Evolved* (Bizarre Creations, 2005), and *Bit.Trip Beat* (Gaijin Games, 2009) – it is impossible for them to avoid the game system. If there is no gameplay, then the thing in question is not a video game; it may instead be an interactive website or a movie or something similar. As soon as the cybertext in question is perfectly systematic, anything it represents has to work within that system. Thus, the video game medium *has* a bias: it is inclined toward representations of religion that are mechanical in character.

Counteracting the Power of Bias

It is worth emphasizing, however, that a bias is not impossible to overcome. Just as it is possible to walk against an incline, it is possible to make a video game that works hard to avoid, or obscure, or repurpose the mechanical elements of any game representation of any given phenomenon. The fictional elements described above are clearly significant. While they might seem like decoration, the nonfunctional art can evoke all kinds of different understandings and interpretations. And this raises perhaps the most important point about the mechanistic bias of video games: it is a bias of *representation,* which is only part of communication. As scholars have pointed out for decades now,[24] communication consists as much of interpretation as it does of messages. In order to be meaningful, a game needs both the game cybertext and at least one player. And the concept of polysemy suggests that where humans are involved, interpretations multiply.[25] What one person understands in a communicative process may be quite different from what another person understands.

The fact is that gamers are a variable lot. Some players love video game artwork, and often play to find as many pretty pictures as they can. Other players are collectors, trying to accumulate things in a game: stats or treasures or experience points or whatever. Still others love narrative and soak up every bit of story they can get. And some gamers are social, focusing on the interactions with other players. The list could go on. The point is that there are many different kinds of players and types of play, as evidenced by some of the different player classifications published by academics, designers, and game enthusiasts.[26] Even these classifications simplify the tremendously complex ways gamers use and understand games.

The reason this is important is that my analysis here assumes certain kinds of interpretations and thus certain kinds of gamers. The mechanical representations of video games may well be ignored, misinterpreted, or purposely reinterpreted by players – especially those who are not particularly systematic thinkers. Players of *Civilization* may impose a narrative on the game, making strategic choices based on a completely personal, idiosyncratic fiction; they may, for instance, decide never to ally with devotees of a particular religion, or avoid declaring war on followers of a faith, even though the game allows it. Likewise, plenty of gamers ignore the cutscenes that provide the more nuanced and organic representations of religion that narratives, such as those in *Dragon Age*, provide.

This is not to say that representation does not matter at all, that the possible range of interpretations is practically limitless. While in theory, anyone can understand anything from any text or cybertext, in practice, genre conventions, cultural traditions, and the choices of the makers of texts constrain the likely interpretations of readers, viewers, listeners, and players. A *Civilization* player is unlikely to think that a cross icon represents the Hindu religion. This is the tension of meaning-making in video games: players with true agency confront preexisting cybertexts full of complicated symbols. Interpretation is the dance of these factors.

The argument of this chapter, then, is not that the designers and players of video games are locked in an iron cage of rational religion when a game chooses to address that subject. Rather, it is worth being aware that, uncorrected by any contrary force, video games have a tendency to mechanize faith, presenting an impoverished vision of what religions mean to adherents.

NOTES

1. Innis, *The Bias of Communication*.
2. Juul, *Half-Real*.
3. Frasca, "Simulation versus Narrative," 231.

4. See Salen and Zimmerman, *Rules of Play*; Juul, *Half-Real*.

5. Joel 2:14 (NIV; emphasis added).

6. See McLuhan, *Understanding Media*.

7. 1 Kings 18:16–46.

8. Newgren, "*Bioshock* to the System."

9. Hayse, "*Ultima IV*: Simulating the Religious Quest."

10. Campbell, "Islamogaming."

11. For example, Parish, "Hallowed Be Thy Game"; and websites such as *Christ and Pop Culture*, http://www.christandpopculture.com.

12. See Eskelinen, "The Gaming Situation"; Aarseth, "Genre Trouble."

13. Juul, *Half-Real*, 6.

14. Jenkins, "Game Design as Narrative Architecture," 119.

15. Bolter and Grusin, *Remediation*.

16. Salen and Zimmerman, *Rules of Play*, 158.

17. *Minecraft – Star Wars – Death Star Run*.

18. Wagner, *Godwired*, esp. ch. 3.

19. Genesis 22:1–19.

20. See, for example, Hall, "Encoding/Decoding."

21. Aarseth, *Cybertext*.

22. Hodge, "Role Playing"; Schut, *Of Games and God*.

23. Juul, *Half-Real*.

24. For example, see Hall, "Encoding/Decoding."

25. Fiske, *Television Culture*.

26. Yee, "Motivations of Play in MMORPGs"; Bartle, "Hearts, Clubs, Diamonds, Spades"; Edwards, "GNS and Other Matters of Role-Playing Theory"; Bateman, Lowenhaupt, and Nacke, "Player Typology in Theory and Practice."

REFERENCES

Aarseth, Espen. *Cybertext: Perspectives on Ergodic Literature*. Baltimore, Md.: Johns Hopkins University Press, 1997.
———. "Genre Trouble: Narrativism and the Art of Simulation." In *First Person: New Media as Story, Performance, and Game*. Edited by Noah Wardrip-Fruin and Pat Harrigan, 45–55. Cambridge, Mass.: MIT Press, 2004.
Bartle, Richard. "Hearts, Clubs, Diamonds, Spades: Players Who Suit MUDs." http://www.mud.co.uk/richard/hcds.htm (accessed September 16, 2012).
Bateman, Chris, Lowenhaupt, Rebecca, and Nacke, Lennart E. "Player Typology in Theory and Practice." Paper presented at the Digital Games Research Association conference, Hilversum, Netherlands, September 2011. http://www.digra.org/dl/db/11307.50587.pdf (accessed January 4, 2013).
Bolter, Jay D., and Grusin, Richard. *Remediation: Understanding New Media*. Cambridge, Mass.: MIT Press, 1999.
Campbell, Heidi. "Islamogaming: Digital Dignity via Alternative Storytellers." In *Halos and Avatars: Playing Video Games with God*. Edited by Craig Detweiler, 63–74. Louisville, Ky.: Westminster John Knox, 2010.
Detweiler, Craig, ed. *Halos and Avatars: Playing Video Games with God*. Louisville, Ky.: Westminster John Knox, 2010.
Edwards, Ron. "GNS and Other Matters of Role-Playing Theory." 2001. http://

www.indie-rpgs.com/articles/1 (accessed December 1, 2012).

Eskelinen, Markku. "The Gaming Situation." *Game Studies: The International Journal of Computer Game Research* 1, no. 1 (July 2001). http://www.gamestudies.org/0101/eskelinen.

Fiske, John. *Television Culture.* New York: Routledge, 1987.

Frasca, Gonzalo. "Simulation versus Narrative: Introduction to Ludology." In *The Video Game Theory Reader.* Edited by Mark J. P. Wolf and Bernard Perron, 221–235. New York: Routledge, 2003.

Hall, Stuart. "Encoding/Decoding." In *Media Studies: A Reader.* Edited by Paul Marris and Sue Thornham, 51–61. New York: New York University Press, 1999.

Hayse, Mark. "*Ultima IV*: Simulating the Religious Quest." In *Halos and Avatars: Playing Video Games with God.* Edited by Craig Detweiler, 34–46. Louisville, Ky.: Westminster John Knox, 2010.

Hodge, Daniel White. "Role Playing: Toward a Theology for Gamers." In *Halos and Avatars: Playing Video Games with God.* Edited by Craig Detweiler, 163–175. Louisville, Ky.: Westminster John Knox, 2010.

Innis, Harold Adams. *The Bias of Communication.* Toronto: University of Toronto Press, 1951.

Jenkins, Henry. "Game Design as Narrative Architecture." In *First Person: New Media as Story, Performance, and Game.* Edited by Noah Wardrip-Fruin and Pat Harrigan, 118–130. Cambridge, Mass.: MIT Press, 2004.

Juul, Jesper. *Half-Real: Video Games between Real Rules and Fictional Worlds.* Cambridge, Mass.: MIT Press, 2005.

McLuhan, Marshall. *Understanding Media.* New York: McGraw-Hill, 1964.

Newgren, Kevin. "*Bioshock* to the System: Smart Choices in Video Games." In *Halos and Avatars: Playing Video Games with God.* Edited by Craig Detweiler, 135–145. Louisville, Ky.: Westminster John Knox, 2010.

Minecraft – Star Wars – Death Star Run. ParadiseDecay, dir. 2011. http://www.youtube.com/watch?v=v0SeJGFi050 (accessed September 15, 2012).

Parish, Jeremy. "Hallowed Be Thy Game." *1UP.com,* March 4, 2005. http://www.1up.com/features/hallowed-thy-game (accessed December 1, 2012).

Salen, Katie, and Zimmerman, Eric. *Rules of Play: Game Design Fundamentals.* Cambridge, Mass.: MIT Press, 2004.

Schut, Kevin. *Of Games and God: A Christian Exploration of Video Games.* Grand Rapids, Mich.: Brazos, 2012.

Wagner, Rachel. *Godwired: Religion, Ritual and Virtual Reality.* New York: Routledge, 2012.

Yee, Nick. "Motivations of Play in MMORPGS." *Daedalus Project.* 2007. http://www.nickyee.com/daedalus/archives/pdf/3-2.pdf (accessed December 1, 2012).

Gameography

Actraiser. Enix, 1991.

Actraiser 2. Enix, 1993.

Age of Empires. Ensemble, 1997.

Age of Empires 2. Ensemble, 1999.

Age of Mythology. Ensemble, 2002.

Alone in the Dark. Bonnell, 1992.

Amnesia: The Dark Descent. Frictional
  Games, 2010.

Arabian Lords. BreakAway Games, 2007.

Assassin's Creed. Ubisoft, 2007–.

Assassin's Creed: Brotherhood. Ubisoft,
  2010.

Asura's Wrath. Capcom, 2012.

Baby Boomer. Color Dreams, 1989.

The Bard's Tale: The Unknown Stories.
  Electronic Arts, 1985.

Bayonetta. Platinum Games, 2009.

The Binding of Isaac. McMillen and
  Himsl, 2011.

Bioshock. 2K Games, 2007.

Bit.Trip Beat. Gaijin Games, 2009.

Black & White. Electronic Arts/Feral
  Interactive, 2001.

Call of Duty. Activision, 2003.

Call of Duty: Black Ops. Activision, 2010.

Call of Duty: Modern Warfare 2. Activision, 2009.

Castlevania. Konami, 1986.

Castlevania II: Simon's Quest. Konami,
  1987.

Civilization IV. Firaxis, 2005.

Civilization V. Firaxis, 2010.

Cosmology of Kyoto. Softedge, 1995.

Cursed Mountain. Deep Silver Vienna,
  2009.

Dance Praise. Digital Praise, 2005.

Dante's Inferno. Electronic Arts, 2010.

Darkfall. Audiovisual Enterprises, 2009.

Deus Ex. Ion Storm, 2000.

Diablo. Blizzard Entertainment, Ubisoft,
  1996.

Diablo III. Activion-Blizzard, 2012.

The Dirge of Cerberus. Square Enix, 2006.

Downpour. Shatsky, Hulett, and Airey,
  2010.

Dragon Age. Electronic Arts, 2009

Dragon Age: Origins. BioWare, 2009.

Dragon Ball Z: Budokai Tenkaichi. Atari,
  2007.

Duck Tales. Capcom, 1989.

Earthbound. Nintendo, 1995.

Elder Scrolls. Bethesda Softworks, 1994–.

El Shaddai: Ascension of the Metatron.
  Ignition Entertainment, 2011.

Enslaved. Namco Bandai Games, 2010.

Europa Universalis. Paradox Entertainment, 2000.

Everquest. Sony Online Entertainment,
  1999.

Fable. Microsoft Studios, 2004.

Fallout 3. Bethesda Softworks, 2008.

Fatal Frame. Shibata, 2001.

Fatal Frame II: Crimson Butterfly. Mayama, 2003.

Fatal Frame III: The Tormented. Kikuchi, 2005.

Fatal Frame IV: The Mask of the Lunar Eclipse. Kikuchi, 2008.

Final Fantasy. Square Enix, 1987.

Final Fantasy III. Square, 1994.

Final Fantasy X. Square Electronic Arts, 2001.

flOw. Thatgamecompany, 2006.

From Dust. Ubisoft Montpelier, 2011.

Geometry Wars: Retro Evolved. Bizarre Creations, 2005.

Get Medieval. Monolith Productions, 1998.

Gods and Kings. Firaxis, 2012.

Guild Wars. NCSoft, 2005.

Guru Meditation. Ian Bogost, 2007.

Halo. Bungie, 2001–2010; 343 Industries, 2011–.

Halo: Reach. Microsoft Studios, 2010.

Hanuman: Boy Warrior. Sony Computer Entertainment Europe, 2009.

Heretic. Raven Software, 1994.

Homecoming. Oertel, 2008.

JESUS: Dreadful Bio-Monster. King Records, 1989.

Journey. Thatgamecompany, 2012.

Journey of Jesus: The Calling. Lightside Games, 2012.

Journey to Wild Divine. Wild Divine, 2001.

Kingdom of Amalur. Electronic Arts, 2012.

Kuma\War. Kuma Reality Games, 2004.

Leela. THQ, 2011.

Left Behind: Eternal Forces. Inspired Media Entertainment, 2006.

The Legend of Zelda. Nintendo, 1986.

Let There Be Smite. Pippin Barr, 2011.

Lineage 2. NCSoft, 2003.

Lufia. Taito, 1993.

Maniac Mansion. Lucasfilm Games, 1990.

Mario Kart Wii. Nintendo, 2008.

Mass Effect. BioWare, 2007.

Might and Magic: Heroes VI. Black Hole Entertainment, 2011.

Minecraft. Mojang, 2010.

Mortal Kombat. Midway Games, 1993.

Mortal Kombat 2. Midway Games, 1994.

Okami. Capcom, 2006.

Origins. Oertel, 2007.

The Path. Tale of Tales, 2009.

Populous. Bullfrog, 1989.

Portal. Valve, 2008.

Quraish. Afkar Media, 2007.

Ra.One: The Game. Sony Computer Entertainment Europe, 2011.

Resistance: Fall of Man. Insomniac Games, 2006.

Rift. Trion Worlds, 2011.

Sam and Max. Telltale Games, 2006.

Second Life. Linden Lab, 2003.

The Secret of Mana. Square, 1993.

Shadowbane. Ubisoft, 2003.

Shattered Memories. Hulett, 2009.

The Shivah. Wadjet Eye Games, 2006.

Silent Hill. Kitao, 1999.

Silent Hill 2. Imamura, 2001.

Silent Hill 3. Yamaoka, 2003.

Silent Hill 4: The Room. Yamaoka, 2004.

Silent Hill: Book of Memories. Hulett, 2012.

SilkRoad Online. Joymax Entertainment, 2005.

Sim City. Maxis, 1989.

The Sims. Maxis, 2000.

Special Force. Solution, 2003.

Special Force 2. W3DTEK, 2007.

Spirit Camera: The Cursed Memoir. Kikuchi, 2012.

Star Wars Jedi Knight: Mysteries of the Sith. LucasArts, 1998.

Star Wars: Knights of the Old Republic. BioWare, 2003.

Tetris. Spectrum Holobyte, 1987.

Tropico. PopTop, 2001.

Ultima. Origin, 1981–2009.

Ultima IV. Origin, 1985.

Ultima IX. Origin, 1999.

War of the Rose. Paradox Interactive, 2012.

Wii Fit Zazen. Nintendo, 2007.

World of Warcraft. Blizzard Entertainment, 2004–.

Zero 4: The Mask of the Lunar Eclipse. Keisuke Kikuchi, 2008.

Zero Wing. Taito, 1989.

Contributors

NATHAN ABRAMS is Professor of Film Studies at Bangor University, Wales. He is the founding editor of *Jewish Film and New Media: An International Journal* and has written widely on U.S. and Jewish culture. His publications include *The New Jew in Film: Exploring Jewishness and Judaism in Contemporary Cinema* (2012); *Norman Podhoretz and Commentary Magazine: The Rise and Fall of the Neo-Cons* (2010); *Jews and Sex* (2008); *Commentary Magazine 1945–1959: "A Journal of Significant Thought and Opinion"* (2006); *Studying Film* (with Ian Bell and Jan Udris; 2001); and numerous articles and chapters.

JASON ANTHONY is a journalist and game designer based in New York City. He works extensively at the intersection of games and religion, and his stories and essays have appeared in *Religion News Service, Boston Review, Christian Century,* and other outlets. His games include a fully gamed seminary chapel service (*In the Cards*), an athletic exploration of the Jewish sabbath (*Shabbat Put!*), and an SMS game of freeze tag exploring the call to prayer as a digital secular ritual (*The Hush*).

HEIDI A. CAMPBELL is Associate Professor of Communication at Texas A&M University, where she teaches media studies. She has researched and published extensively on religion, new media, and digital culture since the mid-1990s. She is author of *Exploring Religious Community Online* (2005) and *When Religion Meets New Media* (2010) and editor of *Digital Religion* (2013). Her work has also appeared in *Handbook on Internet Studies, Journal of the American Academy of Religion, Journal of Computer-Mediated Communication, Journal of Contemporary Religion, Journal of Media and Religion, New Media and Society,* and *The Informa-*

tion Society. She is also Director of the Network for New Media, Religion, and Digital Culture Studies (http://digitalreligion.tamu.edu).

ISAMAR CARRILLO MASSO is a Ph.D. student in new media (games studies) at Bangor University, where she lectures in media and cultural studies and serves as Assistant Editor for the *Journal of Gaming and Virtual Worlds.* She has taught English, literature, and linguistics since 1997 in Venezuela, Taiwan, the Czech Republic, and Oman. She graduated with distinction in 2008 from the University of Reading. Her dissertation was a corpus-based, critical discourse analysis of the portrayal of female characters in *World of Warcraft* and *Diablo.*

RABIA GREGORY is Assistant Professor of Religious Studies at the University of Missouri. Her research focuses on religion and popular culture in late medieval Europe. She is author of *Marrying Jesus: Lay Piety and Learned Devotion in Medieval and Early Modern Europe.*

GREGORY PRICE GRIEVE is Associate Professor of Religious Studies at the University of North Carolina at Greensboro; Director of MERGE: A Network for Collaborative Interdisciplinary Scholarship in UNCG's College of Arts and Sciences; and Co-chair of the American Academy of Religion's section on Religion and Popular Culture. He is author of numerous articles and the monograph *Retheorizing Religion in Nepal* (2007), and co-editor of *Historicizing Tradition in the Study of Religion* (2005). Grieve has been a research fellow at the Asia Research Institute, National University of Singapore, and the Center for Religion and Media at New York University.

PETER LIKARISH is Assistant Professor of Computer Science at Drew University and a visiting scholar at the Palo Alto Research Corporation working with Nick Yee, studying the sociological and psychological nature of online gameplay. His focus is on real-world demographic prediction based on how individuals choose to play MMOGS. He presented the group's findings in 2011 at HotPETS (a venue for hot topics in privacy-enhancing technologies).

SHANNY LUFT is Assistant Professor of Religious Studies at the University of Wisconsin at Stevens Point, where he teaches courses on religion in America, global Christianity, and religion and popular culture. His research explores historical questions about the relationship between religion and leisure, and he has written about amusement parks, evangelical video games, the Protestant debate over the place of leisure in Christian life in the nineteenth century, and conservative Protestant hostility toward Hollywood cinema in the first half of the twentieth century.

KEVIN SCHUT is Associate Professor and Chair of the Media + Communication Department in the School of the Arts, Media + Culture at Trinity Western University in Langley, British Columbia. He is interested in culture and technology and focuses on the study of video games. He has published papers on how the video game medium intersects with diverse topics such as history, mythology, and religion, and is author of *Of Games and God: A Christian Exploration of Video Games* (2012). He loves playing role-playing and strategy games and has spent hundreds of hours in imaginary worlds.

VÍT ŠISLER is Assistant Professor of New Media in the Faculty of Arts at Charles University, Prague. He has published extensively on issues related to Islam and video games in *Communication Yearbook; European Journal of Cultural Studies; Information, Communication and Society; Global Media Journal;* and *Middle East Journal of Culture and Communication.* He is founder and Editor in Chief of *Digital Islam* and Managing Editor of *CyberOrient.* He was a visiting Fulbright scholar at Northwestern University in 2008–2009.

OLIVER STEFFEN is a Ph.D. student at the University of Berne, Switzerland. He graduated with an M.A. in the science of religion from Berne, where he conducted research in the relationship between digital games and religion. His current research project is "Between 'God Mode' and 'God Mood,'" which explores religion in computer games and the meaning of religion for gamers (http://www.god-mode.ch). He regularly reviews religious games for www.ref.ch, an internet portal for Swiss Protestants.

RACHEL WAGNER is Associate Professor of Religion at Ithaca College, New York. Her research is on religion and film, religion in popular culture, and the nature of religion in virtual reality. She is author of *Godwired: Religion, Ritual and Virtual Reality* (2012).

MICHAEL WALTEMATHE is Lecturer in the Evangelical Theological Faculty of Ruhr University, Bochum, in the field of religious education and religious studies. For several years he has been working with computer games and religion, especially the use of computer games in religious education. His theoretical interests include constructivist reflections on religious education and the opportunities to learn in religious plurality. His passion is the game as a phenomenon. He is a member of the Working Group for Religious Education; the Working Group for Phenomenology, Organization, and Technology; and the editorial review boards of *International Journal of Technology and Human Interaction* and *International Society for the Sociology of Religion.*

BRENDA S. GARDENOUR WALTER is Assistant Professor of History at St. Louis College of Pharmacy. She holds a Ph.D. in medieval history from Boston University, where she specialized in the history of medieval medicine and hagiography. She has been a Fulbright scholar in Madrid, an Evelyn Nation Research Fellow at the Huntington Library in California, and a National Endowment for the Humanities fellow at the Wellcome Institute for the History of Medicine in London. Her areas of research include the biological construction of witchcraft in the later Middle Ages, the depiction of the vampire in twentieth-century German cinema, postmodernism and medical ethics, and the role of air in medieval medicine and cosmology. She is co-editor of *Parasites, Worms, and the Human Body in Religion and Culture* (2012) and author of several book chapters.

XENIA ZEILER is Lecturer in South Asian Religions at the University of Bremen, Germany. She studied South Asian history, cultural studies, and Islamic studies at Humboldt University, Berlin; Jawaharlal Nehru University, New Delhi; and the University of Heidelberg. Her research has focused on analyzing transformations and the popular religion of the Hindu Tantric goddess Dhūmāvatī. She has published several articles and book chapters on popular and mainstream Hindu and Tantric religions in contemporary India and on globalized Hinduism and modern mass media.

Index

Page numbers in *italics* indicate illustrations and charts.

Aarseth, Espen, 76, 270
Abrahamic religions, 226. *See also* Christianity; Islam; Judaism
Abrams, Nathan, 10, 16, 18, 49
abstract games, 272
Abu Qatada, 122, 123
Actraiser series, 171, 181–83, 187
Adon Olam, 60
Afghanistan War, 114
After, 220, 221
Age of Empires, 113, 120–22, 128–29, 261
age of gamers, 3, 69, 158
Age of Mythology, 262
agency, 166, 223
agnosticism, 187
agon games, 196
Al-Anfal ("The Spoils of War"), 118
alcohol use in video games, 177
alea games, 196
algorithmic culture, 198
Al-Jāhiīya ("First Encounter"), 122
Alliance, 145–46
allomythic games, 34, 39–43
allopolitical games, 34, 41
Alone in the Dark, 92–93, 97
alter egos, 243
altered states of consciousness, 216
alternative storytelling, 112

Al-wa'd as-sīdiq (*Tale of the Truthful Pledge*), 117
Amakura, Mio, 99
Ameratsu, 38
American Academy of Religion, 6
Amnesia, 223
analysis of games. *See* multimodality
ancestor worship, 265
Andrastrian Chantry (fabricated religion), 176–77, 266, 270
angels, 263
animism, 261–62, 265
anonymity in gaming, 162
Anthony, Jason, 3, 9, 15, 17
apostates, 207
App Store Guidelines, 3–4
Apple, 3–4
"Arab and American Computer War Games" (Machin and Suleiman), 111
Arab world, 7, 11, 15, 110, 116. *See also* Islam
Arabian Lords, 113, 126, 128
Arab-Israeli conflict, 81n1
ARAC (all-races, all class) guilds, 148
architectural elements, 137–38
Asari race, 40
Ashkenazi Judaism, 60
Asia/Asian gaming market, 66, 68–70, 72, 77, 80, 146
As-Salāmu 'Alaykum guild, 41
Assassin's Creed series, 7, 144, 150, 154, 159

Asura's Wrath, 35
Atalanta, 28
Atari, 136
Athame, 40
atheists, 208
Athens, 28
Atkins, B., 59
audiovisual layer of video games, 113,
    114–20, 128
Augustine of Hippo, 261
Aurona Technologies Limited, 71, 74
Australia, 179
authenticity, 5, 39, 114, 233
authority, religious, 10, 39, 66–67, 76–79
avatars: and disposition to act, 224; and
    empowerment, 220, 221; and game
    typologies, 41; and hardcore Christian
    gamers, 163–64; and religious content
    in games, 185–86; and virtual worlds, 151
Avedon, Elliott, 203
Ayyām al-Arab ("The Days of the Arabs")
    stories, 122
Azeroth, 146
Aztec Empire, 32

Baby Boomer, 174
Bainbridge, William Sims, 6, 214
Bainbridge, Wilma Alice, 214
balance in gameplay, 262–63
Balinese cockfights, 31
Bard's Tale, The, 150
Battle of the Trench, 123
Battlefield, 158–59
Bayles, D., 62
Beatrice, 187
Bedouins, 122
belief: and *Actraiser*, 182; and acts of
    faith, 248; and allomythic games, 39;
    and Christian gamers, 155–56, 160; and
    controversies over game content, 70,
    74, 81, 125; creating believable game
    environments, 114, 120; and cultural
    feedback, 171–73; and *Dragon Age*,
    266–67, 271; and Fatal Frame, 101–102;

and game mechanics, 232; and game
    studies field, 7; and Islam, 110, 129–30;
    and Judaism, 47, 48–51; and mechanis-
    tic religion in games, 264; and moral-
    ity in digital games, 224; and multi-
    modal game analysis, 10; and player
    immersion in games, 185–86; and play-
    fulness of gaming, 15; and practiced
    vs. fabricated religions, 176–77; and
    praxic games, 32; and rules of games,
    194–95, 195–97, 198–200, 204, 206,
    208, 209–10; and *Silent Hill*, 92, 95–96;
    and theoptic games, 43
bellatores, 139
Berger, Peter, 246, 248
Bertozzi, Elena, 223
Between Sacred and Profane (Lynch),
    200–201
Bheeman and Hanuman (comic), 73
Bible, 174–75, 181
"Bigger than Jesus" (Zimmerman), 26
Binding of Isaac, The, 186, 269–70, 271
Bioshock, 186, 267
Bit, Trip Beat, 272
Black & White, 42, 220, 224
blasphemy, 80, 186
Blinding Ritual, 98
blood magic, 266
Bogost, Ian, 7, 17, 109, 214, 219
Bolter, Jay, 114, 120
Book of Han, The, 33
Book of Lost Memories, 93
Book of Magic, 174–75, 181
"Born Digital and Born Again Digital"
    (panel), 6
Boxerman, Eddy, 218
boycotts, 76
Boyonetta, 255
Brazil, 70
BreakAway Games, 126
Breath, 261–62
broadband coverage, 70
Buddhism: and *Civilization* series, 124–
    25, 257; and *Fatal Frame*, 89, 100, 101;

and game typologies, 35, 40, 42; and
the gaming market, 66; and neomedievalism, 146; and protests against
game publishers, 81
buffs, 138
bugs, 259–60
Byzantine Empire, 109

Caillois, Roger, 196, 203, 208, 210
Call of Duty series, 154, 158–61
Calvinism, 177
Cambruin, 134
Camera Obscura, 97
Campbell, Heidi, 112
Camtasia Studio, 51
canon in digital game franchises, 96
cargo cults, 39–40
Carlquist, Jonas, 67, 72
Carlson, Rebecca, 175
Carrillo Masso, Isamar, 10, 16, 18, 51–56
Cassidy, Scott Brendan, 67, 72, 73
Castlevania, 181
cathedrals: Manchester Cathedral, 1, 17,
238–39, 250–51; and "neomedieval-
ism," 137–38, 143–44
Catholicism and the Catholic Church,
81, 177–79, 185
censorship: and localization of game
products, 171, 172–75, 175–76; and
multimodality, 48; and Nintendo of
America, 180–81, 184, 186–87; and
non-state actors, 178–79; and religious
content, 177–78
Central Internet Bureau of the Lebanese
Hezbollah movement, 117
Chabon, Michael, 61
Chain World, 26, 27, 38, 44n4
Chaisiri, Richmond Lee, 35
chakra philosophies, 37–38
chance in games, 196, 229
Chandler, Heather, 183
Chanukah, 30, 50–51
Chartres Cathedral, 143–44
chat rooms, 12

cheating, 193, 203–207, 208, 209
Chen, Xinghan (Jenova), 218
Chimaera, 1
China Joy, 68
choice in game play, 210
Choose Your Own Adventure series, 62
Chopra, Deepak, 25–26, 37–38
Christ and Pop Culture, 156, 160
Christian Gamers Online, 156, 162
Christianity: and allomythic games, 39;
Christian gamers, 34, 154–67; and
Civilization series, 124–25, 257; and
fundamentalism, 270; and localiza-
tion of game products, 180–81; and
religious conflict, 263; and Roman
spectacles, 44n12; and sacred games,
28; and *Shadowbane*, 148; and *Silent
Hill*, 96–97
Christmastide (Svyatki), 31
Church of England, 1–2, 5, 18, 238–39, 251
cinema. *See* film and cinema
citations of medieval culture, 136–38, 139,
144, 146, 151
City of God (Augustine of Hippo), 261
civilian casualties in video games, 131n23
civility in gaming, 162
Civilization. See Sid Meier's *Civilization*
series
class divisions, 69
Clementi Game Festival, 68
Clover Studio, 38
cognitive orientation of games, 220–21,
222–23
colonization, 200
Comic-Con, 102
commercialism, 70, 145, 157, 158
communal aspect of gaming, 102, 150
competition, 31–32, 32–33
Computer Bible Games (Conrod), 34
computer religious worlds, 251–53
Confucianism, 25, 124, 257
Conrod, John, 34
conscientious objectors, 207
Conservative Judaism, 60, 61

console games, 71, 74
consumerism, 70, 157, 158
content guidelines, 174
contingency, 222, 234. *See also* chance in games
control confinement, 222–23
conversion, religious, 123, 125, 131n32
Copernicanism, 178
copyright issues, 5
Corliss, Jonathan, 175
Cosmology of Kyoto, 222
Cosplay, 102
Coven of the Blood Rose, 41
crime games, 57–60, 61
Crimson Sacrifice ritual, 99
Critical Play (Flanagan), 195
Crockford, Douglas, 180
Cross and the Controller, The, 156
Crusades, 120, 270
cults, 94
cultural content in games: cultural border zones, 175–76; cultural feedback, 12, 17, 170–75, 185–86; cultural filtering, 172–75; cultural meaning making, 18; cultural odor, 175; cultural significance of gaming, 2; cultural transference, 188; digital culture, 4, 198; significance of religion in games, 2; and stereotypes, 7; and taboos, 173
Cultural Encounters in the Arab World (Sabry), 110
Cursed Mountain, 35
cybertexts, 270

dance and movement notation, 64n21
Dance Dance Revolution, 37
Dance Praise, 37
Daniel and the Lion's Den, 34
Dante Alighieri, 187
Dante's Inferno, 35, 186–87, 261, 262, 270
Darkfall, 136
Darkspawn, 265–66
Dawkins, Richard, 4

De Spectaculis (Tertulian), 44n12
death, 229–30
Decius, 206
definitions of "game," 29, 202–203
definitions of "religion," 198–201, 216
deities in digital games, 261
deity yoga, 42
DeKoven, Bernard, 205–206
Delphi, 28
demographics of gaming population, 3, 50
Demon Tag Ritual, 98
demons, 263
demystification of religion, 255–56
"The Depiction of Arabs in Combat Video Games" (Marashi), 110
Derrickson, Krystina, 112
design flaws, 259–60
Detweiler, Craig, 255, 267
Deus Ex, 225
devotional practices, 32, 142, 144–45, 149
dharma combat, 29
Diablo series, 150, 187
diaspora settings, 67–68, 76–79, 79–80
dice games, 196
didactic games, 29–30, 34–36, 44, 61
"Digital Arabs" (Šisler), 63n1, 126
digital culture, 4, 198
"Digital War Games and Post 9/11 Geographies of Militarism" (Power), 117
Dinshaw, Carolyn, 139
Dionysian festivals, 28
Dirge of Cerberus, The, 172
disempowerment, 222–23, 227, 228, 229–31, 233
divination games, 31, 36–37, 196
"divine as lesson" games, 34–36
Divine Comedy, The, (Dante), 182
divine intercession, 32, 36–37
Divines, 40
dodgeball, 206
dogma, 171
do-it-yourself Judaism, 50
Dovey, Jon, 55–56, 203–204

Dragon Age: and Christian gamers, 163; and emergent play, 271; and fabricated religions, 176; and mechanized play structure, 269–70; and media bias, 271, 273; and narrative of games, 268; and religious content, 265–67

Dragon Ball Z, 170

dragon slaying, 147

draught boards, 195

dreidel, 29, 30

drug use in video games, 177

Duck Tales, 181

Dungeons and Dragons, 162, 260

Durkheim, Emile, 199

Dynamic Difficulty Adjustment (DDA), 218

earnestness, 203–208

Earthbound, 170, 181

Easter Island, 31–32

Eastern Orthodoxy, 32, 271

Eco, Umberto, 135, 139–40

economic impact of gaming, 69

education: and Hinduism, 67; and Islam, 109, 111, 112; and Judaism, 49, 50, 60, 61; medieval religious technologies, 143; and religious content in computer games, 3, 6–7, 249; and typology of game types, 27, 34–35

Egenfeldt-Nielsen, Simon, 113, 195, 202

egg races, 29

eGods (Bainbridge), 6

Egyptian culture, 195

Ehud's Courage and the Cunning Blade, 35

Ekeroth, Jordan, 156–57

El Shaddai, 40, 186, 187

Elder Futhark, 134

Elder Scrolls, 40, 154, 159

Electronic Arts, 136, 187

"Electronic Empire" (Höglund), 110–11

Eliade, Mircea, 199–201

Elijah (prophet), 263–64

emergent play, 268, 270–71

empowerment, 15, 220–21, 227, 228, 233

enclaves, 239, 242, 244, 245, 249, 251–52

Endgame: Syria, 4

Enoch, 40, 96, 187

Enslaved, 35

Entertainment Software Rating Board (ESRB), 177, 179

epistemological reversal, 247–48

epoché of computer worlds, 245–46

escapism, 12–13, 18

Esselink, 172

ethics in gaming: and computer worlds, 250; ethical standards, 165; moral meter games, 224–25; in post-religious age, 57. *See also* morality in game settings

ethnicity, 47, 48–51, 58–59, 180

Ethnographies of the Video Game, 166

Europa Universalis, 270, 271

European Union (EU), 179

evangelicals, 12, 35, 154, 155–65

Evans, Ruth, 144–45

Everquest, 136

evolution of technology, 4–5

external rating boards, 183–85

Fable series, 163

fabricated religions, 176–78

factions, 262

faith, 224, 247, 249, 253, 255, 258, 261

Fallout 3, 250

fantasy role-playing games: and meaningful play, 145–47; and neomedievalism, 135–38, 147–48, 149–51; and religious actions in games, 138–45. *See also* massively multiplayer online role-playing games (MMORPGS)

Fatal Frame series, 10–11, 97–101, 102

feasts and festivals, 30–31, 36

Federal Examination Department for Media Harmful to Young Persons, 176

female characters, 56

feudalism, 139

film and cinema: and Christian gamers, 157; and depictions of religion, 2;

film studies, 47; Hinduism in, 72–73, 75–76, 77, 79–80; and horror game genre, 102; Islam in, 129; Judaism in, 49; sociophenomenological perspective on, 243; as tool of expression, 255; and "transmedia storytelling," 92–93

Final Fantasy series, 159, 174, 176, 181

finite provinces of meaning, 241, 253n8

First Amendment, 5

First Person (Wardrip-Fruin and Harrigan), 194

first-person shooter genre: and depiction of religious spaces, 1, 17, 251–52; examples of, *113*; and free speech, 5; and hardcore Christian gamers, 158; and morality in game settings, 225; and representations of Islam, 114–20, 129; and Wagner's research, 8

Flanagan, Mary, 195

flOw, 218

flow in game play, 217–19, 226–30, 231–32

flower, 218

Fog World, 95

folklore, 97, 101

footraces, 29

forgiveness, 163–64

Forgotten Realms, 260

Forum for Hindu Awakening, 76

Frasca, Gonzalo, 67, 73, 75–76, 124, 258

free speech, 5

free-for-all player-versus-player combat, 147

Friedl, John, 172

From Dust, 42–43, 255, 261–62

"Fun and Games" (Goffman), 205

fundamentalism, 91, 270

funeral games, 28

Gackenbach, Jayne, 217–18

Galilee, Galileo, 178

Galloway, Alexander, 124, 194, 197–98

Game Cultures (Dovey and Kennedy), 55–56, 203–204

Game Developers Conference, 25, 37, 43

Game Localization Handbook, The (Chandler), 183

Game Over (Sheff), 183–84

GameChurch, 156

Gamer Theory (Wark), 125

Gaming (Galloway), 194

Gaming Conference India, 68

gaming culture, 6–7, 68–69

Gauntlet, 136

Gears of War, 164

Geertz, Clifford, 31

gender issues in gaming, 56, 138, 158, 180

Genesis, 43

Geometry Wars, 272

Germany, 176, 179

Get Medieval, 135–36

Geth, 40

Ghassanids, 122

Gilbert, David, 35, 48

Gillespie, Dahlia (game character), 94

global audience for digital games, 80

global diasporas, 76–79

Global Gaming Expo Asia (G2E Asia), 68

Gnosticism, 40, 147, 185

Go, 25, 33, 195

god games, 42, 220–21, 252

"god mode" and "god mood," 216–17, 220–21, 226–30, 228, 231–32

Godwired (Wagner), 144, 255, 259, 267

Goffman, Erving, 205

Golden Rule, 225–26

Goldfarb, Abe, 57

Golem of Prague, 40

Golub, Alex, 151n2

Google Inc., 178–79

Gothic cathedrals, 137–38

Graham, David, 50

graphic novels, 102

Greek culture, 28–30

Gregory, Rabia, 11–12

Grey Wardens, 265–66

Grusin, Richard, 114, 120

Guild Wars, 136

gun violence, 17
Guru Meditation, 223

Half-Real (Juul), 268
Halo series, 7, 9, 154, 159, 161, 197
Halos and Avatars (Detweiler), 6, 255, 267
Hanar, 39–40
handheld digital devices, 8
Hani, 122
Hanuman: Boy Warrior, 10, 35–36, 68–70, 70–73, 73–76, 76–79
haptic feedback, 244
Hardcore Christian Gamer, 154, 156, 163
Haredism, 48–51, 61, 64n8
Harris, Sam, 208
Haunted Forest, 41
haunted magic circle: and Fatal Frame, 11, 97–101; and horror genre, 11, 15; and religious structures in digital games, 88–92; and Silent Hill, 11, 92–97; and transcendence, 102
Hayse, Mark, 7
Heavenville, 26
Hebrew Bible, 96
Helland, Christopher, 4
Hemisphere Games, 218
heresy, 91, 95–96, 207
Heretic, 150
Herfsttij (Huizinga), 140–41, 151n5
Heroes of Might and Magic, 263
hero's journey, 229
hestiastic games, 30–31, 36
Hezbollah, 117–18, 129
hierarchical power, 78, 91, 94, 95, 96
Himuro Mansion, 98, 103n24
Hinasaki, Mafuyu and Miku (game characters), 98–100
Hinduism: Asian and Indian gaming markets, 68–70; and Civilization series, 124, 257; digital gaming in Hindu context, 70–73; and game typologies, 35–36; Hindu Awakening, 82n31; and religious authority in diaspora con-

text, 76–79; representation and simulation in gaming, 73–76; and wedding games, 31
hint systems, 230
Hitchens, Christopher, 4, 208
Hjarvard, Stig, 16
Höglund, Johan, 110–11
holidays, 36
holy sites, 112. See also sacredness
Home Tabernacle, 41
Homo Ludens (Huizinga), 31, 89, 140, 166–67, 194. See also haunted magic circle
Hoover, Stuart, 166
Horde, 145–46
horror: and Cursed Mountain, 35; and disempowerment, 223; and Fatal Frame, 10–11, 97–101, 102; and The Path, 13, 214, 229–30; and Silent Hill, 10–11, 92–97, 102; transcendent horror described, 88–92
Huhtamo, Erkki, 129–30
Huizinga, Johan: on game structure, 3; on hestiastic games, 31; influence on gaming theory, 139–40; on insincere play, 207; and magic circle concept, 7–8, 89, 143, 233; and neomedievalism, 137; and religion/play connection, 139–41; and ritual elements of play, 166–67, 194–95; on rules of games, 194
humor in gaming, 239, 241, 246–50, 251–52
hypertextual elements of digital games, 96

Ibn Ishāq, Muhammad, 122
iconography of video games, 147, 170–71, 180–81. See also symbols and symbolism
Ignatius of Loyola, 42
Iliad, The, 28
imagination in gaming, 264–69
"Imagined Commodities" (Carlson and Corliss), 175

Impaling Ritual, 100
impiety, 36
implicit religion, 12, 216
Importance of Being Earnest, The (Wilde), 192
Index Librorum Prohibitorum ("List of Prohibited Books"), 178
India Gaming Carnival, 68
Inferno (Dante Alighieri), 136
in-game communication technology, 137
Innis, Harold, 256
innovators, religious, 207
insincere play, 196–97, 203–208
interactive worlds, 242, 245
interfaith dialogue, 257
internet: "all your base" meme, 183; and anonymity, 162; and chat programs, 138; and fantasy role-playing games, 143; and Indian gaming, 69, 71, 74, 76–78; and mass-media gaming, 145; and MMORPGs, 150; and online surveys, 168n19; and religion in gaming studies, 2, 66, 267; and secularization, 4; and virtual worlds, 243–44
intertextuality in game design, 52–53, 270
Iraq War, 114–15
Islam: and *Civilization* series, 124, 257, 270; and game typologies, 41; jihad, 121; and religious conflict, 263; representations in video games, 11, 109–10, 110–12, 112–13, 114–20, 120–23, 267; and rules of video games, 124–27; symbols of, 271
"Islamogaming" (Campbell), 112
Istha-deva, 42
Ito, Masahiro, 93
It's a Wonderful Life (1946), 36

James, William, 240, 253
Japanese Buddhism, 40
Japanese culture, 40, 95, 146
Järvinen, Aki, 217
Jenkins, Henry, 92

Jenkins, Jerry B., 34
Jerusalem, 121
Jerusalem Talmud, 44n12
Jesus, 185–86
JESUS: Dreadful Bio-Monster, 173
Jews. *See* Judaism
jihad, 121
Joel (prophet), 261
Journey, 38
Journey of Jesus, 187
Journey to Wild Divine, 223
Judaism: and *The Binding of Isaac*, 270; and *Civilization* series, 124, 257; do-it-yourself Judaism, 50; and dreidel, 29, 30; and game typologies, 35, 40; post-denominational and post-ethnic, 48–51; and protests against game publishers, 81; and religious conflict, 263; in *The Shiva*, 57–60
Judeo-Christian culture, 94, 181–83
Judgment of Paris, 28
judicium dei ("God decides"), 32
"Just Gaming?" (panel), 6
Juul, Jesper, 90, 202–203, 256, 268, 271

Kagura, 100, 101
Kali, 81
kami, 33
karesansui, 219
karma, 222, 224, 225
Kei (game character), 99
Kennedy, Helen, 55–56, 203–204
Khamis, Sahar, 111
Kierkegaard, Søren, 241
Kikuchi, Keisuke, 97
Kinect, 38
Kingdom of Amalur, 146
Kiraigou Ritual, 100
Kirie, 100, 104n29
koans, 33, 43
Kolb, Michael, 249
Konami, 89, 93
Korean gaming, 146
Korean Presbyterian Christianity, 258

Kristeva, Julia, 90
Krogans, 39
Kuma\War, 109, 113, 114–17, 119, 128–29
Kurosawa, Rei, 99
Kusabi (game character), 99, 100–101

Labanotation, 52, 64n21
laboratores, 139
LaHaye, Tim, 34
Lakhmids, 122
Lantz, Frank, 25, 26, 37, 44n4
Lauder, Jack (game character), 57–58, 60–61
Lebanon, 117
Leela, 26, 37
Left Behind, 6–7, 34, 224, 260–61
Legend of Zelda, The, 9, 174–75, 181
Lehdonvirta, Vili, 140
Lehrich, Christopher I., 90
Let There Be Smite, 43
leveling up, 221
Lewis, C. S., 139–40
Life on Screen (Turkle), 242
life-world concept, 240–42, 253nn8, 16
Lightside Games, 187
Likarish, Peter, 12, 15, 17
Limbaugh, Stephen N., Sr., 5
liminality, 100, 221
Lineage 2, 146
Little Red Riding Hood, 214
Little Sisters, 186
live action films, 102
Lobsel Vith, 94, 103n16
localization of game products: and the *Actraiser* series, 181–83; and cultural border zones, 175–76; as cultural feedback filter, 172–75; and external rating boards, 183–85; and fabricated religions, 176–78; and global market for games, 171–72; and Nintendo of America, 180–81; and non-state censorship, 178–79; and religious content, 185–86, 186–88
lockout systems, 180

London Summer Olympics, 27–28
Lord of the Rings, The (Tolkien), 145
Loromir, Archon of Peace, 147, 148
Lovecraft, H. P., 90
Luddites, 176–77
ludic arts, 27
ludological approach to game analysis, 16, 267–69
Lufia, 181
Luft, Shanny, 12, 15–16
Lundgren, Sus, 219, 229
Lynch, Gordon, 200–201

MacAloon, John, 27–28
Machin, David, 111
Mackay, Daniel, 90
magic, 262
magic circle concept, 8, 89, 92, 140–41, 143, 233. *See also* haunted magic circle
Maher, Bill, 208
Make-Make, 32
Mamluks, 121–22
Manchester Cathedral, 1, 17, 238–39, 250–51
Maniac Mansion, 180
Manor of Sleep, 99
Marashi, Ibrahim, 110
Marco Polo, 104n26
Mario Kart Wii, 259
Market Xcel, 82n14
marketing digital games, 59, 82n17, 157, 172–75
martyr videos, 129
Marx, Karl, 4, 261
Mason, Heather, 88
Mass Effect, 39
massively multiplayer online role-playing games (MMORPGS): and comprehensible violence, 145–47; and game typologies, 34; and magic circle concept, 141; and neomedievalism, 11, 136–38, 139–40, 149–51
Material Christianity, 157
Mayan culture, 29

Mayu (game character), 99
McDannell, Colleen, 157
McKie, Patsy, 17–18
mechanized religion, 17, 260–63, 263–64, 267, 271–72
media: and controversial game scenarios, 159–60; and evangelicalism, 157; media bias, 256, 271–73; media studies, 166; and medieval devotional techniques, 149; and neomedievalism, 149; and Rajan Zed, 83n37; and representations of Hinduism, 73, 77–78, 83n37; and representations of Islam, 119–20, 129; and representations of Judaism, 49; sociophenomenological perspective on, 243
Media Archaeology (Huhtamo), 129
mediatization, 16, 69, 76–79
medieval era, 135, 136, 258. *See also* neomedievalism
Medina, 123
meditation, 218–20, 223, 227–29, 232
Meier, Sid, 124, 256–57
Meridian, 148
Metatron, 94, 96
methodologies for game studies. *See* multimodality
mhaibis, 31
Middle East, 109
midrashim, 94
Minakami village, 99
Minazuki, Ruka, 100–101
Minecraft, 269
Mio (game character), 99
Mission 29: Fallujah: Operation al-Fajr, 114–17, 115–16
missionaries, 125
modding games, 164
Modern Warfare 2, 164
Molyneux, Peter, 260
Monopoly, 259
monotheism, 257
morality in game settings: and Christian gamers, 163; and computer religious

worlds, 252; and computer worlds, 250; and disposition to act, 224–26, 227; dualistic conceptions of, 233; moral meter games, 224–25; and *The Path*, 230; and spiritual efficacy, 226–30, 227, 228. *See also* ethics in gaming
Mortal Kombat, 180, 183–85, 186
Mothers Against Violence, 17–18
Motu Mui island, 32
Mount Simeon, 44n12
Moussa, Lateef, 31
Muhammad (prophet), 122
multimodality, 10, 14, 16, 51–56, 63n4
multiplayer games, 161. *See also* massively multiplayer online role-playing games (MMORPGS)
music of video games, 38
Muslims. *See* Islam
Mutsu Province, 97
mystery, 57, 59, 260–61, 263–64
mysticism, 232–33, 244–46
mythography, 135
mythological themes, 71–72, 79–80

narrative: *Dragon Age*, 265–67; and game design, 147–48; game scholarship on, 267–69; and gaming research, 4, 6–7; and Hinduism in video games, 70, 72–73; impact on gameplay, 15; and Islam in video games, 129; narrative layer of video games, 113, 120–23, 124, 128–29
neomedievalism, 11–12, 135–38, 145–51
neo-paganism, 40
Neopets, 41
NES gaming system, 174, 180
Night Journey, The, 223
Nightmare World, 95
nihilists, 204, 208, 209
Nintendo of America, 174, 179–81, 183, 186
Nintendo 3DS, 101
Njepi (Day of Silence), 31
non-player characters, 137

non-state censorship, 178–79
Nordic religions, 148
novelizations of digital games, 102
NYU Game Center, 25

objectionable content, 175–76. See also
    censorship
occult, 92–97
O'Connell, Leah, 30
Okami, 38
Oldenburg, Aaron, 220, 223, 231–32
Olympics, 27–33
omnipotence and omniscience, 233. See
    also "god mode" and "god mood"
On Multiple Realities (Schutz), 240
Ong, Walter, 2
Onigokko, Hidden, 104n26
online conduct, 161–62
online forums, 93, 102
online games, 71, 82n17. See also mas-
    sively multiplayer online role-playing
    games (MMORPGS)
optical feedback, 244
Oracle of Delphi, 257
oratores, 139
Order, the, 11, 88–89, 91, 93–96
order-making role of play, 18, 193, 194–95,
    201–203, 209–10
Orientalism, 15, 110, 121, 126, 129. See also
    Others and Othering
Orland, T., 62
Orochi, 38
Orthodox Judaism, 49, 60, 61
Osmos, 218
Others and Othering: and horror
    genre, 90–91; impact of gameplay, 15;
    Jewishness and Judaism, 48, 56; and
    reciprocity of perspectives thesis, 243;
    and representations of Islam in video
    games, 110, 111, 114–16, 121; and Silent
    Hill, 95–96
Otogirisō, 97
Otto, Rudolph, 90
Owaku, Hiroyuki, 93

Palestinians, 111
Pan Ku, 33
parallel reality games, 34
paramount reality, 13, 239–44, 247–50
Passover, 50–51
Past Life (Waltz), 93
Path, The, 13, 214–15, 215, 226–30, 230–31
Patroclus, 28
Pauline Mediterranean Christianity, 258
pen-and-paper games, 162
Persuasive Games (Bogost), 109
Pew Forum on Religion and Public Life,
    187
Pfeiffer, Jon E., 172
phenomenology, 13, 198–99, 234n6
Piercing of the Soul Ritual, 100
pilgrimages, 142
Pinchbeck, Dan, 221
"Pixel Pashas, Digital Djinns" (Wer-
    ning), 110
play and playfulness: and computer
    religious worlds, 251–53; interrelation-
    ship of religion and media, 149; and
    Schutz's life-world theory, 239–40,
    241–52; and virtual worlds, 151
"The Play is the Thing" (Wagner), 185–86
player-versus-environment games, 136
playing cards, 141–42, 143, 150–51, 202
PlayStation, 41, 66, 71, 74, 218
plot function of religion, 7
poimenic games, 31–32, 36–37
point-and-click games, 62
poker, 25
"The Political Battlefield of Pro-Arab
    Video Games" (Tawil-Souri), 111
political subject matter, 4
polysemy, 272
polytheism, 265
popular culture, 50–51, 157
Populous, 260
portable imagery, 144
Portal, 197
post-denominational Judaism, 48–51
post-ethnic Judaism, 48–51

Power, Marcus, 117
Powers of Horror (Kristeva), 90
praxic games, 32–33, 37–39
prayer, 52, 151
predation games, 223
Presence of the Word, The, (Ong), 2
printing, 142–45, 149, 243
Prismatology (fabricated religion), 176–77
procedural layer of video games, 113, 124–27, 128–30
profane, 199–201
profanity, 164
Project Zero, 97
propaganda, 120
prophets, 207
Protestantism, 129
puzzle games, 219
Pyramid Head, 94

Quarians, 40
quest narratives, 136
Quirkat, 126
Quraish, 113, 122–23, 128
Quran, 118, 131n26

rabbinic Judaism, 61
race issues, 47, 56
Rama, 71–72
Ramadan, 31
Ramayan (television series), 73
Ramayana, 36, 66
Ravan, 80
Randi, James, 208
Ra.One, 67, 79
Rapa Nui, 29
ratings boards, 179
Raynal, Frédéric, 92–93
reality filters, 178–79
real-time strategy games: examples of, 113, 113; and game characters' relationships, 145; and game typologies, 34, 43; and narrative layer, 120–23, 128; religion as strategic tool, 224–26, 260–61

reciprocity of perspectives thesis, 243
Reform Judaism, 29, 48–51, 60, 61
regulatory issues, 175
Rei, 100
Reichmuth, Philipp, 110
religious authority, 78
religious content in games: and computer worlds, 250; and localization of game products, 185–86; and marketing of games, 187; religious conflict, 134, 147–48, 263; religious spaces, 1, 17, 90, 137–38, 143–44, 238–39, 250–51; religious strategies, 11, 120–23, 256–57, 260–61; religious syncretism, 95; religious values, 164–65; ritual, 6, 12–14, 96, 97–101, 194–95, 259; symbolism, 214; transcendence, 90–91, 102
Remediation (Bolter and Grusin), 114
remediation, 114, 120, 129, 268
representation: and the game interface, 56; and *Hanuman: Boy Warrior,* 73–76; impact of gameplay, 15; and Islam in video games, 110–12; and Judaism, 49; and media bias, 272
Resistance: Fall of Man, 1, 2, 5, 13, 17–18, 238, 251
Revelation (biblical), 34
revelation, religious, 247
Richard the Lionheart, 121
riddles, 33
Rift, 197
"Rights of Passage" (Steiner), 175
Rise of Islam, 126
rites of passage, 204
ritual: and Christian gamers, 12; and *Fatal Frame,* 11, 97–101; and "God modes/moods," 13; and hardcore Christian gamers, 166–67; and "Just Gaming?" panel, 6; ritual spaces, 90; ritual theory, 221; and rules of games, 194–95; and *Silent Hill,* 96; and spiritual efficacy, 216, 234; and systematic nature of gaming systems, 259
Road to Emmaus, 41

Rohrer, Jason, 26, 27, 38

"The Role of 'New' Arab Satellite Channels in Fostering Intercultural Dialogue" (Khamis), 111

role-playing games (RPGs), 34, 40, 162–63, 221, 265–67, 269. *See also* massively multiplayer online role-playing games (MMORPGs)

Roman spectacles, 44n12

Rope Maidens, 98

Rudy, Kathryn, 142

rules: and definitions of religion, 198–201; and demystification of religion, 256; didactic games, 29–30; and empowerment in gaming, 220; "god mode" and "god mood," 216–17; and insincere play, 203–208; and meditative gaming, 216–17; and moral issues in games, 225; and narrative, 268; order-making function of, 193, 194–95, 201–203, 209–10; and procedural layer of games, 128, 130; and religious gaming, 195–98, 209–10; and representation of Islam and Muslims, 124–27; and representations of Islam in video games, 127; and spiritual efficacy, 226, 227, 228, 228; and systematic nature of gaming systems, 259–60

Rules of Play (Salen and Zimmerman), 89–90, 197–98

Russian divination games, 31

Sabry, Tarik, 110

sacredness: and cultural Othering, 15; and definitions of religion, 199; and digital game types, 34, 36–38; and disempowerment, 222; and horror genre, 88–90, 92–95, 100–101, 102; and implicit religion, 12; and rules, 195; "Sacred Digital Guidelines," 5; sacred games, 27–28, 30–31, 32–33; sacred spaces, 5–9, 11, 143–44; sacred/profane distinction, 200–201, 263

Sae (game character), 99

Sakuya, 100

Salen, Katie, 89–90, 95, 197–98, 202, 205

Salvatore, R. A., 146

Sam and Max, 176

Samael, 94

Samyn, Michaël, 214, 215, 230–31

Sanatan Sanstha, 76, 82n31

Sassanid Empire, 109

Scandinavian religions, 147

Scholtz, Clifford, 7

Schut, Kevin, 13, 17, 18

Schutz, Alfred: computer worlds as enclaves, 242–46, 249, 251–52; and "life-world" concept, 240–42, 253n8; and "paramount reality," 13, 239; and playfulness/humor, 246–47

science fiction, 39

Scientology, 177

ScreenCap, 53

Second Life, 9, 41

"*Second Life* and the Sacred" (Derrickson), 112

Secret of Mana, The, 181

Secret Yiddish Policemen's Union, The, (Chabon), 61

secularism, 4–5, 8, 187

Sega Genesis, 183

self-censorship, 177

self-representation, 110–12

semiotic approaches to game study, 47, 62

September 11 terrorist attacks, 109, 111, 114

Serious Man, A, (2009), 61

server architectures, 137

sexual content in video games: and cultural feedback, 186; and industry self-censorship, 177; and localization of game products, 180; and marketing of games, 187

shabbos laws, 35

Shadowbane, 11–12, 134–36, 146–48, 150

Shaiban tribe, 122

shamanic trances, 42

Shamgar-Handelman, Lea, 44
Sheff, David, 183–84
Shia Islam, 109, 116
Shibata, Makoto, 97, 103n24
Shinto rituals, 101
Shintoism: and *Civilization* series, 257;
    and *Fatal Frame*, 11, 97, 99–101; and
    game typologies, 33, 38; and horror
    genre, 88–89; and religious signifiers,
    101; and *Silent Hill*, 95
Shiva, The, 57–60
shock experiences, 241, 245
Shri Ramayan Pracharini Sabha, 76
Shrine Maiden, 100–101
Sid Meier's *Civilization* series: and emer-
    gent play, 270–71; and game typolo-
    gies, 43; and Islam, *113*, 124–28, 129;
    and mechanized religion, 270; and
    media bias, 273; religion as strategic
    tool, 256–57, 260
signifiers, 89, 101, 119–20
Sikhism, 257
Silent Hill (2006), 92, 93
Silent Hill Heaven, 96
Silent Hill Omnibus, 93
Silent Hill Revelation 3D (2012), 92, 93
Silent Hill series: "Birth Memo," 103n15;
    "Creation Memo," 103n16; and film,
    102; and horror genre, 88–92; religious
    themes in, 92–97; and religious tran-
    scendence, 101; rules and rituals of,
    10–11
Silent Hill Wiki, 96
SilkRoad Online, 146
Sillestor, 147
Sim City, 42, 220–21
Simmel, Georg, 198–99
Sims, The, 255
simulation, 67, 73–76, 124, 258–60
sincerity, 196–97, 203–208
single-player role-plying games, 146
Sinner's Reward (Waltz), 93
Šisler, Vít, 7, 11, 15, 63n1, 81n1, 126
Sita, 71–72

skill games, 219
Smite, 81
Smith, Jonas Heide, 195, 202
Smith, Jonathan Z., 156, 199
Sniderman, Stephen, 30, 207–208, 209
Social Gaming Asia Summit, 68
"Social Realism in Gaming" (Galloway),
    124
sociophenomenological approach, 13,
    239–40, 243
Sony: and flow-based games, 218; and
    game rating systems, 184; and reli-
    gious controversies, 1, 5, 17–18, 36, 71,
    74–76, 79, 238; and technical critiques
    of games, 74
Soul Stones, 148
Sound of Music, The, (1965), 36
Special Force series, *113*, 117–18, 128
Spirit Camera: The Cursed Memoir, 101
Spiritual Exercises, 42
spirituality: and Christian gamers, 12;
    and devotional practices, 42–43; and
    horror, 102; and Judaism, 50; and
    mysticism, 13; and nature of play, 2;
    in pre-digital games, 25; and ritual
    game space, 90; spiritual efficacy, 13,
    16, 215–26, 227, 228, 234; and the super-
    natural, 91–92
Spiro, Melford, 172
splinter groups, religious, 207
spoilsports, 204, 207–208
spoken text, 51–56, *52, 53,* 59–60. *See also*
    narrative
sportsmanship, 160
St. Louis County, 5
Star Wars series, 223, 224, 248–49, 250
Steffen, Oliver, 13, 15
Steiner, Christopher, 175
stereotypes, 7, 15, 59–60, 62, 121
Stevens, Brett, 221
Stone, Russell (game character), 35, 48,
    57–60, 60–61
Strangling Ritual, 88, 98
Suits, Bernard, 203, 205, 209

Suleiman, Usama, 111
Sumo, 33
Sunni Islam, 109, *115–16*, 116
Super Nintendo Entertainment System
    (SNES), 183
Superbowl Sunday School, 30
supernatural elements: and horror genre,
    88, 90–91, 93, 97, 101, 102; supernatural
    powers, 13–14, 255
sūra, 131n26
Sūrat rasūl Allāh ("Life of Allah's Mes-
    senger"), 122
surveys of gamers, 156–57, 158–59, 161–65,
    167n12, 168n19
Sūrya, 72
suspension of disbelief, 204
Sutton-Smith, Brian, 203–204
swings, ritual, 195
symbols and symbolism: and cultural
    feedback, 12, 170–71; and cultural
    meaning making, 18; impact on game-
    play, 14–15; and Islam in video games,
    110; and localization of game prod-
    ucts, 180–81; and mechanized play
    structure, 269–70; and neomedieval-
    ism, 138, 149; and *The Path*, 214; and
    religious content in games, 2, 4; and
    Schutz's "paramount reality," 239–40,
    250
syncretism, religious, 95

Takamine, Junsei, 98
Tale of Tales, 214
Talmudic tradition, 59
Tanakh, 35, 94
Tangata Manu, 31–32
Taoism, 33, 35–37, 124, 257, 270
Tatoo (software), 52
Tatooed Priestess, 99–100
Tawil-Souri, Helga, 111
Team Silent, 93, 95
Teamspeak, 138
technical critiques of games, 74
technological advance, 124–25

technology, 262
Tecmo, 89, 97, 101
television, 75, 119–20
Tengriism, 257
terms-of-use agreements, 143
terrorism, 111
Tertulian, 44n12
Tetris, 219, 272
Tetris Defense, 56
Tevinter Imperium, 265–66
text elements of gameplay, 62, 171–72
Thatgamecompany, 218
theoptic games, 34, 42
Thomas, Günter, 216, 219
Thornham, Helen, 166
Three Kingdoms period, 146
Tibetan Book of the Dead, 35
Tibetan Buddhism, 29
time perspectives, 244
Tolkien, J. R. R., 140, 145
topoi, 129–30
Tosca, Susana Pajares, 195, 202
Tower of Babel, 182
Toyama, Keiichiro, 93
trial by combat, 32
Transana, 51–52, *52*, 55, *55*
transcendence, 90–91, 102
translation, 170–72, 175, 183, 187
transmedia storytelling, 92–93, 102
Tree of Life, 135, 148
triflers, 204–206, 208, 209
trinitarian religion, 94
Tropico, 261
Tsuboyama, Masashi, 93
Turkle, Sherry, 242
turn-based games, *113*, 124
Turner, Victor, 221
Tweed, Thomas, 199
two-dimensional single-player RPGs, 150
typology of game types: audiovisual,
    narrative, and procedural layers, *113*,
    114–20, 120–23, 124–27, 128–30; and
    digital religious games, 39–43, 195–98;
    Greek roots, 26–27, 27–39

ulama, 29
Ullamaliztli games, 32
Ultima series, 224, 267
Understanding Video Games (Egenfeldt-
    Nielsen, Smith, and Tosca), 113, 195
United Kingdom, 1
United States of America: and children's
    games, 104n26; and cultural feedback
    filters, 170, 173, 174, 178, 180, 187, 188n9;
    and Hinduism, 67, 70, 74, 76, 78–79,
    82n31; and Islam, 109; and Judaism,
    49–50
Universal Society of Hinduism, 36, 67,
    74–76, 76–79, 81, 82n31
unscripted narration, 137
U.S. Supreme Court, 5, 174

vajrayana Buddhism, 42
Valtiel, 94, 96
variation in game content, 170–89
Vedic India, 195
Ventrilo, 138
video game systems, 258–60
"Video Games, Video Clips, and Islam"
    (Šisler), 112
"Videogames of the Oppressed" (Fra-
    sca), 124
Viola, Bill, 223
violent content in video games: and
    Christian gamers, 163; and cultural
    feedback, 186; and hardcore Christian
    gamers, 159; and industry self-censor-
    ship, 177; and marketing of games, 187;
    and MMORPGS, 138, 139, 145–47; and
    morality in game settings, 226; and
    Othering, 56
virtuality: and life-world concept,
    242–44, 251–52; and representation of
    religious spaces, 240; virtual worlds,
    197; virtually religious communities,
    142; and Zen game genre, 219
vocabulary of gaming, 145
voice elements of gameplay, 171–72
voiceover-internet-protocol chat, 138

Wagner, Rachel: on earnestness in
    gameplaying, 12–13; on escapism
    in digital games, 8; on game struc-
    ture, 3; on legal/religious conflicts,
    18; on religion in gaming context,
    15; on religion/play connection,
    140, 142, 144–45, 269; on religious
    content in games, 185–86, 255; on
    rules, 259
Waltemathe, Michael, 13
Walter, Brenda Gardenour, 10–11, 15
Waltz, Tom, 93
War of the Roses, 136
Wark, McKenzie, 125, 129
Weber, Max, 4, 78
WeiQi (Go), 25, 33, 195
Werning, Stephan, 110
Western Christianity, 95
Western religions, 91
Wicca, 41
Wii, 35
Wii Fit Zazen, 223
Wilde, Oscar, 192
Wired magazine, 26, 44n4
Witches Tower, 41
Wittgenstein, Ludwig, 202
Wolfpack, 134
Wong Tai Sin temple, 36–37
woodcuts, 141–42, 149, 151
Woolsley, Ted, 174
World Cyber Games, 68
World of Warcraft, 9, 145–46, 151n2,
    162–63, 197
World Tree, 134, 135
world-building, 137

X-Files, The, 104n24
Xuchilbara, 94, 103n16

Yae (game character), 99, 100
Yamaoka, Akira, 93
Yevonites (fabricated religion), 176–77
Yin and Yang, 33
yoga, 38

Zed, Rajan, 74–76, 77–79, 83n37

Zeiler, Xenia, 10, 15, 18

Zelig, Amos (game character), 57, 59–61

Zen and Zen games, 29, 33, 195, 218–19,
    232

Zen Buddhism, 232

Zero series, 97, 99, 104n28

Zero Wing, 183

Zimmerman, Eric: and definitions
    of play, 194, 197–98, 202, 203; on
    emergent play, 268; and Game De-
    velopers Conference, 25–26, 43; and
    game typologies, 38; and insincere
    play, 205; on ritual sphere of play,
    89–90, 95

Zoroastrianism, 257, 270

CPSIA information can be obtained at www.ICGtesting.com
Printed in the USA
LVOW01s2117150414

381825LV00019B/66/P